MySQL 8 for Big Data

Effective data processing with MySQL 8, Hadoop, NoSQL APIs, and other Big Data tools

Shabbir Challawala

Jaydip Lakhatariya

Chintan Mehta

Kandarp Patel

BIRMINGHAM - MUMBAI

MySQL 8 for Big Data

First published: October 2017

Production reference: 1161017

Published by Packt Publishing Ltd.
Livery Place
35 Livery Street
Birmingham
B3 2PB, UK.
ISBN 978-1-78839-718-6

www.packtpub.com

Credits

Authors
Shabbir Challawala
Jaydip Lakhatariya
Chintan Mehta
Kandarp Patel

Copy Editor
Tasneem Fatehi

Reviewers
Ankit Bhavsar
Chintan Gajjar
Nikunj Ranpura
Subhash Shah

Project Coordinator
Manthan Patel

Commissioning Editor
Amey Varangaonkar

Proofreader
Safis Editing

Acquisition Editor
Aman Singh

Indexer
Rekha Nair

Content Development Editor
Snehal Kolte

Graphics
Tania Dutta

Technical Editor
Sagar Sawant

Production Coordinator
Shantanu Zagade

About the Authors

Shabbir Challawala has over 8 years of rich experience in providing solutions based on MySQL and PHP technologies. He is currently working with KNOWARTH Technologies. He has worked in various PHP-based e-commerce solutions and learning portals for enterprises. He has worked on different PHP-based frameworks, such as Magento E-commerce, Drupal CMS, and Laravel.

Shabbir has been involved in various enterprise solutions at different phases, such as architecture design, database optimization, and performance tuning. He has been carrying good exposure of Software Development Life Cycle process thoroughly. He has worked on integrating Big Data technologies such as MongoDB and Elasticsearch with a PHP-based framework.

I am sincerely thankful to Chintan Mehta for showing confidence in me writing this book. I would like to thank KNOWARTH Technologies for providing the opportunity and support to be part of this book. I also want to thank my co-authors and PacktPub team for providing wonderful support throughout. I would especially like to thank my mom, dad, wife Sakina, lovely son Mohammad, and family members for supporting me throughout the project.

Jaydip Lakhatariya has rich experience in portal and J2EE frameworks. He adapts quickly to any new technology and has a keen desire for constant improvement. Currently, Jaydip is associated with a leading open source enterprise development company, KNOWARTH Technologies (`www.knowarth.com`), where he is engaged in various enterprise projects.

Jaydip, a full-stack developer, has proven his versatility by adopting technologies such as Liferay, Java, Spring, Struts, Hadoop, MySQL, Elasticsearch, Cassandra, MongoDB, Jenkins, SCM, PostgreSQL, and many more.

He has been recognized with awards such as Merit, Commitment to Service, and also as a Star Performer. He loves mentoring people and has been delivering training for Portals and J2EE frameworks.

I am sincerely thankful to my splendid co-authors, and especially to Mr. Chintan Mehta, for providing such motivation and having faith in me. I would like to thank KNOWARTH for constantly providing new opportunities to help me enhance myself. I would also like to appreciate the entire team at Packt Publishing for providing wonderful support throughout the project.

Finally, I am utterly grateful to my parents and my younger brother Keyur, for supporting me throughout the journey while authoring. Thank you my friends and colleagues for being around.

Chintan Mehta is the co-founder at KNOWARTH Technologies (www.knowarth.com) and heads Cloud/RIMS/DevOps. He has rich progressive experience in Systems and Server Administration of Linux, AWS Cloud, DevOps, RIMS, and Server Administration on Open Source Technologies. He is also an AWS Certified Solutions Architect-Associate.

Chintan's vital role during his career in Infrastructure and Operations has also included Requirement Analysis, Architecture design, Security design, High-availability and Disaster recovery planning, Automated monitoring, Automated deployment, Build processes to help customers, performance tuning, infrastructure setup and deployment, and application setup and deployment. He has also been responsible for setting up various offices at different locations, with fantastic sole ownership to achieve Operation Readiness for the organizations he had been associated with.

He headed Managed Cloud Services practices with his previous employer and received multiple awards in recognition of very valuable contributions made to the business of the group. He also led the ISO 27001:2005 implementation team as a joint management representative. Chintan has authored *Hadoop Backup and Recovery Solutions* and reviewed *Liferay Portal Performance Best Practices* and *Building Serverless Web Applications*.

He has a Diploma in Computer Hardware and Network from a reputed institute in India.

I have relied on many people, both directly and indirectly, in writing this book. First, I would like to thank my co-authors and the wonderful team at PacktPub for this effort. I would like to especially thank my wonderful wife, Mittal, and my sweet son, Devam, for putting up with the long days, nights, and weekends when I was camped out in front of my laptop. Many people have inspired and made contributions to this book and provided comments, edits, insights, and ideas, especially Krupal Khatri and Chintan Gajjar. There were several things that could have interfered with my book. I also want to thank all the reviewers of this book.
Last, but not the least, I want to thank my mom and dad, friends, family, and colleagues for supporting me throughout the writing of this book.

Kandarp Patel leads PHP practices at KNOWARTH Technologies (www.knowarth.com). He has vast experience in providing end-to-end solutions in CMS, LMS, WCM, and e-commerce, along with various integrations for enterprise customers. He has over 9 years of rich experience in providing solutions in MySQL, MongoDB, and PHP-based frameworks. Kandarp is also a certified MongoDB and Magento developer.

Kandarp has experience in various Enterprise Application development phases of the Software Development Life Cycle and has played prominent role in requirement gathering, architecture design, database design, application development, performance tuning, and CD/CI.

Kandarp has a Bachelor of Engineering in Information Technology from a reputed university in India.

I would like to acknowledge Chintan Mehta for guiding me through the various stages of the roller-coaster ride while writing the book. I would like to thank KNOWARTH Technologies for providing me the opportunity to be a part of this book. I would also like to thank my splendid co-authors and PacktPublishing team for providing wonderful support throughout the journey.
Last, but not the least, I want to thank my mom and dad, and my wife Jalpa, for continuously supporting and encouraging me throughout the writing of the book. I dedicate my first book to my lovely princesses, Jayna and Jaisvi.

About the Reviewers

Ankit Bhavsar is a senior consultant at KNOWARTH Technologies (www.knowarth.com) and leads the team working on Enterprise Resource Planning Solutions. He has rich knowledge in Java, JEE, MySQL, PostgreSQL, Apache Spark, and many more open source tools and technologies utilized in building enterprise-grade applications.

Ankit has played dynamic roles during his career in Development and Maintenance of Astrology Portal's Content Management and Enterprise Resource Planning Solutions, which includes Object-Oriented Programming, Technical Architecture analysis, design, and development, as well as Database design, development and enhancement, process, and data and object modeling in a variety of applications and environments to provide technical and business solutions to clients.

Ankit has a Masters of Computer Application from North Gujarat University.

> First, I would like to thank my co-reviewers and the wonderful team at Packt Publishing for this effort. I would also like to thank Subhash Shah and Chintan Mehta. I also want to thank all the authors of this book. Last, but not least, I want to thank my mom, friends, family, and colleagues for supporting me throughout the reviewing of this book.

Chintan Gajjar is a consultant at KNOWARTH Technologies (www.knowarth.com). He has rich progressive experience in advanced Javascript, NodeJS, BackboneJS, AngularJS, Java, and MongoDB, and also provides enterprise services such as Enterprise Portal Development, ERP Implementation, and Enterprise Integration services in Open Source Technologies.

Chintan's vital role during his career in enterprise services has also included Requirement Analysis, Architecture design, UI Implementation, Build processes to help customers, following best practices in development and processes, and development to deployment processes with great ownership, to develop the reality of a customer's idea and his organizations he had been associated with.

Chintan has played dynamic roles during his career in Development Enterprise Resource Planning Solutions, worked on development of **single page application** (**SPA**) also worked on mobile application which including NodeJS, MongoDB and AngularJS. Chintan received multiple awards in recognition to very valuable contribution made to team and the business of the company. Chintan has contributed in book *Hadoop Backup and Recovery Solutions*. Chintan has completed **Master in Computer Application** (**MCA**) degree from Ganpat University.

I would like to thank co-reviewers and the wonderful team at Packt Publishing for this effort. I would also like to thank Subhash Shah, Chintan Mehta, and Ankit Bhavsar and colleagues for supporting me throughout the reviewing of this book. I also want to thank all the authors of this book.

Nikunj Ranpura has rich progressive experience in Systems and Server Administration of Linux, AWS Cloud, Devops, RIMS, Networking, Storage, Backup, and Security and Server Administration on Open Source Technologies. He adapts quickly to any technology and has a keen desire for constant improvement. He is also an AWS Certified Solutions Architect-Associate.

Nikunj has played distinct roles in his career, such as Systems Analyst, IT Manager, Managed Cloud Services Practice Lead, Infrastructure Architect, Infrastructure Developer, DevOps Architect, AWS Architect, and support manager for various large implementations. He has been involved in creating solutions and consulting to build SAAS, IAAS, and PAAS services on cloud.

Currently, Nikunj is associated with a leading open source enterprise development company, KNOWARTH Technologies, as a lead consultant, where he takes care of enterprise projects with regards to requirement analysis, architecture design, security design, high availability, and disaster recovery planning to help customers, along with leading the team.

Nikunj graduated from Bhavnagar University and has done CISCO and UTM firewall certifications as well. He has been recognized with two awards for his valuable contribution to the company. He is also a contributor on Stack Overflow. He can be contacted at `ranpura.nikunj@gmail.com`.

I would like to thank my family for their immense support and faith in me throughout my learning stage. My friends have developed the confidence in me to a level that makes me bring the best out of myself. I am happy that God has blessed me with such wonderful people around me, without whom my success as it is today would not have been possible.

Subhash Shah is a software architect with over 11 years of experience in developing web-based software solutions based on varying platforms and programming languages. He is an object-oriented programming enthusiast and a strong advocate of free and open source software development, and its use by businesses to reduce risk, reduce costs, and be more flexible. His career interests include designing sustainable software solutions. The best of his technical skills include, but are not limited to, requirement analysis, architecture design, project delivery monitoring, application and infrastructure setup, and execution process setup. He is an admirer of writing quality code and test-driven development.

Subhash works as a principal consultant at KNOWARTH Technologies Pvt Ltd. and heads ERP practices. He holds a degree in Information Technology from Hemchandracharya North Gujarat University.

It is a pleasure to hold the reviewer badge. I would like to thank the Packt Publishing team for offering such an opportunity. I would like to thank my family for supporting me throughout the course of reviewing this book. It would have been difficult without them understanding my priorities and being a source of inspiration. I want to thank my colleagues for their constant support and help. Finally, I want to thank the authors for writing such useful and detailed content.

www.PacktPub.com

For support files and downloads related to your book, please visit `www.PacktPub.com`. Did you know that Packt offers eBook versions of every book published, with PDF and ePub files available? You can upgrade to the eBook version at `www.PacktPub.com` and as a print book customer, you are entitled to a discount on the eBook copy. Get in touch with us at `service@packtpub.com` for more details. At `www.PacktPub.com`, you can also read a collection of free technical articles, sign up for a range of free newsletters and receive exclusive discounts and offers on Packt books and eBooks.

`https://www.packtpub.com/mapt`

Get the most in-demand software skills with Mapt. Mapt gives you full access to all Packt books and video courses, as well as industry-leading tools to help you plan your personal development and advance your career.

Why subscribe?

- Fully searchable across every book published by Packt
- Copy and paste, print, and bookmark content
- On demand and accessible via a web browser

Customer Feedback

Thanks for purchasing this Packt book. At Packt, quality is at the heart of our editorial process. To help us improve, please leave us an honest review on this book's Amazon page at https://www.amazon.in/dp/1788397185.

If you'd like to join our team of regular reviewers, you can email us at customerreviews@packtpub.com. We award our regular reviewers with free eBooks and videos in exchange for their valuable feedback. Help us be relentless in improving our products!

Table of Contents

Preface

With the organizations handling large amounts of data on a regular basis, MySQL has become a popular solution to handle this *Structured Big Data*. In this book, you will see how **Database Administrators (DAs)** can use MySQL to handle billions of records and load and retrieve data with performance comparable or superior to commercial DB solutions with higher costs.

Many organizations today depend on MySQL for their websites, and Big Data solutions for their data archiving, storage, and analysis needs. However, integrating them can be challenging. This book will show how to implement a successful Big Data strategy with Apache Hadoop and MySQL 8. It will cover real-time use case scenarios to explain integration and achieving Big Data solutions using different technologies such as Apache Hadoop, Apache Sqoop, and MySQL Applier.

The book will have discussion on topics such as features of MySQL 8, best practices for using MySQL 8, and NoSQL APIs provided by MySQL 8, and will also have a use case on using MySQL 8 for managing Big Data. By the end of this book, you will learn how to efficiently use MySQL 8 to manage data for your Big Data applications.

What this book covers

Chapter 1, *Introduction to Big Data and MySQL 8*, provides an overview of Big Data and MySQL 8, their importance, and life cycle of big data. It covers the basic idea of Big Data and its trends in the current market. Along with that, it also explains the benefits of using MySQL, takes us through the steps to install MySQL 8, and acquaints us with newly introduced features in MySQL 8.

Chapter 2, *Data Query Techniques in MySQL 8*, covers the basics of querying data on MySQL 8 and how to join or aggregate data set in it.

Chapter 3, *Indexing your data for High-Performing Queries*, explains about indexing in MySQL 8, introduces the different types of indexing available in MySQL, and shows how to do indexing for faster performance on large quantities of data.

Chapter 4, *Using Memcached with MySQL 8*, provides an overview of Memcached with MySQL and informs us of the various advantages of using it. It covers the Memcached installation steps, replication configuration, and various Memcached APIs in different programming languages.

Chapter 5, *Partitioning High Volume Data*, explains how high-volume data can be partitioned in MySQL 8 using different partitioning methods. It covers the various types of partitioning that we can implement in MySQL 8 and their use with Big Data.

Chapter 6, *Replication for building highly available solutions*, explains implementing group replication in MySQL 8. Chapter talks about how large data can be scaled and replicating of data can be faster using different techniques of replication.

Chapter 7, *MySQL 8 Best Practices*, covers the best practices of using MySQL 8 for Big Data. It has all the different kinds of dos and don'ts for using MySQL 8.

Chapter 8, *NoSQL API for Integrating with Big Data Solutions*, explains integration of NoSQL API for acquiring data. It also explains NoSQL and its various APIs in different programming languages for connecting NoSQL with MySQL.

Chapter 9, *Case Study: Part I - Apache Sqoop for Exchanging Data between MySQL and Hadoop*, explains how bulk data can be efficiently transferred between Hadoop and MySQL using Apache Sqoop.

Chapter 10, *Case Study: Part II - Realtime event processing using MySQL applier*, explains real-time integration of MySQL with Hadoop, and reading binary log events as soon as they are committed and writing them into a file in HDFS.

What you need for this book

This book will guide you through the installation of all the tools that you need to follow the examples. You will need to install the following software to effectively run the code samples present in this book:

- MySQL 8.0.3
- Hadoop 2.8.1
- Apache Sqoop 1.4.6

Who this book is for

This book is intended for MySQL database administrators and Big Data professionals looking to integrate MySQL and Hadoop to implement a high performance Big Data solution. Some previous experience with MySQL will be helpful.

Conventions

In this book, you will find a number of text styles that distinguish between different kinds of information. Here are some examples of these styles and explanations of their meanings.

Code words in text, database table names, folder names, filenames, file extensions, pathnames, dummy URLs, user input, and Twitter handles are shown as follows: "We can include other contexts through the use of the include directive."

A block of code is set as follows:

```
[default]
exten => s,1,Dial(Zap/1|30)
exten => s,2,Voicemail(u100)
exten => s,102,Voicemail(b100)
exten => i,1,Voicemail(s0)
```

When we wish to draw your attention to a particular part of a code block, the relevant lines or items are set in bold:

```
[default]
exten => s,1,Dial(Zap/1|30)
exten => s,2,Voicemail(u100)
exten => s,102,Voicemail(b100)
exten => i,1,Voicemail(s0)
```

Any command-line input or output is written as follows:

```
# cp /usr/src/asterisk-addons/configs/cdr_mysql.conf.sample
/etc/asterisk/cdr_mysql.conf
```

New terms and **important** words are shown in bold. Words that you see on the screen, for example, in menus or dialog boxes, appear in the text like this: "Clicking the **Next** button moves you to the next screen".

Warnings or important notes appear in a box like this.

 Tips and tricks appear like this.

Reader feedback

Feedback from our readers is always welcome. Let us know what you think about this book--what you liked or disliked. Reader feedback is important for us as it helps us develop titles that you will really get the most out of.

To send us general feedback, simply email us at feedback@packtpub.com and mention the book's title in the subject of your message.

If there is a topic that you have expertise in and you are interested in either writing or contributing to a book, see our author guide at www.packtpub.com/authors.

Customer support

Now that you are the proud owner of a Packt book, we have a number of things to help you get the most from your purchase.

Downloading the example code

You can download the example code files for this book from your account at http://www. packtpub.com. If you purchased this book elsewhere, you can visit http://www.packtpub. com/support and register to have the files emailed directly to you.

You can download the code files by following these steps:

1. Log in or register to our website using your email address and password.
2. Hover the mouse pointer on the **SUPPORT** tab at the top.
3. Click on **Code Downloads & Errata**.

4. Enter the name of the book in the **Search** box.
5. Select the book for which you're looking to download the code files.
6. Choose from the drop-down menu where you purchased this book from.
7. Click on **Code Download**.

You can also download the code files by clicking on the **Code Files** button on the book's webpage at the Packt Publishing website. This page can be accessed by entering the book's name in the **Search** box. Note that you need to be logged in to your Packt account.

Once the file is downloaded, make sure that you unzip or extract the folder using the latest version of:

- WinRAR / 7-Zip for Windows
- Zipeg / iZip / UnRarX for Mac
- 7-Zip / PeaZip for Linux

The code bundle for the book is also hosted on GitHub at `https://github.com/PacktPublishing/MySQL-8-for-Big-Data`. We also have other code bundles from our rich catalog of books and videos available at `https://github.com/PacktPublishing/`. Check them out!

Downloading the color images of this book

We also provide you with a PDF file that has color images of the screenshots/diagrams used in this book. The color images will help you better understand the changes in the output. You can download this file from `https://www.packtpub.com/sites/default/files/downloads/MySQL8forBigData_ColorImages.pdf`.

Errata

Although we have taken every care to ensure the accuracy of our content, mistakes do happen. If you find a mistake in one of our books, maybe a mistake in the text or the code, we would be grateful if you could report this to us. By doing so, you can save other readers from frustration and help us improve subsequent versions of this book. If you find any errata, report them by visiting `http://www.packtpub.com/submit-errata`, selecting your book, clicking on the **Errata Submission Form** link, and entering the details of your errata. Once your errata are verified, your submission will be accepted and the errata will be uploaded to our website or added to any list of existing errata under the Errata section of that title.

To view the previously submitted errata, go to `https://www.packtpub.com/books/content/support` and enter the name of the book in the search field. The required information will appear under the Errata section.

Piracy

Piracy of copyrighted material on the Internet is an ongoing problem across all media. At Packt, we take the protection of our copyright and licenses very seriously. If you come across any illegal copies of our works in any form on the Internet, do provide us with the location address or the website name immediately, so that we can pursue a remedy.

Contact us at `copyright@packtpub.com` with a link to the suspected pirated material.

We appreciate your help in protecting our authors and our ability to bring you valuable content.

Questions

If you have a problem with any aspect of this book, you can contact us at `questions@packtpub.com`, and we will do our best to address the problem.

1
Introduction to Big Data and MySQL 8

Today we are in the age of digitalization. We are producing enormous amounts of data in many ways--social networking, purchasing at grocery stores, bank/credit card transactions, emails, storing data on clouds, and so on. One of the first questions that comes to mind is: are you getting the utmost out of the collected data? For this data tsunami, we need to have appropriate tools to fetch data in an organized way that can be used in various fields such as scientific research, real-time traffic, fighting crime, fraud detection, digital personalization, and so on. All this data needs to be captured, stored, searched, shared, transferred, analyzed, and visualized.

Analysis of structured, unstructured, or semi-structured ubiquitous data helps us discover hidden patterns, market trends, correlations, personal preferences, and so on. With the help of the right tools to process and analyze, data organization can result in much better marketing plans, additional revenue opportunities, improved customer service, healthier operational efficiency, competitive benefits, and much more.

Every company collects data and uses it; however, to potentially flourish, a company needs to use data more effectively. Every company must carve out direct links to produced data, which can improve business either directly or indirectly.

Okay, now you have Big Data, which is generally being referred to as a large quantity of data, and you are doing analysis--is this what you need? Hold on! The other most critical factor is to successfully monetize the data. So, get ready and fasten your seatbelts to fly in understanding the importance of Big Data!

In this chapter we will learn about below points to find out Big Data's role in today's life and basic installation steps for MySQL 8:

- Importance of Big Data
- Life cycle of Big Data
- What is structured database
- MySQL's basics
- New feature introduced in MySQL 8
- Benefits of using MySQL 8
- How to install MySQL 8
- Evolution of MySQL for Big Data

The importance of Big Data

The importance of Big Data doesn't depend only on how much data you have, it's rather what you are going to do with the data. Data can be sourced and analyzed from unpredictable sources and can be used to address many things. Let's see use cases with real-life importance made on renowned scenarios with the help of Big Data.

The following image helps us understand a Big Data solution serving various industries. Though it's not an extensive list of industries where Big Data has been playing a prominent role in business decisions, let's discuss a few of the industries:

Social media

Social media content is information, and so are engagements such as views, likes, demographics, shares, follows, unique visitors, comments, and downloads. So, in regards to social media and Big Data, they are interrelated. At the end of the day, what matters is how your social media-related efforts contribute to business.

 I came across one wonderful title: *There's No Such Thing as Social Media ROI - It's Called Business ROI.*

One notable example of Big Data possibilities on Facebook is providing insights about consumers lifestyles, search patterns, likes, demographics, purchasing habits, and so on. Facebook stores around 100PBs of data and piles up 500TB of data almost daily. Considering the number of subscribers and data collected, it is expected to be more than 60 zettabytes in the next three years. The more data you have, the more analysis you can have with sophisticated precision approaches for better **Return on Investment** (**ROI**). Information fetched from social media is also leveraged when targeting audiences for attractive and profitable ads.

Facebook has a service called **Graph Search**, which can help you do advanced searches with multiple criteria. For instance, you can search for *people of male gender living in Ahmedabad who work with KNOWARTH Technologies*. Google also helps you refine the search. Such searches and filters are not limited to these; it might also contain school, political views, age, and name. In the same way, you can also try for hotels, photos, songs, and more. So here, you have the business ROI of the Facebook company, which provides Facebook ad services which can be based on specific criteria such as regions, interests, or other specific features of user data. Google also provides a similar platform called **Google AdWords**.

Politics

The era of Big Data has been playing a significant role in politics too; political parties have been using various sources of data to target voters and better their election campaigns. Big Data analytics also made a significant contribution to the 2012 re-election of Barack Obama by enhancing engagement and speaking about the precise things that were significant for voters.

Narendra Modi is considered one of the most technology and social media-savvy politicians in the world! He has almost 500 million views on Google+, 30 million followers on Twitter, and 35 million likes on Facebook! Narendra Modi belongs to the **Bhartiya Janta Party (BJP)**; Big Data analysis carried major responsibility for the BJP party and its associates for their successful Indian General Election in 2014, using open source tools that helped them get in direct touch with their voters. BJP reached their fluctuating voters and negative voters too, as they kept monitoring social media conversations and accordingly sent messages and used tactics to improve their vision for the election campaign.

Narendra Modi made a statement about *prioritizing toilets before temples* seven months earlier, after which the digital team closely monitored social media conversations around this. It was noticed that at least 50% of users were in line with the statement. This was when the opportunity to win the hearts of voters was converted to the mission of Swacch Bharat, which means hygienic India. The results were astonishing; BJP party support rose to around 30% in merely 50 hours.

Science and research

Did you know that with the help of Big Data, human genome decoding, which actually took 10 years to process, is now decoded in hardly a day, and there is almost a 100 times reduction in cost predicted by Moore's Law? Back in the year 2000, when the **Sloan Digital Sky Survey (SDSS)** started gathering astronomical data, it was with a rate of around 200 GB per night, which, at that time, was much higher than the data collected in astronomy history.

National Aeronautics and Space Administration (NASA) uses Big Data extensively considering the huge amount of science and research done. NASA gathers data from across the solar system to reveal unknown information about the universe; its massive collection of data is a prominent asset for science and research, and has been a benefit to humankind in diverse ways. The way NASA fetches data, stores it, and uses it in effective ways is enormous. There are so many use cases of NASA that it would be difficult to elaborate here!

Power and energy

One of the leading energy management companies that helps improve energy consumption with the help of Big Data predictive analysis, which helps build stronger relationships and retaining of customers. This company connects with more than 150 utilities and serves more than 35 million household customers to improve energy usage and reduce costs and carbon emissions. It also provides analytical reports to utility providers, from more than 10 million data points each day, for a holistic overview of usage for analysis. Household customers get these reports in invoices, which provide areas where energy usage can be reduced and directly helps consumers optimize energy costs.

Fraud detection

When it comes to security, fraud detection, or compliance, then Big Data is your soulmate, and precisely if your soulmate helps you in identifying and preventing issues before they strike, then it becomes a sweet spot for business. Most of the time, fraud detection happens a long time after the fraud has happened, when you might have already been damaged. The next steps would be obviously to minimize the impact and improve areas that could help you prevent this from being repeated.

Many companies who are into any type of transaction processing or claims are using fraud detection techniques extensively. Big Data platforms help them analyze transactions, claims, and so on in real-time, along with trends or anomalous behavior to prevent fraudulent activities.

The **National Security Agency** (**NSA**) also does Big Data analytics to foil terrorist plans. With the help of advanced Big Data fraudulent techniques, many security agencies use Big Data tools to predict criminal activity, credit card fraud, catch criminals, and prevent cyber attacks, among others. Day by day, as security, compliance, and fraud change their patterns, accordingly security agencies and fraud transaction techniques are becoming richer to keep a step ahead for such unwanted scenarios.

Healthcare

Nowadays, a wrist-based health tracker is a very common thing; however, with the help of Big Data, it not only shows your personal dashboard or changes over time, but also gives you relevant suggestions based on the medical data it collects to improve your diet, and analytic facts about people like you. So, from simple wrist-based health trackers, there are a lot of signs that can improve the healthcare of a patient. Companies providing these kinds of services also analyze how health is impacted by analyzing trends. Gradually, such wearables are also being used in Critical Care Units to quickly analyze the trend of doctors' immediate remediations.

By leveraging data accumulated from government agencies, social services files, accident reports, and clinical data, hospitals can help evaluate healthcare needs. Geographical statistics based on numerous factors, from population growth and disease rate to enhancing the quality of human life, are compared to determine the availability of medical services, ambulances, emergency services, pandemic plans, and other relevant health services. This can unbox probable environmental hazards, health risks, and trends that are being done by few agencies on a regular basis to forecast flu epidemics.

Business mapping

Netflix has millions of subscribers; it uses Big Data and analytics about a subscriber's habits based on age, gender, and geographical location to customize, which has proven to generate more business as per its expectations.

Amazon, back in 2011, started awarding $5 to its customers who use the Amazon Price Check Mobile App--scanning products in the store, grab a picture, and searching to find the lowest prices. It also had a feature to submit the in-store price for the products. It was then Big Data's role to have all the information on products could can be compared with Amazon products for price comparison and customer trends, and accordingly plan marketing campaigns and offers based on valuable data that was collected to dominate a rapidly developing e-commerce competitive market.

McDonalds has more than 35,000 local restaurants that cater to around 75 million customers in more than 120 countries. It uses Big Data to gain insights to improve customer experience and offers McDonalds key factors such as menu, queue timings, order size, and the pattern of orders by customers, which helps them optimize the effectiveness of their operations and customization based on geographical locations for lucrative business.

There are many real-world Big Data use cases that have changed humanity, technology, predictions, health, science and research, law and order, sports, customer experience, power and energy, financial trading, robotics, and many more fields. Big Data is an integral part of our daily routine, which is not evident all the time, but yes, it plays a significant role in the back to what we do in many ways. It's time to start looking in detail at how the life cycle of Big Data is structured, which would give an inside story of many areas that play a significant role in getting data to a place that might be used for processing.

The life cycle of Big Data

Many organizations are considering Big Data as not only just a buzzword, but a smart system to improve business and get relevant marked information and insights. Big Data is a term that refers to managing huge amounts of complex unprocessed data from diverse sources like databases, social media, images, sensor-driven equipment, log files, human sentiments, and so on. This data can be in a structured, semi-structured, or unstructured form. Thus, to process this data, Big Data tools are used to analyze, which is a difficult and time-intensive process using traditional processing procedures.

The life cycle of Big Data can be segmented into **Volume**, **Variety**, **Velocity**, and **Veracity**--commonly known as the **FOUR V's OF BIG DATA**. Let's look at them quickly and then move on to the four phases of the Big Data life cycle, that is, collecting data, storing data, analyzing data, and governing data.

The following illustrates a few real-world scenarios, which gives us a much better understanding of the four Vs defining Big Data:

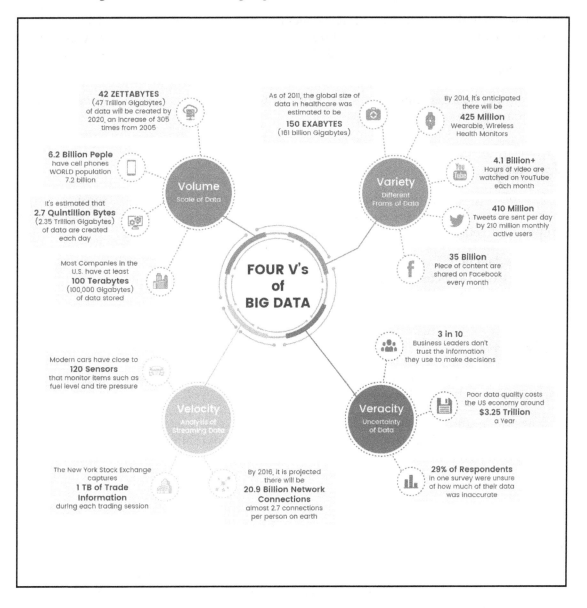

Volume

Volume refers to the vast amount of data generated and stored every second. The size of data in enterprises is not in terabytes--it does an accrual of zettabytes or brontobytes. New Big Data tools are now generally using distributed systems that might be sometimes diversified across the world.

The amount of data generated across the globe by year 2008 is expected to be generated in just a minute by year 2020.

Variety

Variety refers to several types and natures of data such as click streams, text, sensors, images, voice, video, log files, social media conversations, and more. This helps people who scrutinize it to effectively use it for insights.

70% of the data in the world is unstructured such as text, images, voice, and so on. However, earlier structured data was popular for being analyzed, as it fits in files, databases, or such traditional data storing procedures.

Velocity

Velocity refers to the speed of the data generated, ingested, and processed to meet the demands and challenges that exist in the pathway towards evolution and expansion.

New age communication channels such as social media, emails, and mobiles have added velocity to the data in Big Data. To scrutinize around 1TB of trading event information every day for fraud detection is a time sensitive process, where sometimes every minute matters to prevent fraud. Just think of social media conversations going viral in a matter of seconds; analysis helps us get trends on such platforms.

Veracity

Veracity refers to the inconsistency of data that can be found; it can affect the way data is being managed and handled effectively. Managing such data and making it valuable is where Big Data can help.

Quality and accuracy has been a major challenge when we talk about Big Data, as that's what it's all about. The amount of Twitter feeds is an appropriate use case where hashtags, typos, informal text, and abbreviations abound; however, we daily come across scenarios where Big Data does its work in the backend and lets us work with this type of data.

Phases of the Big Data life cycle

The effective use of Big Data with exponential growth in data types and data volumes has the potential to transform economies useful business and marketing information and customer surplus. Big Data has become a key success mantra for current competitive markets for existing companies, and a game changer for new companies in the competition. This all can be proven true if **VALUE FROM DATA** is leveraged. Let's look at the following figure:

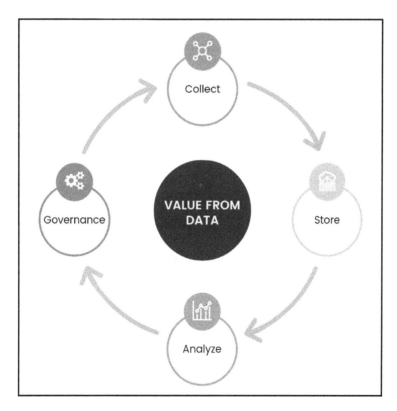

As this figure explains, the Big Data life cycle can be divided into four stages. Let's study them in detail.

Collect

This section is key in a Big Data life cycle; it defines which type of data is captured at the source. Some examples are gathering logs from the server, fetching user profiles, crawling reviews of organizations for sentiment analysis, and order information. Examples that we have mentioned might involve dealing with local language, text, unstructured data, and images, which will be taken care of as we move forward in the Big Data life cycle.

With an increased level of automating data collection streams, organizations that have been classically spending a lot of effort on gathering structured data to analyze and estimate key success data points for business are changing. Mature organizations now use data that was generally ignored because of either its size or format, which, in Big Data terminology, is often referred to as unstructured data. These organizations always try to use the maximum amount of information whether it is structured or unstructured, as for them, data is value.

You can use data to be transferred and consolidated into Big Data platform like **HDFS** (**Hadoop Distributed File System**). Once data is processed with the help of tools like Apache Spark, you can load it back to the MySQL database, which can help you populate relevant data to show which MySQL consists.

With the amount of data volume and velocity increasing, Oracle now has a NoSQL interface for the InnoDB storage engine and MySQL cluster. A MySQL cluster additionally bypasses the SQL layer entirely. Without SQL parsing and optimization, Key-value data can be directly inserted nine times faster into MySQL tables.

Store

In this section, we will discuss storing data that has been collected from various sources. Let's consider an example of crawling reviews of organizations for sentiment analysis, wherein each gathers data from different sites with each of them having data uniquely displayed.

Traditionally, data was processed using the **ETL** (**Extract**, **Transform**, and **Load**) procedure, which used to gather data from various sources, modify it according to the requirements, and upload it to the store for further processing or display. Tools that were every so often used for such scenarios were spreadsheets, relational databases, business intelligence tools, and so on, and sometimes manual effort was also a part of it.

The most common storage used in Big Data platform is HDFS. HDFS also provides **HQL** (**Hive Query Language**), which helps us do many analytical tasks that are traditionally done in business intelligence tools. A few other storage options that can be considered are Apache Spark, Redis, and MongoDB. Each storage option has their own way of working in the backend; however, most storage providers exposes SQL APIs which can be used to do further data analysis.

There might be a case where we need to gather real-time data and showcase in real time, which practically doesn't need the data to be stored for future purposes and can run real-time analytics to produce results based on the requests.

Analyze

In this section, we will discuss how these various data types are being analyzed with a common question starting with *what if...?* The way organizations have evolved with data also has impacted new metadata standards, organizing it for initial detection and reprocessing for structural approaches to be matured on the value of data being created.

Most mature organizations reliably provide accessibility, superiority, and value across business units with a constant automated process of structuring metadata and outcomes to be processed for analysis. A mature data-driven organization's analyzing engine generally works on multiple sources of data and data types, which also includes real-time data.

During the analysis phase, raw data is processed, for which MySQL has Map/Reduce jobs in Hadoop, to analyze and give the output. With MySQL data lying in HDFS, it can be accessed by the rest of the ecosystem of Big Data platform-related tools for further analysis.

Governance

Value for data cannot be expected for a business without an established governance policy in practice. In the absence of a mature data governance policy, businesses can experience misinterpreted information, which could ultimately cause unpredictable damages to the business. With the help of Big Data governance, an organization can achieve consistent, precise, and actionable awareness of data.

Data governance is all about managing data to meet compliance, privacy, regulatory, legal, and anything that is specifically obligatory as per business requirements. For data governance, continuous monitoring, studying, revising, and optimizing the quality of the process should also respect data security needs. So far, data governance has been taken with ease where Big Data is concerned; however, with data growing rapidly and being used in various places, this has drawn attention to data governance. It is gradually becoming a must-considerable factor for any Big Data project.

As we have now got a good understanding of the life cycle of Big Data, let's take a closer look at MySQL basics, benefits, and some of the excellent features introduced.

Structured databases

Many organizations use a structured database to store their data in an organized way with the formatted repository. Basically, data in a structured database has a fixed field, predefined data length, and defines what kind of data is to be stored such as numbers, date, time, address, currency, and so on. In short, the structure is already defined before data gets inserted, which gives a cleaner idea of what data can reside there. The key advantage of using a structured database is data being easily stored, queried, and analyzed.

An unstructured database is the opposite of this; it has no identifiable internal structure. It can have a massive unorganized agglomerate or various objects. Mainly, the source of structured data is machine-generated, which means information generated from the machine and without human intervention, whereas unstructured data is human-generated data. Organizations use structured databases for data such as ATM transactions, airline reservations, inventory systems, and so on. In the same way, some organizations use unstructured data such as emails, multimedia content, word processing documents, webpages, business documents, and so on.

Structured databases are traditional databases that used by many enterprises for more than 40 years. However, in the modern world, data volume is becoming bigger and bigger and a common need has taken its place--data analytics. Analytics is becoming difficult with structured databases as the volume and velocity of digital data grows faster by the day; we need to find a way to achieve such needs in an effective and efficient way. The most common database that is used as a structured database in the open source world is MySQL. You will learn how to achieve this structured database as Big Data that makes complex analysis easy. First, let's look into some insights of MySQL in the next section.

Basics of MySQL

MySQL is a well-known open source structured database because of its performance, easiness to use, and reliability. This is the most common choice of web applications for a relational database. In the current market, thousands of web-based applications rely on MySQL including giant industries like Facebook, Twitter, and Wikipedia. It has also proven the database choice for **SaaS** (**Software as a Service**) based applications like SugarCRM, Supply Dynamics, Workday, RightNow, Omniture, and Zimbra. MySQL was developed by MySQL AB, a Swedish company, and now it is distributed and supported by Oracle Corporation.

MySQL as a relational database management system

Data in a relational database is stored in an organized format so that information can be retrieved easily. Data will be stored in different tables made up of rows and columns. However, the relationship also can be built between different tables that efficiently store huge data and effectively retrieve the selected data. This provides database operations with tremendous speed and flexibility.

As a relational database, MySQL has capabilities to establish relationships with different tables such as one to many, many to one, and one to one by providing primary keys, foreign keys, and indexes. We can also perform joins between tables to retrieve exact information like inner joins and outer joins.

SQL (**Structured Query Language**) is used as an interface to interact with the relational data in MySQL. SQL is an **ANSI** (**American National Standard Institute**) standard language which we can operate with data like creation, deletion, updating, and retrieval.

Licensing

Many industries prefer open source technology for their flexibility and cost-saving features, while MySQL has put its footprint in the market by becoming the most popular relational database for web applications. Open source means that you can view the source of MySQL and customize it based on your needs without any cost. You can download the source or binary files from its site and use them accordingly.

The MySQL server is covered under the **GNU** (**General Public License**), which means that we can freely use it for web applications, study its source code, and modify accordingly. It also has the enterprise edition as well with advanced features included. Many enterprises purchase enterprise support from MySQL to get assistance on various issues.

Reliability and scalability

MySQL has great reliability to perform well without requiring extensive troubleshooting due to bottlenecks or other slowdowns. It also incorporates a number of performance-enhanced mechanisms such as index support, load utilities, and memory caches. MySQL uses InnoDB as a storage engine, which provides highly efficient ACID-compliant transactional capabilities that assure high performance and scalability. To handle the rapidly growing database, MySQL Replication and cluster helps scale out the database.

Platform compatibility

MySQL has great cross-platform availability that makes it more popular. It is flexible to run on major platforms such as RedHat, Fedora, Ubuntu, Debian, Solaris, Microsoft Windows, and Apple macOS. It also provides **Application Programming Interface** (**APIs**) to interconnect with various programming languages such as C, C++, C#, PHP, Java, Ruby, Python, and Perl.

Releases

Here is a list of major releases of MySQL so far:

- Version 5.0 GA was released on 19th October, 2005
- Version 5.1 GA was released on 14th November, 2008
- Version 5.5 GA was released on 3rd December, 2010
- Version 5.6 GA was released on 5th February, 2013
- Version 5.7 GA was released on 21st October, 2015

Now it's time for the major version release--MySQL 8--which was announced on 12th September, 2016 and is still in the development milestone mode. Let's see what's new in this latest release.

New features in MySQL 8

The MySQL database development team has recently announced its major release as MySQL 8 **Development Milestone Release** (**DMR**) with significant updates and fixes for problems that were much needed in this change of Big Data.

You might be wondering why it's 8 after 5.7! Did the intermediate versions, that is, 6 and 7, missed out? Of course this was not the case; actually 6.0 was preserved as part of the changeover to a more frequent and timely release while 7.0 for the clustering version of MySQL.

Let's see some exciting features introduced in this latest version, as depicted in the following diagram:

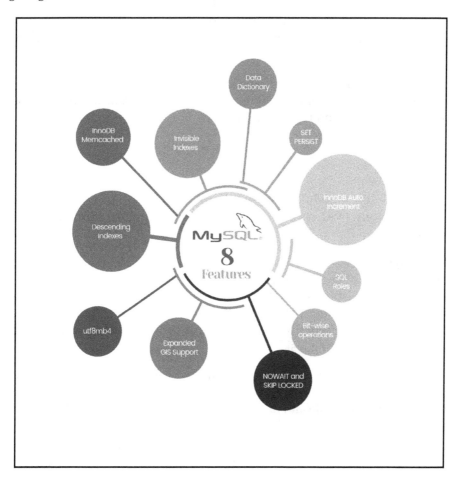

It's time to look at MySQL 8 features in detail, which makes us excited and convinced about the reasons for a major version upgrade of MySQL.

Transactional data dictionary

Up until the previous version, the MySQL data dictionary was stored in different metadata files and non-transactional tables, but from this version, it will have a transactional data dictionary to store the information about the database. No more `.frm`, `.trg`, or `.par` files. All information will be stored in the database, which removes the cost of performing heavy file operations. There were numerous issues with filesystem metadata storage like the vulnerability of the filesystem, exorbitant file operations, difficult to handle crash recovery failures, or replication; it was also difficult to add new feature-related metadata. Now this upgrade has made it simple by storing information in a centralized manner, and will have improved performance as this data dictionary object can be cached in memory, similar to other database objects.

This data dictionary will have data that is needed for SQL query execution such as catalog information, character sets, collations, column types, indexes, database information, tables, store procedures, functions and triggers, and so on.

Roles

In MySQL 8, the privileges module has been improved by introducing roles, which means a collection of permissions. Now we can create roles with a number of privileges and assign to multiple users.

The problem with the previous version was that we were not able to define generic permissions for a group of users and each user has individual privileges. Suppose if there are 1,000 users already existing that have common privileges, and you want to remove the write permissions for all of these 1,000 users, what would you have done in the previous version? You would take the lengthy approach of updating each and every user, right? Arrgh... that's a time-consuming task.

Now with MySQL 8, it is easy to update any change in privileges. Roles will define all the required privileges and this role will be assigned to those 1,000 users. We just need to make any privilege changes in the role and all users will automatically inherit the respective privileges.

Roles can be created, deleted, grant or revoked permission, granted or revoked from the user account, and can specify the default role within the current session.

InnoDB auto increment

MySQL 8 has changed the auto-increment counter value store mechanism. Previously, it was stored in the memory, which was quite difficult to manage during server restarts or server crashes. However, now the auto-increment counter value is written into the redo log whenever the value gets changed and, on each checkpoint, it will be saved in the system table, which makes it persistent across the server restart.

With the previous version, updating the auto-increment value may have caused duplicate entry errors. Suppose if you updated the value of auto-increment in the middle of the sequence with a larger than the current maximum value, then but subsequent insert operations could not identify the unused values, which could cause a duplicate entry issue. This has been prevented by persisting the auto-increment value, hence subsequent insert operations can get the new value and allocate it properly.

If server restart happened, the auto-increment value was lost with the previous version as it was stored in memory and InnoDB needed to execute a query to find out the maximum used value. This has been changed, as the newer version has the capability to persist its value across the server restart. During the server restart, InnoDB initializes the counter value in memory using the maximum value stored in the data dictionary table. In case of server crashes, InnoDB initializes the auto-increment counter value that is bigger than the data dictionary table and the redo log.

Supporting invisible indexes

MySQL 8 provides you with a feature to make indexes invisible. These kind of indexes cannot be used by the optimizer. In case you want to test the query performance without indexes, using this feature you can do so by making them invisible rather than dropping and re-adding an index. This is a pretty handy feature when indexing is supposed to be dropped and recreated on huge datasets.

All indexes are visible by default. To make them invisible or visible, `INVISIBLE` and `VISIBLE` keywords are used respectively, as described in the following code snippet:

```
ALTER TABLE table1 ALTER INDEX ix_table1_col1 INVISIBLE;
ALTER TABLE table1 ALTER INDEX ix_table1_col1 VISIBLE;
```

Improving descending indexes

Descending indexes existed in version 5.7 too, but they were scanned in reverse order, which caused performance barriers. To improve performance, MySQL 8 has optimized this and scanned descending indexes in forward order, which has drastically improved performance. It also brings multiple column indexes for the optimizer when the most efficient scan order has ascending order for some columns, and descending order for other columns.

SET PERSIST

Server variables can be configured globally and dynamically while the server is running. There are numerous system variables that we can set using `SET GLOBAL`:

```
SET GLOBAL max_connections = 1000;
```

However, such settings will be lost after server restart. To avoid this, MySQL 8 has introduced the `SET PERSIST` variant, which preserves variables across a server restart:

```
SET PERSIST max_connections = 1000;
```

Expanded GIS support

Until the previous version, it supported only one coordinate system, a unitless 2D place that was not referenced to a position on earth. Now MySQL 8 has added support for a **Spatial Reference System** (**SRS**) with geo-referenced ellipsoids and 2D projections. SRS helps assign coordinates to a location and establishes relationships between sets of such coordinates. This spatial data can be managed in data dictionary storage as the `ST_SPATIAL_REFERENCE_SYSTEMS` table.

The default character set

The default character set has been changed from latin1 to UTF8. UTF8 is the dominating character set, though it hadn't been a default one in prior versions of MySQL. Along with the character set default, collation has been changed from latin1_swedish_ci to utf8mb4_800_ci_ai. With these changes globally accepted, character sets and collations are now based on UTF8; one of the common reasons is because there are around 21 different languages supported by UTF8, which makes systems provide multilingual support.

Extended bit-wise operations

In MySQL 5.7, bit-wise operations and functions were working for BigInt (64-bit integer) data types only. We needed to pass BIGINT as an argument and it would return the result as BIGINT. In short, it had maximum range up to 64 bits to perform operations. A user needs to do conversion to the BIGINT data type in case they want to perform it on other data types. This typecasting was not feasible for data types larger than 64 bits as it would truncate the actual value, which resulted in inaccuracy of data.

MySQL 8 has improved bit-wise operations by enabling support for other binary data types such as Binary, VarBinary, and BLOB. This makes it possible to perform bit-wise operations on larger than 64-bit data. No more typecasting needed! This allows the taking of arguments and returning results larger than 64 bits.

InnoDB Memcached

Multiple get operations are now possible with the InnoDB Memcached plugin, which will really help in improving the read performance. Now, multiple key value pairs can be fetched in a single Memcached query. Frequent communication traffic has also been minimized as we can get multiple data in a single shot. We will be referring the Memcached plugin in detail in Chapter 4, *Using Memcached with MySQL 8*.

Range queries are also supported by the InnoDB Memcached plugin. It simplifies range searches by specifying a particular range and retrieves values within this range.

NOWAIT and SKIP LOCKED

When rows are locked by other transactions that you are trying to access, then you need to wait for that transaction to release the lock on the same row so that you can access it accordingly. To avoid waiting for the other transaction, InnoDB has added support of the NOWAIT and SKIP LOCKED options. NOWAIT will return immediately with an error in case the requested row is locked rather than going into the waiting mode, and SKIP LOCKED will skip the locked row and never wait to acquire the row lock. Hence, SKIP LOCKED will not consider the locked row in the resulting set:

```
SELECT * FROM table1 WHERE id = 5 FOR UPDATE NOWAIT;
SELECT * FROM table1 FOR UPDATE SKIP LOCKED;
```

Benefits of using MySQL

Whether you are a developer or an enterprise, you would obviously choose the technology that provides good benefits and results when compared to other similar products. MySQL provides numerous advantages as the first choice in this competitive market. It has various powerful features available that make it a more comprehensive database. Let's now go through some benefits of using MySQL.

Security

The first thing that comes to mind is securing data, because nowadays data has become precious and can impact business continuity if legal obligations are not met; in fact, it can be so bad that it can close down your business in no time. MySQL is the most secure and reliable database management system used by many well-known enterprises such as Facebook, Twitter, and Wikipedia. It really provides a good security layer that protects sensitive information from intruders. MySQL gives access control management so that granting and revoking required access from the user is easy. Roles can also be defined with a list of permissions that can be granted or revoked for the user. All user passwords are stored in an encrypted format using plugin-specific algorithms.

Scalability

Day by day, the mountain of data is growing because of extensive use of technology in numerous ways. Due to this, load average is going through the roof. For some cases, it is unpredictable that data cannot exceed up to some limit or number of users will not go out of bounds. Scalable databases would be a preferable solution so that, at any point, we can meet unexpected demands to scale. MySQL is a rewarding database system for its scalability, which can scale horizontally and vertically; in terms of data and load of application queries across multiple MySQL servers is quite feasible. It is pretty easy to add horsepower to the MySQL cluster to handle the load.

An open source relational database management system

MySQL is an open source database management system that makes debugging, upgrading, and enhancing the functionality fast and easy. You can view the source and make the changes accordingly and use it in your own way. You can also distribute an extended version of MySQL but it requires a license for this.

High performance

MySQL gives high speed transaction processing with optimal speed. It can cache the results, which boosts read performance. Replication and clustering enables for better concurrency and manages the workload. Database indexes also accelerate the performance of SELECT query statements for large amounts of data. To enhance performance, MySQL 8 has included indexes in performance schema to speed up data retrieval.

High availability

Today, in the world of competitive marketing, an organization's key point is to have their system up and running. Any failure or downtime directly impacts business and revenue; hence, high availability is a factor that cannot be overlooked. MySQL is quite reliable and has constant availability using cluster and replication configurations. Cluster servers instantly handle failures and manage the failover part to keep your system available almost all the time. If one server gets down, it will redirect the user's request to another node and perform the requested operation.

Cross-platform capabilities

MySQL provides cross-platform flexibility that can run on various platforms such as Windows, Linux, Solaris, OS 2, and so on. It has great API support for the all major languages, which makes it very easy to integrate with languages like PHP, C++, Perl, Python, Java, and so on. It is also part of the **LAMP** (**Linux Apache MySQL PHP**) server that is used worldwide for web applications.

It's now time to get our hands dirty and take a look at MySQL 8; let's start with the installation of MySQL 8 on a Linux platform in our case. We prefer MySQL 8 on a Linux operating system as that has been a common use case across many organizations. You are able to use it on other platforms that MySQL supports, such as Windows, Solaris, HP-UNIX, and so on. Linux provides various ways to install the MySQL server, as follows:

- RPM package
- YUM repository
- APT repository
- SLES repository
- Debian package
- TAR package
- Compiling and installing from the source code

We will install MySQL 8 with an RPM-based Linux distribution provided by Oracle; however, you can choose either of the approaches mentioned here. Let's see how to obtain and install it using the RPM package.

Installing MySQL 8

Let's first see from where to download MySQL 8 and a basic understanding of package structures to choose which one is appropriate. We start by obtaining MySQL 8 and will then quickly glance through installation and verification.

Obtaining MySQL 8

Download the RPM package of the MySQL Community Server from its download page (`https://dev.mysql.com/downloads/mysql/8.0.html`). There are various variants available based on the operating system and its architecture version. It comes with different packages that can be described by the package name. The following syntax is followed by the package name:

```
packageName-version-distribution-archType.rpm
```

Package Name: Name of the package, like `myql-community-server`, `mysql-community-client`, `mysql-community-libs`

Version: Describes the version-particular package

Distribution: This says the package is intended for which Linux distribution based on its abbreviation

Abbreviation	Linux distribution
el6, el7	Red Hat Enterprise Linux/Oracle Linux/CentOS 6, 7
fc24, fc25	Fedora 24 or 25
sles12	SUSE Linux Enterprise Server 12
solaris11	Oracle Solaris 11

Arch Type: Describes the processor type for which the package was built, like x86_64, i686, and so on

MySQL 8 installation

Once you have the RPM packages, just install it using the following command. This will place the required files and folder under the system directories:

```
rpm -vih <package-name>.rpm
```

For the standard installation, it requires only `mysql-community-common`, `mysql-community-libs`, `mysql-community-client`, and `mysql-community-server` packages. Look at the following screenshot for the installation process:

```
[root@ip-172-31-43-204 tmp]# rpm -ivh mysql-community-common-8.0.1-0.1.dmr.el6.x86_64.rpm
warning: mysql-community-common-8.0.1-0.1.dmr.el6.x86_64.rpm: Header V3 DSA/SHA1 Signature, key ID 5072e1f5: NOKEY
Preparing...                          ################################# [100%]
Updating / installing...
   1:mysql-community-common-8.0.1-0.1.################################# [100%]
[root@ip-172-31-43-204 tmp]# rpm -ivh mysql-community-libs-8.0.1-0.1.dmr.el6.x86_64.rpm
warning: mysql-community-libs-8.0.1-0.1.dmr.el6.x86_64.rpm: Header V3 DSA/SHA1 Signature, key ID 5072e1f5: NOKEY
Preparing...                          ################################# [100%]
Updating / installing...
   1:mysql-community-libs-8.0.1-0.1.dm################################# [100%]
[root@ip-172-31-43-204 tmp]# rpm -ivh mysql-community-client-8.0.1-0.1.dmr.el6.x86_64.rpm
warning: mysql-community-client-8.0.1-0.1.dmr.el6.x86_64.rpm: Header V3 DSA/SHA1 Signature, key ID 5072e1f5: NOKEY
Preparing...                          ################################# [100%]
Updating / installing...
   1:mysql-community-client-8.0.1-0.1.################################# [100%]
[root@ip-172-31-43-204 tmp]# rpm -vih mysql-community-server-8.0.1-0.1.dmr.el6.x86_64.rpm
warning: mysql-community-server-8.0.1-0.1.dmr.el6.x86_64.rpm: Header V3 DSA/SHA1 Signature, key ID 5072e1f5: NOKEY
Preparing...                          ################################# [100%]
Updating / installing...
   1:mysql-community-server-8.0.1-0.1.################################# [100%]
```

After the successful installation, just check its version to validate if it's installed properly and can be accessible:

```
[root@ip-172-31-43-204 tmp]# mysql --version
mysql  Ver 8.0.1-dmr for Linux on x86_64 (MySQL Community Server (GPL))
[root@ip-172-31-43-204 tmp]#
```

The next step is to reset the temporary password during post-installation. MySQL will restrict you to use the database before changing this temporary password. A temporary password will be generated by MySQL and available in its log file. To retrieve a temporary password, you need to open the `/var/log/mysql/mysqld.log` file and search for the `temporary password` keyword.

Copy this and try to connect to MySQL with the following command:

```
[root@ip-172-31-43-204 tmp]# mysql -u root -p
Enter password:
Welcome to the MySQL monitor.  Commands end with ; or \g.
Your MySQL connection id is 8
Server version: 8.0.1-dmr

Copyright (c) 2000, 2017, Oracle and/or its affiliates. All rights reserved.

Oracle is a registered trademark of Oracle Corporation and/or its
affiliates. Other names may be trademarks of their respective
owners.

Type 'help;' or '\h' for help. Type '\c' to clear the current input statement.

mysql>
```

As shown in the preceding screenshot, you will land on a MySQL command prompt, where you can execute the following query to reset the password:

```
ALTER USER 'root'@'localhost' IDENTIFIED BY '<NEW_PASSWORD>';
```

MySQL service commands

Let's look at a few MySQL basic commands:

- To start the MySQL service, perform the following command:

  ```
  service mysqld start
  ```

- To stop the MySQL service, perform the following command:

  ```
  service mysqld stop
  ```

- To check the status of MySQL service whether it is running or not, perform the following command:

  ```
  service mysqld status
  ```

Evolution of MySQL for Big Data

Most enterprises have used MySQL as a relational database for many decades. There is a large amount of data stored, which is used either for transactions or analysis on the data that is collected and generated, and this is where Big Data analytic tools need to be implemented. This is now possible with MySQL integration with Hadoop. Using Hadoop, data can be stored in a distributed storage engine and you can also implement the Hadoop cluster for the distributed analytical engine for Big Data analytics. Hadoop is most preferred for its massive parallel processing and powerful computation. With the combination of MySQL and Hadoop, it is now possible to have real-time analytics where Hadoop can store the data and work in parallel with MySQL to show the end results in real time; this helps address many use cases like GIS information, which has been explained in the *Introducing MySQL 8* section of this chapter. We have seen the Big Data life cycle previously where data can be transformed to generate analytic results. Let's see how MySQL fits in to the life cycle.

The following diagram illustrates how MySQL 8 is mapped to each of the four stages of the Big Data life cycle:

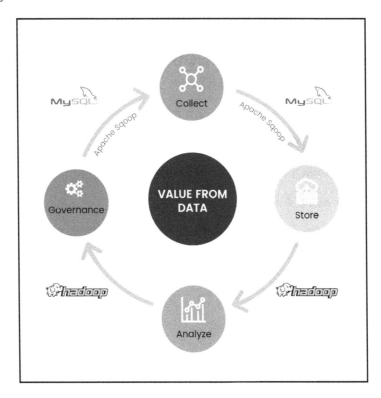

Acquiring data in MySQL

With the volume and velocity of data, it becomes difficult to transfer data in MySQL with optimal performance. To avoid this, Oracle has developed the NoSQL API to store data in the InnoDB storage engine. This will not do any kind of SQL parsing and optimization, hence, key/value data can be directly written to the MySQL tables with high speed transaction responses without sacrificing ACID guarantees. The MySQL cluster also supports different NoSQL APIs for Node.js, Java, JPA, HTTP/REST, and C++. We will explore this in detail later in the book, however, we need to keep in mind that using the NoSQL API, we can enable the faster processing of data and transactions in MySQL.

Organizing data in Hadoop

The next step is to organize data in the Hadoop filesystem once the data has been acquired and loaded to MySQL. Big Data requires some processing to produce analysis results where Hadoop is used to perform highly parallel processing. Hadoop is also a highly scalable distributed framework and is powerful in terms of computation. Here, the data is consolidated from different sources to process the analysis. To transfer the data between MySQL tables to HDFS, Apache Sqoop will be leveraged.

Analyzing data

Now it's time for analyzing data! This is the phase where MySQL data will be processed using the map reduce algorithm of Hadoop. We can use other analysis tools such as Apache Hive or Apache Pig to do similar analytical results. We can also perform custom analysis that can be executed on Hadoop, which returns the results set with the data analyzed and processed.

Results of analysis

The results that were analyzed from our previous phases are loaded back into MySQL, which can be done with the help of Apache Sqoop. Now MySQL has the analysis result that can be consumed by business intelligence tools such as Oracle BI Solution, Jasper Soft, Talend, and so on or other traditional ways using web applications that can generate various analytical reports and, if required, do real-time processing.

This is how MySQL fits easily into a Big Data solution. This architecture makes structured databases handle the Big Data analysis. To understand how to achieve this, refer to `Chapter 9`, *Case study: Part I - Apache Sqoop for Exchanging Data between MySQL and Hadoop*, and `Chapter 10`, *Case study: Part II - Realtime event processing using MySQL applier*, which cover a couple of real-world use cases where we discuss using MySQL 8 extensively and solving business problems to generate value from data.

Summary

In this chapter, we discussed Big Data and its importance in various industries. We also looked into different Big Data segments and their life cycle phases including collecting, storing, analyzing, and governance. We discussed structured databases and why we require a structured database for Big Data. We looked at major features of the MySQL database and explored the newly added features in the MySQL 8 version. Then, we discussed the major benefits of using MySQL and learned how to install MySQL 8 in the Linux system using the RPM package. Finally, we understood how MySQL can be used in Big Data analysis and how it can fit within the Big Data life cycle phases with the help of Hadoop and Apache Sqoop.

In the next chapter, you will learn different query techniques with MySQL 8 including joins and aggregating datasets.

2
Data Query Techniques in MySQL 8

In Chapter 1, *Introduction to Big Data and MySQL 8*, we saw an overview of big data and MySQL 8 along with new features of MySQL 8 followed by the installation of MySQL 8. In this chapter, we will explore data query techniques. This chapter assumes that you have gone through the previous chapter and are familiar with MySQL 8 and how to install MySQL 8.

In this chapter, we will cover the following important topics for MySQL 8 query techniques:

- Overview of SQL
- Database storage engines and types
- Select statements in MySQL
- Insert and update statements in SQL
- Transactions in MySQL
- Aggregating data in MySQL 8
- JSON Data Type and selecting and updating in JSON Data Type

Before we move on to the details, let's have an overview of SQL with respect to MySQL.

Overview of SQL

Structured Query Language (**SQL**) is used to manipulate, retrieve, insert, update, and delete data in **relational database management system** (**RDBMS**). To make it simpler, SQL tells the database what to do and exactly what it needs. SQL is a standard language that all RDBMS systems such as MySQL, MS Access, MS SQL, Oracle, Postgres, and others use.

Using SQL, the user can access, define and manipulate the data from MySQL. We can leverage SQL modules, libraries, and precompilers to embed with the other languages which help in creating/dropping databases and tables, manage view, stored procedures, function etc. in a database. Using SQL, we can also manage permissions on tables, procedures and different views.

The following are a few important SQL commands that we explain in detail later in the chapter:

- **SELECT**: Extracts data from a database
- **UPDATE**: Updates data from a database
- **DELETE**: Removes existing records from a database
- **INSERT INTO**: Add new information into a database
- **CREATE DATABASE**: Creates a new database
- **ALTER DATABASE**: Modifies or change characteristics of a database
- **DROP DATABASE**: Delete a database
- **CREATE TABLE**: Creates a new table
- **ALTER TABLE**: Modifies or change characteristics of a table
- **DROP TABLE**: Deletes a table
- **CREATE INDEX**: Creates an index
- **DROP INDEX**: Remove an index

Database storage engines and types

Let's have a look at different storage engine of MySQL database. This is an important section to understand before we jump into data query techniques, as storage engines play an important role in data query techniques. MySQL stores data in the database as a subdirectory. In each database, data is stored as tables and each table definition information is being stored in a file with extension as `.frm` with the same name as the table name. Suppose if we create a new table as `admin_user` then it will store all table definition related information in `admin_user.frm` file.

We can see information related to a table with the use of SHOW TABLE STATUS command. Let's try to execute this command for `admin_user` table and pull the information.

```
mysql> SHOW TABLE STATUS LIKE 'admin_user' \G;
*************************** 1. row ***************************
       Name: admin_user
     Engine: InnoDB
    Version: 10
 Row_format: Dynamic
       Rows: 2
Avg_row_length: 8192
Data_length: 16384
Max_data_length: 0
Index_length: 16384
  Data_free: 0
Auto_increment: 3
Create_time: 2017-06-19 14:46:49
Update_time: 2017-06-19 15:15:08
 Check_time: NULL
  Collation: utf8_general_ci
   Checksum: NULL
Create_options:
    Comment: Admin User Table
1 row in set (0.00 sec)
```

This command shows that this is an InnoDB table with the column name `Engine`. There is additional information that you can refer for other purposes like the number of rows, index length, and so on.

The storage engine helps to handle different SQL operations for the various table types. Each storage engine has its own advantages and disadvantages. The choice of storage engine would always depend on the needs. It is important to understand features of each storage engine and choose the most appropriate one for your tables to maximize the performance of the database. In MySQL 8, whenever we create a new table then default storage engine is set as InnoDB.

We can say plug and play kind of storage engine architecture used by MySQL Server because we can easily load and unload the storage engines from the MySQL Server. We can see all supported storage engines with the help of SHOW ENGINES command. This will provide enough information as the storage engine is supported by MySQL Server or not, what is the default storage engine used by MySQL Server. Let's execute this command and pull that information.

```
mysql> SHOW ENGINES \G;
*************************** 1. row ***************************
      Engine: InnoDB
     Support: DEFAULT
     Comment: Supports transactions, row-level locking, and foreign keys
Transactions: YES
          XA: YES
  Savepoints: YES
*************************** 2. row ***************************
      Engine: MRG_MYISAM
     Support: YES
     Comment: Collection of identical MyISAM tables
Transactions: NO
          XA: NO
  Savepoints: NO
*************************** 3. row ***************************
      Engine: MEMORY
     Support: YES
     Comment: Hash based, stored in memory, useful for temporary tables
Transactions: NO
          XA: NO
  Savepoints: NO
*************************** 4. row ***************************
      Engine: BLACKHOLE
     Support: YES
     Comment: /dev/null storage engine (anything you write to it disappears)
Transactions: NO
          XA: NO
  Savepoints: NO
*************************** 5. row ***************************
      Engine: MyISAM
     Support: YES
     Comment: MyISAM storage engine
Transactions: NO
          XA: NO
  Savepoints: NO
*************************** 6. row ***************************
      Engine: CSV
     Support: YES
     Comment: CSV storage engine
```

```
 Transactions: NO
           XA: NO
   Savepoints: NO
*************************** 7. row ***************************
       Engine: ARCHIVE
      Support: YES
      Comment: Archive storage engine
 Transactions: NO
           XA: NO
   Savepoints: NO
*************************** 8. row ***************************
       Engine: PERFORMANCE_SCHEMA
      Support: YES
      Comment: Performance Schema
 Transactions: NO
           XA: NO
   Savepoints: NO
*************************** 9. row ***************************
       Engine: FEDERATED
      Support: NO
      Comment: Federated MySQL storage engine
 Transactions: NULL
           XA: NULL
   Savepoints: NULL
9 rows in set (0.00 sec)
```

InnoDB

In MySQL 8, **InnoDB** is the default storage engine broadly used out of all other available storage engines. InnoDB was released with MySQL 5.1 as a plugin in 2008 and this is considered as default storage engine from the version 5.5 and later. InnoDB has been taken over by Oracle Corporation in October 2005, from the *Innobase Oy*, which is a Finland-based company.

InnoDB tables support ACID-compliant commits, rollback, and crash recovery capabilities to protect user data. It also supports row-level locking, which helps with better concurrency and performance. InnoDB stores data in clustered indexes to reduce I/O operations for the all SQL select queries based on the primary key. InnoDB also supports FOREIGN KEY constraints that allows better data integrity for the database. The maximum size of an InnoDB table can scale up to 256 TB, which should be good enough to serve many big data use cases.

Important notes about InnoDB

Executing a simple statement like `SELECT count(*) FROM [table name]` without having indexes in place would be very slow as it does a full table scan to retrieve data. If you want to use count query frequently in the InnoDB table, it is suggested you create triggers on insert and delete operations, after which you can increase or decrease counters when records are inserted or deleted, which would help you achieve better performance.

 MySQL Dump, which is used to take backup, is too slow with InnoDB. You can turn on the flags--opt--compress during `mysqldump`, which actually compresses data before taking a dump of your MySQL database/table.

InnoDB is a **multiversion concurrency control** (**MVCC**) storage engine that keeps information of old versions of changed rows to support the transaction and rollback features, which comes in very handy in case of data integrity or failure.

To optimize InnoDB table performance, the following are a few settings that we can use in `my.cnf` settings. However, it would vary based on your environment and databases.

- `innodb_open_files=300`: This defines the maximum number of open files which it can keep open while working with the `innodb_file_per_table` mode.
- `innodb_buffer_pool_size = 128M`: This specifies the pool size in memory which can be used to cache the indexes and table data. This is one of the important aspects to tune the InnoDB table. We can increase this value based on RAM size on the server.
- `innodb_thread_concurrency = 8`: This setting is used for a number of concurrent threads to be used to process the request that is derived based on the number of CPUs available.

MyISAM

MyISAM was the default storage engine for MySQL prior to 5.5 1. MyISAM storage engine tables do not support ACID-compliant as opposed to InnoDB. MyISAM tables support table level locking only, so MyISAM tables are not transaction-safe. MyISAM tables are optimized for compression and speed. MyISAM is generally used when you need to have primarily read operations with minimal transaction data. The maximum size of a MyISAM table can grow up to 256 TB, which helps in use cases like data analytics.

Important notes about MyISAM tables

MyISAM supports full-text indexing, which can help in complex search operations. Using full-text indexes, we can index data stored in BLOB and TEXT data types. We will have a detailed look at full-text indexing in Chapter 3, *Indexing your data for high-performing queries*.

Due to low overhead, MyISAM uses a simpler structure, which provides good performance; however, it cannot help much for good performance when there is a need for better concurrency and use cases that don't fit the need for heavy read operations. The most common performance problem of MyISAM is table locking, which can stick your concurrent queued queries as it locks the table for any other operation till the earlier one is not executed.

A MyISAM table doesn't support transactions and foreign keys. It seems that because of these constraints, MySQL 8's system schema tables now use InnoDB tables instead of MyISAM tables.

Memory

A memory storage engine is generally known as a heap storage engine. It is used for extremely fast access to data. This storage engine stores data in the RAM so that it wouldn't need I/O operations. As it stores data in the RAM, all data is lost upon server restart. This table is basically used for temporary tables or the lookup table. This engine supports table-level locking, which limits high write concurrency.

Important notes about memory tables are as follows:

- As memory table stores data in the RAM, which has a very limited storage capacity; if you try to write too much data into the memory table, it will start swapping data into the disk and then you lose the benefits of the memory storage engine.
- These tables don't support TEXT and BLOB data types, even such data types might not be required as it has limited storage capacity.
- This storage engine can be used to cache the results; lookup tables, for example, or postal codes and state names.
- Memory tables support B-tree indexes and Hash indexes.

Archive

This storage engine is used to store large amounts of historical data without any indexes. Archive tables do not have any storage limitations. The archive storage engine is optimized for high insert operations and also supports row-level locking. These tables store data in a compressed and small format. The archive engine does not support DELETE or UPDATE operations; it only allows INSERT, REPLACE, and SELECT operations.

Blackhole

This storage engine accepts data but does not store it. It discards data after every INSERT instead of storing it.

The following example shows the BLACKHOLE table process:

```
mysql> CREATE TABLE user(id INT, name CHAR(10)) ENGINE = BLACKHOLE;
Query OK, 0 rows affected (0.07 sec)
mysql> INSERT INTO USER VALUES(1,'Kandarp'),(2,'Chintan');
Query OK, 2 rows affected (0.00 sec)
Records: 2 Duplicates: 0 Warnings: 0
mysql> SELECT * FROM USER;
Empty set (0.00 sec)
```

Now what is the use of this storage engine? Why would anybody use it? Why would we run an INSERT query that doesn't insert anything into the table?

This engine is useful for replication with large amount of servers. A blackhole storage engine acts as a filter server between the master and slave server, which do not store any data but only apply replicate-do-* and replicate-ignore-* rules and write a binlogs. These binlogs are used to perform replication in slave servers. We will discuss this in detail in Chapter 7, *Replication for building highly available solutions*.

CSV

The CSV engine stores data in the `.csv` file type using the comma-separated values format. This engine extracts data from the database and copies it to `.csv` out of the database. If you create a CSV file from the spreadsheet and copy it into the MYSQL data folder server, it can read the data using the select query. Similarly, if you write data in the table, an external program can read it from the CSV file. This storage engine is used for the exchange of data between software or applications. A CSV table does not support indexing and partitioning. All columns in the CSV storage engine need to be defined with the `NOT NULL` attribute to avoid errors during table creation.

Merge

This storage engine is also known as a `MRG_MyISAM` storage engine. This storage engine merges a MyISAM table and creates it to be referred to a single view. For a merge table, all columns are listed in the same order. These tables are good for data warehousing environments.

The following example shows you how to create merge tables:

```
mysql> CREATE TABLE user1 (id INT NOT NULL AUTO_INCREMENT PRIMARY KEY, name
CHAR(20)) ENGINE=MyISAM;
mysql> CREATE TABLE user2 (id INT NOT NULL AUTO_INCREMENT PRIMARY KEY, name
CHAR(20)) ENGINE=MyISAM;
mysql> INSERT INTO user1 (name) VALUES ('abc'),('xyz');
mysql> INSERT INTO user2 (name) VALUES ('def'),('pqr');
mysql> CREATE TABLE user (id INT NOT NULL AUTO_INCREMENT, name CHAR(20),
INDEX(id))ENGINE=MERGE UNION=(user1,user2);
```

The table is used to manage log-related tables, generally. You can create different months of logs in separate MyISAM tables and merge these tables using the merge storage engine.

MyISAM tables have storage limit for the operating system but a collection of MyISAM (merge) tables do not have storage limits. So using a merge table would allow you to split data into multiple MyISAM tables, which can help in overcoming storage limits.

With the MERGE table, it is difficult to do partitioning hence it is not supported by MERGE tables and we cannot implement partition on MERGE table or any MyISAM table.

Federated

The FEDERATED storage engine allows you to create a single database on multiple physical servers. It opens a client connection to another server and executes queries against a table there, retrieving and sending rows as needed. It was originally marketed as a competitive feature that supported many enterprise-grade proprietary database servers, such as Microsoft SQL Server and Oracle, but that was always a stretch, to say the least. Although it seemed to enable a lot of flexibility and neat tricks, it has proven to be a source of many problems and is disabled by default. However, we can enable it by starting the MySQL Server binary with `--federated` option.

Let's create a `FEDERATED` table.

```
CREATE TABLE user_federated (
id INT(20) NOT NULL AUTO_INCREMENT,
name VARCHAR(32) NOT NULL DEFAULT '',
PRIMARY KEY (id),
INDEX name (name))
ENGINE=FEDERATED DEFAULT CHARSET=latin1
CONNECTION='mysql://remote_user:[password]@remote_host:port/federated/table
';
```

The connection field contains information mentioned as follows for your ready reference:

- `remote_user`: A username of remote MySQL Server
- `password`: A password of remote MySQL Server
- `remote_host`: A hostname of the remote server
- `port`: Port number of the remote server
- `federated`: Remote server database name
- `table`: Remote server database table name

NDB cluster

NDB cluster (also known as **NDB**) is an in-memory storage engine offering high availability and data persistence features.

The NDB cluster storage engine can be configured with a range of failover and load-balancing options, but it is easiest to start with the storage engine at the cluster level. NDB Cluster uses the NDB storage engine that contains a complete set of data, which is dependent only on other datasets available within the cluster.

The Cluster portion of the NDB Cluster is configured independently of the MySQL servers. In an NDB Cluster, each part of the cluster is considered to be a node.

The following diagram will help you understand which store engine you need to use for your requirement:

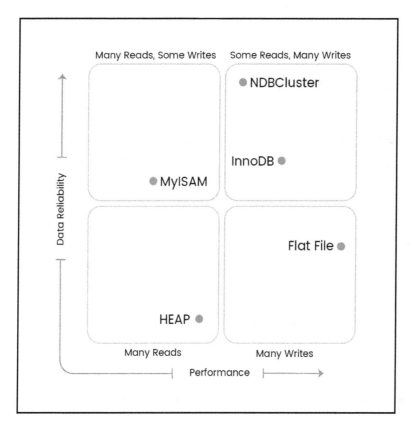

Each store engine has its own advantage and usability:

- **Search Engine**: NDBCluster
- **Transactions data**: InnoDB
- **Session data**: MyISAM or NDBCluster
- **Localized calculations**: Memory
- **Dictionary**: MyISAM

Now you have a better idea about various storage engines along with different use cases, which will help you choose based on your needs. Let's now have a look at Data manipulation statements used to fetch, save, and update data.

Select statement in MySQL 8

The Select statement is used to retrieve data from single or multiple tables:

```
SELECT field 1, field 2, field 3 from table_name [WHERE Clause] [GROUP BY
{col_name }] [HAVING where_condition] [ORDER BY {col_name}  {ASC | DESC},
...] [LIMIT{OFFSET M}{LIMIT N}]
```

This is the common syntax used to retrieve data from a single table:

- Fields one and two are the column names of the table. To fetch all columns from the table, the * expression can be used.
- table_name indicates the table name from where data needs to be retrieved.
- The WHERE clause can be used to specify any condition in a single and multiple column.
- The Group BY function is used with aggregate functions to group the result sets.
- The HAVING clause is needed after GROUP BY to filter based on conditions for a group of rows or aggregates. If we use the HAVING clause without GROUP BY, it would act similarly to the WHERE clause.
- The ORDER BY clause is used to sort the table result sets in ascending or descending order.
- LIMIT is used to constrain the number of rows returned by the SELECT statement.

Let's go through each clause.

WHERE clause

The following code block has the general syntax for the select query with the WHERE clause:

```
SELECT FIELD1, FIELD2, FIELD3,...FIELDn from TABLE_NAME1 ,TABLE_NAME2
[WHERE condition1 [AND [OR]] condition2...
```

The WHERE clause is an optional part of the SELECT command. You can use AND or OR to specify conditions. The WHERE clause can also be used with DELETE and UPDATE query, which we will discuss soon in this chapter.

Here is the list of operators used with the where clause for conditions. Let's take an example of a table schema to understand these operations. Let's create a table called users with schema mentioned here having id, first_name, last_name, address, city, state, zip, login_attempts, contact_number, email, username, and password:

```
CREATE TABLE `users` (
 `id` int(10) unsigned NOT NULL AUTO_INCREMENT,
 `first_name` varchar(255),
 `last_name` varchar(255),
 `address` varchar(255),
 `city` varchar(50),
 `state` varchar(2),
 `zip` varchar(10),
`login_attempts` int(10),
 `contact_number` varchar(20),
 `email` varchar(191),
 `username` varchar(191),
 `password` varchar(255),
 PRIMARY KEY (`id`)
) ENGINE=InnoDB PRIMARY KEY (`id`) AUTO_INCREMENT=0 DEFAULT CHARSET=utf8mb4
COLLATE=utf8mb4_unicode_ci;
```

Equal To and Not Equal To

Equal To (=) checks whether the values of the two fields are equal or not. If it matches, then the condition becomes true and fetches for further processing. If it doesn't match, then condition should be Not Equal which would revert the way of Equal To. It would fetch data based on the condition that doesn't match.

For example, the following query is used to retrieve all records with the city matching New York:

```
SELECT * FROM `users` WHERE `city` = 'New York';
```

Greater than and Less than

Greater than (>) checks whether the value of the left field is greater than the value of the right field. If yes, then the condition becomes true. Less than (<) checks whether the value of the left field is less than the value of the right field. We can also use >/< and equals together.

For example, the following query is used to retrieve all records with login attempts more than the value 2:

```
SELECT * FROM `users` WHERE `login_attempts` > 2;
```

LIKE

The LIKE operator provides an easy way to search records with the different patterns in a column. We can use wildcards characters in a query to build various patterns. There are basically two kinds of wildcard which are mostly use. Let's see each of them with the example.

- % **(Percentage)**: Use this wildcard to search zero or more occurrences of any character. Suppose if we want to search users whose username starts with 'a' then we can use this wildcard just like below query.

    ```
    select * from users where username like 'a%';
    ```

    In case where we want to search users whose username starts from 'a' and ends with 's' then the query with % wildcard will be like this.

    ```
    select * from user where username like 'a%s';
    ```

- _ **(Underscore)**: Use this wildcard where we want to search records with the pattern where any character can take place where we have specified underscore (_). Suppose we want to search users whose username ends with dmin and we are not sure about the first character. Hence below query will search results whose username's first character can be any but it should end with dmin.

    ```
    select * from users where username like '_dmin';
    ```

Make sure that it would consider exactly one character for one underscore. Hence in this case user with username as `"aadmin"` will not be considered because query has mentioned only one wildcard character with the underscore.

IN/NOT IN

The IN operator is used to compare multiple values in the `where` clause. For example, the following query is used to find all users that have city either `new york` or `chicago`:

```
select * from users where city IN ('new york','chicago')
```

NOT IN works in reverse, for example, find all users that do not have city either `new york` or `chicago`:

```
select * from users where city NOT IN ('new york','chicago');
```

BETWEEN

The `BETWEEN` can be used in a case where we want to fetch records which comes under the certain range. This range can be any like text, dates or numbers. Suppose if we want to search users whose created date is between 1st July to 16th July, 2017 then below query can help us with the `BETWEEN` clause.

```
select * from users where created_at BETWEEN '2017-07-01 00:00:00' AND
'2017-07-16 00:00:00';
```

Same way, we can also define the range in number to search users who belong to that particular range. Like if we want students whose marks are between 70 to 80 then `BETWEEN` can be used to define the range.

ORDER BY clause

The `ORDER BY` helps us in retrieving records in an ordered manner. This provides sorted data on a particular column in an ascending or a descending manner. By default, it will sort in ascending order but we can also explicitly specify the sorting manner with `ASC` and `DESC` keyword. If we specify `ASC` then it will sort in an ascending order while `DESC` keyword will sort in descending order. Here is the query which will find all users in a sorted manner in an ascending order on city column.

```
SELECT * FROM users ORDER BY city ASC;
```

Sorting in multiple columns is also possible using `ORDER BY` clause. We can pass multiple columns as shown in below query where we have ordered by `city` and `username` column.

```
SELECT * FROM users ORDER BY city, username;
```

LIMIT clause

Using `LIMIT` clause we can retrieve only some amount of rows from the large data chunks. It helps to limit the number of rows returned as a result set. Suppose there are thousands of rows exists in a table but we require only 10 records then this clause helps to fetch only 10 records instead of fetching thousands of records. This really helps to tune the performance while searching on large datasets.

We can pass either one or two arguments with the LIMIT clause. In case of two arguments, one will be an offset which specifies the offset of the first row to return. While the second argument will be count which specifies the maximum number of rows to be returned. This both argument should be zero or in a positive manner. Check the below query where we have fetched rows from the user table starting from the 5th row up to the 10 records.

```
SELECT * FROM users limit 5 , 10;
```

If we specify only one argument with the `LIMIT` clause then the argument will be considered as the number of rows. For example, the following query is used to retrieve 10 rows from the users table:

```
SELECT * FROM users limit 10;
```

As of now, we have seen retrieving data from a single table; if we want to retrieve data from multiple tables, `JOIN` and `UNION` keywords are used.

SQL JOINS

Join is used to retrieve data from multiple tables. For example, if there are two tables, **order** and **customer**, and we want to retrieve data, it is possible using the `JOIN` clause.

The different types of JOIN are as follows:

- `INNER JOIN`: Returns only those records which have matching values in both tables.
- `CROSS JOIN`: Returns only those records which are have matching values in either the left or right table.
- `LEFT JOIN`: This will returns all records from the left table and only matching records from the right table.
- `RIGHT JOIN`: This will returns all records from the right table and only matching records from the left table.

The following figure illustrates the example that we looked at briefly:

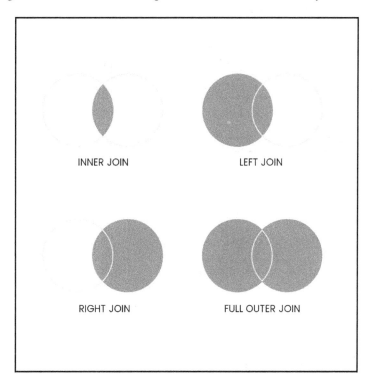

INNER JOIN

This join returns records matching in both tables and returns relevant records. For example, the Order table used in any Ecommerce applications:

order_id	customer_id	order_amount	order_date	ship_id
1001	2	7	2017-07-18	3
1002	37	3	2017-07-19	1
1003	77	8	2017-07-20	2

For example, the Customer table used in ecommerce application which consists Customer data:

customer_id	name	country	city	postal_code
1	Alfreds Futterkiste	Germany	Berlin	12209
2	Ana Trujillo	Mexico	México D.F.	05021
3	Antonio Moreno	Mexico	México D.F.	05023

The following query would fetch all order records with customer details. As the customer IDs 37 and 77 are not present in the customer table, it will fetch only the matching rows excluding customer IDs 37 and 77:

```
SELECT order.order_id, customer.name
FROM order
INNER JOIN customer ON order.customer_id = customer.customer_id;
```

LEFT JOIN

LEFT JOIN retrieves all the records from the left table while only matching records from the right table. If we use the customer and order table example with left join, it will fetch all records from the order table even if there are no matches in the right table (customer). To fetch all order details for the customer, the following query can be used:

```
SELECT order.order_id, customer.name
FROM order
LEFT JOIN customer ON order.customer_id = customer.customer_id;
```

RIGHT JOIN

RIGHT JOIN fetches all records from the right and common records from the left table. If we use the customer and order table example with right join, it will fetch all records from the customer table even if there are no matches in the left table (order). To fetch all customer details with order, the following query can be used:

```
SELECT order.order_id, customer.name
FROM order
RIGHT JOIN customer ON order.customer_id = customer.customer_id;
```

CROSS JOIN

The CROSS JOIN returns all records where there is a match in either the left or right table records. If we take the order and customer table example, it will return five rows with customer and order details:

```
SELECT order.order_id, customer.name FROM order OUTER_JOIN customer ON
order.customer_id = customer.customer_id;
```

UNION

The UNION keyword is used to combine the results from multiple select queries into a single table. Each SELECT statement used in a UNION query must have the same number of columns and each column must require a similar data type. The column names from the first SELECT statement are used as the columns for the results returned.

For example, the Employee table:

employee_id	name	city	postal_code	country
1	Robert	Berlin	12209	Germany
2	Mac	México D.F.	5021	Mexico
3	Patel	México D.F.	5023	Mexico

For example, Contractor table:

contractor_id	name	City	postal_code	country
1	Dave	Berlin	12209	Germany
2	Robert	México D.F.	5021	Mexico
3	Patel	México D.F.	5023	Mexico

The column names from the first SELECT statement are used as the columns for the results returned as shown in following example.

```
SELECT 'Employee' As Type, name, city, country FROM Employee
UNION
SELECT 'Contractor', name, city, country FROM Contractor;
```

The following example of UNION removes duplicate rows from the result; if we don't want to remove duplicate rows, the ALL keyword can be used:

```
SELECT country FROM Employee UNION SELECT country FROM Contractor;
```

This query returns two rows from the preceding table--Germany and Mexico. To fetch all rows from both these tables, we can use the ALL keyword as follows:

```
SELECT country FROM Employee UNION ALL SELECT country FROM Contractor;
```

Subquery

A Select statement under the select statement is called a **subquery**. This sub statement can be used to select the column or in conditional cases. A subquery can also be nested within another query statement like INSERT, UPDATE, or DELETE.

The following query returns a set of users who are located in Ahmedabad using a subquery:

```
SELECT firstName, lastName FROM users
WHERE city IN
(SELECT city FROM cities WHERE city = 'Ahmedabad');
```

Optimizing SELECT statements

Select queries are used to retrieve data in dynamic web pages, so tuning these statements provides good performance which is quite important. Here are some considerations to optimize queries:

- Make sure that you have indexes in tables. Indexes always help to speed up the filtering and the retrieval of results. We can specify indexes in where clause of the `select` query.
- Indexes also minimize the number of full table scanning for a huge table.
- Tunning on *InnoDB buffer pool, MyISAM key cache,* and the *MySQL query cache* helps to cache the results which will be faster retrieval for the repetitive results. We can adjust the size of the cache memory so that it provides faster access by providing results from the cache only.
- Adjust the size and properties of the memory areas that MySQL uses to cache for the InnoDB buffer pool, MyISAM key cache, and the MySQL query cache, which helps run repeated select queries faster.
- We should use `WHERE` instead of `HAVING` if we are not using `GROUP BY` or other aggregate functions like `COUNT()`, `MIN()`, `MAX()`, `AVG()`, and so on.
- Use `EXPLAIN` to analyze your query for where clauses, join clauses, and indexes.

Now let's take a look at how `EXPLAIN` is useful for the optimization of the query performance:

```
EXPLAIN SELECT * FROM `sales_order_item` i
INNER JOIN sales_order o ON i.order_id = o.entity_id
INNER JOIN catalog_product_entity p ON p.sku = i.sku
INNER JOIN customer_entity c ON c.entity_id = o.customer_id
WHERE i.order_id = 42
```

The following is the output of the query executed:

```
*************************** 1. row ***************************
id: 1
select_type: SIMPLE
table: o
partitions: NULL
type: const
possible_keys: PRIMARY,SALES_ORDER_CUSTOMER_ID
key: PRIMARY
key_len: 4
ref: const
rows: 1
filtered: 100.00
```

```
    Extra: NULL
*************************** 2. row ***************************
    id: 1
    select_type: SIMPLE
    table: c
    partitions: NULL
    type: const
possible_keys: PRIMARY
    key: PRIMARY
    key_len: 4
    ref: const
    rows: 1
    filtered: 100.00
    Extra: NULL
*************************** 4. row ***************************
    id: 1
    select_type: SIMPLE
    table: p
    partitions: NULL
    type: ref
possible_keys: CATALOG_PRODUCT_ENTITY_SKU
    key: CATALOG_PRODUCT_ENTITY_SKU
    key_len: 195
    ref: ecommerce.i.sku
    rows: 1
    filtered: 100.00
    Extra: Using index condition
4 rows in set (0.01 sec)
```

In the preceding output, `possible_keys` shows which INDEXES apply to this query and KEY tells us which of these was actually used. In our example each JOIN uses the Index key, we should try to avoid the NULL value of the key by creating the index. The ROWS field tells us how many rows are scanned in the query executed to be identified, and should be reduced for better query performance as this would minimize data transfer.

Insert, replace, and update statements in MySQL 8

Insert, replace, and update statements are used to insert or modify data in the database. Let's take a look at them one by one.

Insert

`INSERT` inserts new rows into an existing table; the following is the syntax to add new rows to a table:

```
INSERT [INTO] tbl_name [(field_name1, field_name2...)] {VALUES | VALUE}
({value of filed 1},value of filed 2,...),(...),...
```

The following inserts new users into the user table:

```
Insert INTO user (first_name,last_name,email,password) VALUES
("Robert","Dotson","RuthFDotson@teleworm.us","17500917b5cd7cefdb57e87ce7348
5d3"),
("Ruth","Uselton","DarronAUselton@armyspy.com","17500917b5cd7cefdb57e87ce73
485d3");
```

Update

`UPDATE` modifies data into an existing table; the following is the syntax to add new rows to a table:

```
UPDATE table_reference  SET field_name1="value" [, field_name2="value"] ...
[WHERE where_condition]
[ORDER BY ...]
[LIMIT row_count]
```

The following `UPDATE` statement is used to update the first name in the users table:

```
UPDATE users set first_name = "abc" where email =
"DarronAUselton@armyspy.com";
```

Replace

`REPLACE()` replaces all the occurrences of a substring within a string. We can use the `REPLACE` statement with the `UPDATE` or `SELECT` statement.

```
REPLACE(str, find_string, replace_with)
```

The following MySQL statement replaces all the occurrences of K with SA within the column country from the users table, for those rows in which the column value of country is INDIA during select:

```
SELECT city,country, REPLACE(country,'K','SA') FROM user WHERE
country='INDIA';
```

The following MySQL statement replaces all the occurrences of `INDIA` with `UK` within the column country:

```
UPDATE user set country = replace(country, 'INDIA', 'UK');
```

Transactions in MySQL 8

Transaction is a logical unit of one or more Insert, Update, and Delete statements. Transaction is useful when you want to do multiple operations on the database. Either all the changes that are successful would be committed, unsuccessful ones would be undone, or errors generated during execution would perform transactions rolled back. The InnoDB storage engine supports the rollback of transactions. The goal of the InnoDB storage model is to combine the best properties of a multi-versioning database with two-phase locking. InnoDB performs locking at the row level and runs queries as non-locking for consistent reads by default for better performance and integrity of data.

Let's take an example to understand where transaction is useful. Consider a banking database. Suppose a bank customer want to transfers money from his account to another account. Generally, SQL statements will be divided into five parts using a transaction:

- Transaction start
- Debit from customer account
- Credit in another customer account
- Recording the transaction logs
- Transaction commit

The SQL statement from the customer account would be as follows:

```
UPDATE sb_accounts SET balance = balance - 1000 WHERE account_no = 932656 ;
```

The SQL statement to credit to another customer account would be as follows:

```
UPDATE sb_accounts SET balance = balance + 1000 WHERE account_no = 932600 ;
```

The SQL statement to record details of the transaction journal would be as follows:

```
INSERT INTO journal VALUES
(100896, 'Transaction on Benjamin Hampshair a/c', '26-AUG-08' 932656,
932600, 1000);
```

The SQL statement to complete the transaction would be as follows:

```
COMMIT WORK;
```

In between all these steps, if some error occurs, like server unavailable, then transaction rollback would happen, which means Insert and Update queries executed would be rolled back.

Aggregating data in MySQL 8

Generally, it happens that data you want is not always available in the database. To generate data, such as getting a total count of orders or sum of price for all orders, MySQL provides many built-in aggregate functions that you can use to represent loaded data to perform calculations in MySQL statements. Data aggregation values can be sums, counting, averages, and so forth. Aggregate functions are all about fetching data from one column of a table, performing calculations on several rows, and returning the required value as an outcome.

As per the ISO standard, there are mainly the following listed aggregate functions:

- Minimum
- Maximum
- Average
- Count
- Sum

The importance of aggregate functions

For businesses, there would be several requirements at each level for each of the diversified functions to produce aggregated data to visualize. Top executives of companies would be concerned with having a holistic view of the whole organization; however, a manager would be limited to knowing specific department numbers. An individual doesn't necessary need such details. All these might have variations of having slicing and dicing at each level, and numerous calculations.

We can do these with the help of aggregate functions. Let's understand an example of an e-commerce portal database. An e-commerce portal might need various data such as average price, total count of products, sum of total sales of a product, maximum buy price, and lowest buy price; these are pretty much unlimited. However, they can be sliced and diced to further details based on business needs.

Before we go into details for each function, there some SQL clauses that are very important to understand.

GROUP BY clause

The `GROUP BY` clause uses to group the records with the identical values. It will form a group of common values by one or more columns and returns a single result. This is being widely used where we want to use some aggregation functions like `COUNT`, `MAX`, `MIN`, `SUM`, and `AVG`. This clause will come after the WHERE clause as shown in below syntext of the SELECT query.

```
SELECT <field(s)> FROM <table_name> WHERE <condition> GROUP BY
<column_name(s)> ORDER BY <column_name(s)>;
```

Let's see an example to get the total number of companies in each country.

```
SELECT COUNT(companyID), country FROM Companies GROUP BY country;
```

HAVING clause

The `HAVING` clause uses to fetch the results with a condition based on the different aggregate functions. Suppose if we want to retrieve records which depend on some of the operations like sum, average, count, max, min etc then this clause will help us. This clause removes the limit of `WHERE` clause because `WHERE` clause cannot be used with the aggregate function. Have a look at the below syntax to find the place of HAVING clause in a select query.

```
SELECT column_name(s) FROM table_name WHERE condition GROUP BY
column_name(s) HAVING condition ORDER BY column_name(s);
```

Let's see an example by fetching the total number of companies in each country. This only includes country where more than 3 companies exist.

```
SELECT COUNT(companyId), country FROM Companies GROUP BY Country
HAVING COUNT(companyId) > 5;
```

Minimum

The `MIN` aggregate function returns the lowest value from the data being loaded.

The following is an example to find the lowest price of a product from a table named products by filtering the price column:

```
SELECT MIN(price) lowest FROM products;
```

Maximum

The MAX aggregate function returns the highest value from the data being loaded.

The following is an example to find the highest price of a product from a table named products by filtering the price column:

```
SELECT MAX(price) highest FROM products;
```

Average

The AVG aggregate function returns the average value from the data being loaded, which ignores the NULL value.

The following is an example to find the average price of a product from a table named products by filtering the price column:

```
SELECT AVG(price) average FROM products;
```

Count

The COUNT aggregate function returns the count from the data being loaded. The following is an example to find the count of products from a table named products:

```
SELECT COUNT(*) AS Total FROM products;
```

Sum

The SUM aggregate function returns the sum from the data being loaded, which ignores the NULL value.

The following is an example to find the sum of total sales of each product from a table named orders grouped by productcode:

```
SELECT productcode, sum(price * quantity)
total FROM orders GROUP by productcode;
```

You can also see further details like the product name with the help of joins.

The following is an example to find the sum of total sales of each product from a table named orders grouped by `productcode`. To get `productname`, we would match `productname` in the products table:

```
SELECT P.productCode, P.productName, SUM(price * quantity) total FROM
orders O INNER JOIN products  P ON O.productCode = P.productCode GROUP by
productCode ORDER BY total;
```

JSON

In MySQL 5.7, the JSON functionality was introduced that allows you to get dataset results in JSON data format, virtual columns, and, tentatively, 15 SQL functions that allow you to search and use JSON data on the server side. In MySQL 8, there are additional aggregation functions that can be used in JSON objects/arrays to represent loaded data in a further optimized way. The following are the two JSON aggregation functions that were introduced in MySQL 8:

- `JSON_OBJECTAGG()`
- `JSON_ARRAYAGG()`

Let's take an example of an e-commerce platform where we will create a few tables and data to understand both these functions.

First, let's create a table for products as follows:

```
CREATE TABLE `products` ( `id` int(11) NOT NULL AUTO_INCREMENT,
`pname` varchar(75) DEFAULT NULL,
 `pmanufacturer` varchar(75) DEFAULT NULL,
 `pprice` int(10) DEFAULT NULL,
 PRIMARY KEY (`id`)) ENGINE=InnoDB DEFAULT CHARSET=latin1;
```

Now let's create a table for attributes:

```
CREATE TABLE `attr` (
`id` int(11) NOT NULL AUTO_INCREMENT,
`pname` varchar(120) DEFAULT NULL,
`pdesc` varchar(256) DEFAULT NULL,
PRIMARY KEY (`id`)
) ENGINE=InnoDB DEFAULT CHARSET=latin1;
```

Now, we are almost done creating tables; the last one is a table for value, as shown in the following code:

```
CREATE TABLE `value` ( `p_id` int(11) NOT NULL, `attr_id` int(11) NOT NULL,
`values` text, PRIMARY KEY (`p_id`,`attr_id`)) ENGINE=InnoDB DEFAULT
CHARSET=latin1;
```

We now need a few entries in the tables, which we would be referring to for JSON examples.

Let's insert data into the tables that we created--attribute, value, and products--as shown in the following code:

```
INSERT INTO attr(id, pname) VALUES (1, "color"),
(2, "material"),
(3, "style"),
(4, "bulb_type"),
(5, "usage"),
(6, "cpu_type"),
(7, "cpu_speed"),
(8, "weight"),
(9, "battery_life"),
(10, "fuel_type");

INSERT INTO products(id, pname, pmanufacturer, pprice) VALUES
(1, "LED Desk Lamp", "X", 26);

INSERT INTO products(id, pname, pmanufacturer, pprice) VALUES
(2, "Laptop", "Y", 800);

INSERT INTO products(id, pname, pmanufacturer, pprice) VALUES
(3, "Grill", "Z", 300);

INSERT INTO value VALUES
(2, 1, "blue"),
(2, 6, "quad core"),
(2, 7, "3400 mhz"),
(2, 8, "2,1 kg"),
(2, 9, "9h");

INSERT INTO value VALUES (3, 1, "black"),
(3, 8, "5 kg"),
(3, 10, "gas");
```

JSON_OBJECTAGG

`JSON_OBJECTAGG()` reads two columns or expressions and shows them as a key and a value, respectively, in a single JSON object. A `NULL` key would cause an error while duplicate keys would be ignored. The following is an example of this:

```
mysql> SELECT id, col FROM table;
+------+----------------------------------------+
| id   | col                                    |
+------+----------------------------------------+
|    1 | {"key1": "value1", "key2": "value2"}   |
|    2 | {"keyA": "valueA", "keyB": "valueB"}   |
+------+----------------------------------------+
2 rows in set (0.00 sec)
mysql> SELECT JSON_OBJECTAGG(id, col) FROM table;
+------------------------------------------------------------+
| JSON_OBJECTAGG(id, col)                                    |
+------------------------------------------------------------+
| {"1": {"key1": "value1", "key2": "value2"}, "2": {"keyA":  "valueA",
"keyB": "valueB"}}
|------------------------------------------------------------+
row in set (0.00 sec)
```

Now let's connect with our sample data; you want to retrieve all products that consist of all the keys and values attributes as a JSON object by leveraging data from the `products`, `attr`, and `value` tables with the help the `JSON_OBJECTAGG` aggregate function. You must have noticed that the `products` table has structured data and, if we take a closer look at the `attr` and `value` tables, they consist of semi-structured data. The following is an example output of `JSON_OBJECTAGG` aggregate function:

```
SELECT JSON_OBJECT("key", p.id,
            "title", p.pname,
            "manufacturer", p.pmanufacturer,
            "price", p.pprice,
            "specifications", JSON_OBJECTAGG(a.name, v.value)) as product
FROM products as p JOIN value as v ON p.id=v.p_id JOIN attr as a ON
a.id=v.attr_id GROUP BY v.p_id;
+----------------------------------------------------+
|product
|
+----------------------------------------------------+</strong>
  "key": 1,
  "price": 26,
  ";title": "LED Desk Lamp",
  "manufacturer": "X",
  "specifications": {
```

```
      "color": "black",
      "style": "classic",
      "usage": "Indoor use only",
      "material": "plastic",
      "bulb_type": "LED"
   "key": 2,
   "price": 800,
   "title": "Laptop",
   "manufacturer": "Y",
   "specifications": {
      "color": "blue",
      "weight": "2,1 kg",
      "cpu_type": "quad core",
      "cpu_speed": "3400 mhz",
      "battery_life": "9h"
   "key": 3,
   "price": 300,
   "title": "Grill",
   "manufacturer": "Z",
   "specifications": {
      "color": "black",
      "weight": "5 kg",
      "fuel_type": "gas"
+---------------------------------------------------------------+
3 rows in set (0,01 sec
```

JSON_ARRAYAGG

The JSON_ARRYAGG function reads a column or expression as an argument and shows the output as a single JSON array after aggregating results. The following is an example of ordering of the elements in an array which would be undetermined.

```
mysql> SELECT col FROM table;
+-------------------------------------+
| col                                 |
+-------------------------------------+
| {"key1": "value1", "key2": "value2"} |
| {"keyA": "valueA", "keyB": "valueB"} |
+-------------------------------------+
2 rows in set (0.00 sec)

myysql> SELECT JSON_ARRAYAGG(col) FROM table;
+-------------------------------------------------------------+
| JSON_ARRAYAGG(col)                                          |
+-------------------------------------------------------------+
| [{"key1": "value1", "key2": "value2"}, {"keyA": "valueA", "keyB":
```

```
"valueB"}]
|+--------------------------------------------------------------+
1 row in set (0.00 sec)
```

Now let's connect with our sample data; you want to retrieve all products that consist of possible keys and values attributes by leveraging data from the `products`, `attr`, and `value` tables with the help of the `JSON_ARRYAGG` aggregate function. The following is an example output of the `JSON_ARRAYAGG` aggregate function:

```
SELECT p.id, JSON_ARRAYAGG(a.pname) as prod_attributes
FROM products as p JOIN value as v ON p.id=v.p_id
     JOIN attr as a ON a.id=p_id
GROUP BY v.p_id;
+---+-------------------------------------------------------------+
| id | prod_attributes                                           |
+---+-------------------------------------------------------------+
|  1 | ["color", "style", "usage", "material", "bulb_type"]
|
|  2 | ["cpu_type", "weight", "color","cpu_speed", "battery_life"]
|
|  3 | ["color", "fuel_type", "weight"]
|
+---+-------------------------------------------------------------+
3 rows in set (0,01 sec)
```

Let's consider that we need to create a new schema using these functions. This will help if you want to migrate with the new schema. The following is an example of the query and its output:

```
CREATE TABLE all_product AS (SELECT p.id, p.pname, p.pmanufacturer,
p.pprice,JSON_OBJECTAGG(a.name, v.value) as semi_data
FROM products as p JOIN value as v ON p.id=v.p_id
JOIN attr as a ON a.id=v.attr_id GROUP BY v.p_id);
SELECT * FROM all_product;
+----+-----------------+--------------+-------+--------------------------------
----------------------------------------------------------------+
+----+-----------------+--------------+-------+--------------------------------
----------------------------------------------------------------+
|  1 | LED Desk Lamp | X              |   26 | {"color": "black", "style":
"classic", "usage": "Indoor use only", "material": "plastic",
"bulb_type":"LED"} |
|  2 | Laptop          | Y              |  800 | {"color": "blue", "weight":
"2,1 kg", "cpu_type": "quad core", "cpu_speed": "3400 mhz", "battery_life":
"9h"} |
|  3 | Grill           | Z              |  300 | {"color": "black", "weight":
"5 kg", "fuel_type": "gas"}
|
```

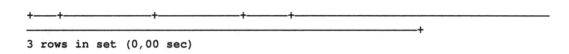

```
+——+———————+——————————+———+——+——————————————————————
————————————————————————————————————+
3 rows in set (0,00 sec)
```

Summary

By now, you have learned the different database engines available in MySQL 8 and their applications. We established how to create tables, modify existing tables, and how to add/remove columns from an existing table. We also understood how to drop tables and databases. We learned in detail about different filter criteria available in MySQL. After that, we explored the different joins available in MySQL 8 and how to use joins in a query to fetch meaningful data from the database in a single query. We explored how database transactions work in MySQL and the importance of transactions in real-life scenarios. Lastly, we understood how to use aggregate functions in MySQL and learned the usage of different aggregate functions such as group by, having, min(), max(), avg(), sum(), and count(), and how to store JSON information in the database.

In the next chapter, you will learn how indexing works in MySQL 8, the new features introduced related to indexing, different types of indexing, and how to use indexing on your tables.

3

Indexing your data for High-Performing Queries

In the previous chapter, you learned to apply queries on your data stored in the MySQL database. You learned the different syntax of the select query, how to join tables, and how to apply aggregate functions on the table.

In this chapter, you will learn below topics on what is indexing and different types of indexes:

- MySQL indexing
- MySQL index types
- Indexing JSON data

Let's assume that we have a database table that has more then 50 lakh records of email addresses and you want to fetch one record out of this table. Now, if you write a query to fetch an email address, MySQL will have to check in each and every row for the values matching your queried email address. If MySQL takes one microsecond to scan one record, then it will take around five seconds to load just one record and, as the number of records increases in a table, the time taken will also increase exponentially, which would affect performance!

Fortunately, current relational database technology features have solutions to quickly retrieve information from large datasets. Indexes can be defined on tables that retrieve information from the table quickly without scanning the entire table. Indexes are actually pointers to the rows in the table. Defining an index on a table does not require any change in the actual definition of the table; indexes can be created independently. We can define one or more indexes or one index on more than one column based on how we are going to manipulate and retrieve data from the tables.

The following figure is a simple example of indexing the record. On the right-hand side table, records are stored as per the new entry and each new record is inserted at the end of the table. So when you want to search for records containing a particular word, the database engine has to scan the entire table to get the matching records. However, if this data is sorted properly inside columns, DB engines can easily locate the records and return results.

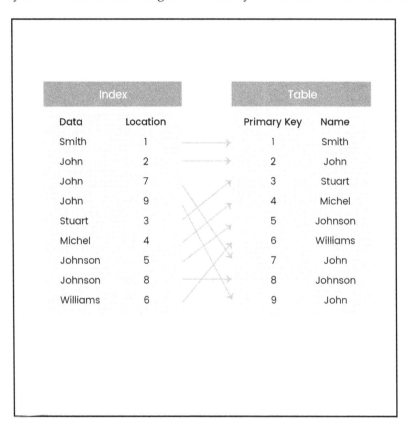

MySQL indexing

MySQL supports various indexes on its tables for the faster access of records. Before we define indexes on the tables, it is important to know when we need to index data, and it's also equally important to select the proper field to create indexes.

The following list shows when to use indexing:

- When grouping based on a specific column is required
- When sorting on a specific column is required
- When you need to find the minimum and maximum values from the table
- When we have a large dataset and need to find a few records based on certain conditions frequently
- When you need to fire a query that has a join between two or more tables

Index structures

There are different structures used by various indexing methods to store the index information in the database:

- Bitmap indexes
- Sparse indexes
- Dense indexes
- B-Tree indexes
- Hash indexes

Let's quickly go through each of these indexes.

Bitmap indexes

As the name suggests, a Bitmap index stores column information as a bit. Bitmap indexing is used when there is low cardinality in unique values in the columns. For example, the gender field in a table can have two values--male or female. Now all the rows of table can have either male or female as the value.

So here the question is what is actually stored in the Bitmap indexes? Each row in the bitmap index table has two values--either zero or one--and each row of the index table has as many bits as the number of rows that exist in the table. There is one Bitmap index for each of the unique values of columns. So in general, a Bitmap index uses an array of bits and, when searching records, it uses the bit-wise operation to locate and return the records.

We will not be discussing much on Bitmap indexes; currently, MySQL 8 does not support bitmap indexes.

Sparse indexes

In a Sparse index, all searched records are not stored in the database; only one record per block is stored in the index in a sorted manner. If the queried record is not found in the index, the database will do a sequential search in that record block to find out the queried records. This behavior is slower than the Dense index as a Sparse index stores only a few records in the index, and the size of the index is lower than the Dense index.

Dense indexes

In a Dense index, the index is available for each and every searched record available in the database. As all searched records are directly available from the index, it becomes very fast, but will consume much more disk space because of its single-level behavior.

B-Tree indexes

B-Tree is the most widely used indexing structure across the RDBMS. MySQL's InnoDB database engine uses B-tree index structures. B-tree is a self-balancing tree data structure that stores data in the lowest level node in a sorted order. Due to its structure, a B-tree algorithm searching in a B-tree data structure returns the results in logarithmic time. All values in B-tree indices are stored at the same level.

The highest level node in a B-tree data structure is called the root node while the lowest node is called the leaf node. The root node may point to the leaf node or refer to the leaf node. Referring to the leaf node contains pointers to the leaf node or another referring leaf node. Leaf nodes store actual data while referring leaf nodes contain pointers to another non-leaf node or actual data.

In a B-tree data structure, each of the root, leaf, or non-leaf node consists of linked listing. A referencing or internal node consists of a minimum key of the child page, which is referred to along with the page number of the child page. As each node in a B-tree is a doubly-linked list, each node also contains a reference to the next and previous node at the same level.

The level of the internal node or child node increases as soon as all the space at the leaf node is used. Once all leaf nodes are filled up, one new page is created and the root node points to the new page and the child node splits into two.

Whenever an index is created in the database, values of the key is sorted and indexed in the B-tree structure. When a key is created on more than one column, then, at the time of search, MySQL will start looking into the index table with the leftmost column of the index.

On the users table that we created in `Chapter 2`, *Data query techniques in MySQL 8*, let's apply indexes on the `first_name` and `last_name` columns:

```
CREATE INDEX idx_firstname_lastname ON users(first_name, last_name);
```

So let's say we need all user records where the first name is `Vivek` and the last name is `Patel`:

```
SELECT * from users where first_name = 'Vivek' and last_name = 'Patel';
```

When we apply the preceding select query, MySQL B-tree indexing will first look for the `first_name` column for matching records with `Vivek` and then for the second column, `last_name`, for matching records with `Patel`:

```
SELECT * from users where last_name = 'Patel' and first_name = 'Vivek';
```

Whereas, if you apply the select statement with a reverse condition, MySQL will not look into the index table to search the data and will do a full table scan, which can be a heavy operation depending on your data.

So it is very important to create indexes depending on the query that you are going to use frequently. We will understand more about the indexing table when see different types of indexing used in MySQL 8 later in this chapter.

B-tree indexes are used in MySQL for comparison operations such as =, >, <. >=, and <=.

The following figure is an example of how a B-tree index looks. Here, each node on the same level is linked to an other along with intermediate and leaf nodes:

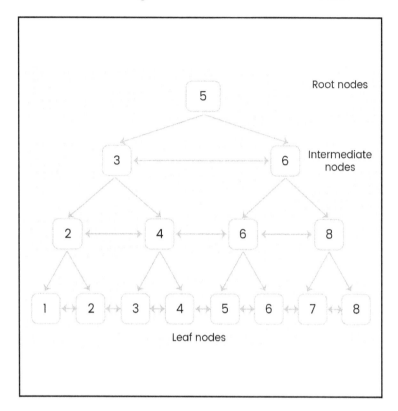

Hash indexes

Hash indexes behave differently from B-tree data structures. A Hash index performs much faster than B-tree indexes. It uses key value pairs to index the data. Hash indexes only allow equal comparison operators such as = or <=> where only value comparisons are done. It doesn't support operators where range comparison is required, such as >, <, >=, or <=. In range comparison, a B-tree structure performs in log(n) time, whereas in such conditions, a Hash index can take O(n) time, which might not be a right fit for many use cases.

In MySQL 8, Hash indexes are only supported on Memory and NDB database engines. It is not supported in MyISAM or InnoDB database engines.

Hash index cannot be used on the order by clause. The Hash structure uses the whole index key value to search, unlike B-tree, where the leftmost columns can be used to query.

Creating or dropping indexes

Creating an index in MySQL is quite similar to any other RDBMS. The following is the syntax used to create an index with all the possible parameters:

```
CREATE [UNIQUE|FULLTEXT|SPATIAL] INDEX index_name
[index_type]
ON tbl_name (index_col_name,...)
[index_option]
[algorithm_option | lock_option] ...
```

UNIQUE | FULLTEXT | SPATIAL

These are the type of indexes that we can define in MySQL 8. The SPATIAL index is available only in InnoDB and MyISAM database engines. Defining the SPATIAL index on other databases will result in an error.

Index_col_name

Index_col_name is the name of the column where we need to define an index as mentioned in the following snippet.

```
index_col_name: col_name [(length)] [ASC | DESC]
```

With the index column name, you can define the length of the index column, order of the index, and whether the index needs to be created in ascending or descending order. When you are using a string type column such as char, varchar, or text, you can define the actual length of the column. The following is an example query to create an index on the first_name column of the users table with an index on the first 15 characters of the query:

```
CREATE INDEX idx_first_name ON users(first_name(15));
```

Index_options

Following are various index options available, each of them has been explained further.

```
index_option:
KEY_BLOCK_SIZE [=] value |
index_type |
WITH PARSER parser_name |
COMMENT 'string'
| {VISIBLE | INVISIBLE}
index_type: USING
```

```
{BTREE | HASH}
```

KEY_BLOCK_SIZE

You can also specify the size of the index block using `KEY_BLOCK_SIZE`. This parameter is not supported at index level with the InnoDB database engine.

With Parser

This is a full text index option and can be used to define the parsing algorithm available as a plugin in MySQL for full text searching.

COMMENT

You can specify comments for the index created for understanding or self-explanatory purposes. The maximum size for the comment option is 1,024 characters in MySQL 8.

VISIBILITY

This is to change or mention the visibility of the index in the table. An Invisible index is treated as a hidden index and is not used by the MySQL optimizer to index the data. It is available for any storage engine.

index_type

You can define the index type on the storage engine. The following is a list of storage engines on which you can define `index_type`. Index type cannot be used with the FULL TEXT or SPATIAL indexes. When an index type that is not supported by MySQL is used, then MySQL will automatically use the default index type on the table.

STORAGE ENGINE NAME	INDEX TYPE
InnoDB	BTREE
MyISAM	BTREE
Memory/HEAP	HASH, BTREE
NDB	HASH, BTREE

algorithm_option

Algorithm option is used to identify how a table is rebuilt when the index is modified. When Algorithm is set to INPLACE, a built-in technique and methodology is used to rebuild the index when the table definition is modified.

```
algorithm_option:
ALGORITHM [=] {DEFAULT|INPLACE|COPY}
```

If the Algorithm option is COPY, then while altering the table definition, it uses the method to copy the table internally and rebuild indexes.

If the default algorithm is used, then MySQL will automatically choose the algorithm based on the available option.

lock_option

To manage the level of concurrent operations on table when it is getting altered **LOCK** clause is useful.

```
lock_option:
LOCK [=] {DEFAULT|NONE|SHARED|EXCLUSIVE}Index_col_name
```

If lock_option is set to SHARED, then, in parallel, other queries are permitted to be executed during table altering operations. If lock_option is set to NONE, then other DDL operations are permitted during table altering operations. If lock_option is set to EXCLUSIVE, then MySQL will first wait for any existing read/write operations to be completed and then get the lock, which blocks further read/write operations until the execution of the indexing query operation is completed for further use.

The following is a simple example of creating and dropping indexes from the database table, assuming that we have an employee table that has the columns, employee_id, firstname, email_address, and joining_date:

```
CREATE TABLE IF NOT EXISTS `employee` (
`employee_id` int(11) NOT NULL,
`firstname` varchar(50) NOT NULL,
`email_address` varchar(100) NOT NULL,
`joining_date` datetime NOT NULL
) ENGINE=InnoDB DEFAULT CHARSET=latin1 COMMENT='Employee Meta data
information' AUTO_INCREMENT=1 ;
```

Now, let's define a primary key for `employee_id`, which is always going to be unique, not null, and never repetitive:

```
ALTER TABLE `employee` ADD PRIMARY KEY (`employee_id`);
```

Additionally, the employee `email_address` always needs to be unique so that we can define a unique key on the `email_address` column:

```
ALTER TABLE `employee` ADD UNIQUE KEY `unique_email_address`
(`email_address`);
```

Now, often we may need a list of employees filtered and sorted by their `joining_date`. So we define an index on the joining date to make the query faster:

```
ALTER TABLE `employee` ADD KEY `idx_joining_date` (`joining_date`);
```

To drop an index from a table, the following syntax is used:

```
DROP INDEX INDEX_NAME on tbl_name;
```

When to avoid indexing

So far you have learned different indexing structures and how to create or drop indexes in MySQL 8. Indexing can really boost the performance of your query, but there are cases when creating an index does not improve the performance of the query or can even have adverse effects on query performance.

When the cardinality of the table is very low, unnecessarily creating an index may actually not have much benefit. The reason is that MySQL will do a full table scan if, with indexing, it has to scan 30% of records. In such cases, we should avoid creating any indexes on the table.

Creating an index requires additional disk space. Also, when an index is created, MySQL has to update the index table every time a row is inserted, updated, or deleted. So creating too many indexes on a table can actually have drastic effects on the insert/update queries and it can become slower.

MySQL 8 index types

In the previous topics, you learned different index structures and how to create indexes on a table. Now let's see different indexes in detail that are available in MySQL and their importance.

When you create a table in MySQL, there are five types of index options available:

- PRIMARY
- UNIQUE
- COLUMN
- FULLTEXT
- SPATIAL

You can choose any of these indexes on your table based on your database design; the frequency of data and columns used in the query would accordingly help you define where indexes need to be applied.

Defining a primary index

The primary key is used to identify each row uniquely. The column on which the primary key is defined is unique in nature and contains not null values. In the following section, you will learn how to use the primary key and the difference between a surrogate key and natural key.

Primary indexes

Every InnoDB table contains one special index to identify each row uniquely. This column is also referred to as a clustered index. A clustered index is synonymous to a primary key in most cases.

Whenever a primary key is defined, MySQL uses it as a clustered index. If there is no primary key defined, then MySQL will check whether any unique index is defined having not null values. If any relevant columns are found, than MySQL will use that column as a clustered index.

If there is no primary key or unique key, MySQL will internally create a hidden column with unique row ID values and define a clustered index on that column, which will be used internally by MySQL for secondary indexes. Each unique row ID consists of 6 bytes, which is increased based on new data populated. Ideally, you should always define a primary key on a column. If you see no columns as unique, then you can always create an auto increment numeric primary key on your table, which can be used as a clustered index.

All indexes other than clustered indexes are considered secondary indexes. On each secondary index, one column is stored of a clustered index that helps locate the record and access it faster. It also means that if a primary key is long, the secondary index will consume relatively more disk space.

Natural keys versus surrogate keys

When the primary key of a table is made of actual data, it is called a **natural key**. Natural keys are made from one or more columns in the table.

Sometimes when you want to generate data at runtime, the primary key is created using auto-increment values, which is called a **surrogate key**.

Let's go through the following example to understand this better:

```
CREATE TABLE users (
email_address VARCHAR(255) NOT NULL PRIMARY KEY,
first_name VARCHAR(100) NULL,
last_name VARCHAR(100) NULL
) ENGINE=InnoDB;
```

We will have following data format populated in the users table:

email_address	first_name	last_name
User1@mail.com	Firstname1	Lastname1
User2@mail.com	Firstname2	Lastname2
User3@mail.com	Firstname3	Lastname3
User4@mail.com	Firstname4	Lastname4

Here, we have set email as the primary key, which is a natural key, and indexing on this table will help when you search a user by the primary key.

What if we have a few users not having an email address associated with them? In that case, we cannot use the primary key on the `email_address` column. We can create another column that is an auto increment value and can be set as a primary key. We can set a unique key on the `email_address` column that will allow null values inside the `email_address` field; however, it will put on a constraint that the `email_address` must be unique for each user. This will help accommodate the primary key requirement along with data consistency:

```
CREATE TABLE users (
user_id INT(11) NOT NULL AUTO_INCREMENT PRIMARY KEY,
email_address VARCHAR(255) NULL DEFAULT NULL,
first_name VARCHAR(100) NULL,
last_name VARCHAR(100) NULL,
UNIQUE(email_address)
) ENGINE=InnoDB;
```

Surrogate keys are numeric in most cases and do not have any relationship with the data stored in the tables, whereas natural keys are made up of one or more columns from the data. While searching, surrogate keys do not provide any meaningful data but act as a natural key that is stored using actual values, which helps us provide relevant values queried from the table.

Natural keys can be non-numeric and can use more than one column, which obviously might consume comparatively more disk space to create indexes. When natural keys are used, it can also have an effect on join queries to fetch data from a table, which is not the scenario when using surrogate keys.

Unique keys

A unique key is used to define constraints on a column where all values in the given column must be non-repetitive. Unique keys, like primary keys, must have all values be unique. However, unique keys allow NULL values inside the columns. We can define a unique key on a group of columns or a single column.

As stated earlier, a unique key can be used as a clustered key if values inside the unique key are not null and there are no primary keys defined on the table.

The following is an example of creating a unique key:

```
ALTER TABLE users ADD UNIQUE INDEX unique_email_address(`email_address`);
```

Dropping a unique key is the same as dropping any column index:

```
ALTER TABLE users DROP INDEX unique_email_address;
```

Defining a column index

An index is used to increase the performance of the select query. An index can be defined on one or more columns. There are multiple options available to create the column index based on the requirement and usage of the select query. The following are the different column indexes available in MySQL 8 and their usage.

Composite indexes in MySQL 8

Many times we have more than one field where we actually need to define an index to achieve high performance from the query on large datasets. When an index is created on more than one column of a table, it is called a **composite index**. MySQL allows composite indexes on up to 16 columns.

Let's consider the following table definition:

```
CREATE TABLE users (
email_address VARCHAR(255) NOT NULL PRIMARY KEY,
first_name VARCHAR(100) NOT NULL,
last_name VARCHAR(100) NOT NULL,
INDEX idx_user_fullname(first_name,last_name)
);
```

Here, `idx_user_fullname` is the composite index consisting of `first_name` and `last_name`. Now, when we use the following query to find the users by name, it will use the `idx_user_fullname` composite index:

```
SELECT * from users where first_name = 'John' and last_name = 'Cena';
```

If we use following query too, than also it would use composite index:

```
SELECT * from users where first_name = 'John';
```

Consider another operator like OR in the SQL statement:

```
SELECT * from users where first_name = 'John' or first_name = 'Michael';
```

If we use following query too, than also it would use composite index.

```
SELECT * from users where first_name = 'John' and (last_name = 'Cena' or
last_name = 'Michael');
```

All the preceding queries will return output using composite indexing for desired results.

However, while using a composite index, if the following queries are used with a small change to the column order in the query, MySQL will not use the index to search the results from the table and will do a full table scan. Hence, we recommend that you ensure that the database design and queries are in sync to optimally benefit from indexing:

```
SELECT * from users where last_name = 'John' and first_name = 'Cena';
```

If we use following query too, than also it would use composite index:

```
SELECT * from users where last_name = 'Cena';
```

Consider another operator like OR in the SQL statement:

```
SELECT * from users where last_name = 'Cena' or last_name = 'Stuart';
```

If we use following query too, than also it would use composite index:

```
SELECT * from users where last_name = 'Cena' and (first_name = 'Alex' or
first_name = John);
```

Covering index

When an index is created on fields of a table that are required in the query, it is called a **covering index**. Creating covering indexes can result in faster performance.

There are time when we need the select query, where the number of fields in columns and number of filters are the same. In such cases, if we define the index on the filter criteria, then results can be directly acquired from the index. In turn, this operation can be very fast and produce a quick output.

```
ALTER TABLE users ADD INDEX idx_first_name_last_name (first_name,
last_name);
```

Now apply the select query on this user table as follows:

```
SELECT first_name, last_name from users where first_name = 'John' and
last_name = 'Cena';
```

As we can see, both filter parameters and select parameters are the same. So MySQL will return output from the index data itself.

Invisible indexes

Invisible indexes are introduced in MySQL 8, as we have seen in `Chapter 1`, *Introduction to Big Data and MySQL 8*. Making an index invisible will tell the MySQL optimizer that it does not need to use that index in the query:

```
ALTER TABLE users ALTER INDEX email_address INVISIBLE;
```

The preceding query will make an index on `email_address` invisible. When making indexes invisible, MySQL will still maintain the index table on `email_address` or on insert or update operations. Invisible indexes can be used in cases where we want to measure the performance of the queries that we have created and check whether the indexing is being used in the query or not.

A primary key of a table cannot be made invisible. If there is no primary key defined on the table and if there is a unique key defined on any other column of the table, then MySQL will consider a unique non-null column as primary and will not allow invisible indexing on these columns.

Descending indexes

Like invisible indexes, descending indexes are also an enhanced feature of MySQL 8 and were not present in earlier versions of MySQL.

Descending indexes allow you to create an index in reverse order, which performs very fast on the query when sorting is used on columns in a descending manner. It can reduce the output of the query to a certain extent.

Let's understand descending order in more detail with an example. We will consider the following data for the users table:

email_address	first_name	last_name	registered_date
alex@mail.com	Alex	Lastname1	2017-04-04 11:23:53
john@mail.com	John	Lastname2	2017-03-06 15:14:34
stuart@mail.com	Stuart	Lastname3	2017-03-04 10:12:12
lynda@mail.com	Lynda	Lastname4	2017-04-04 10:23:53

If we want users sorted in descending order by their registration date but ascending by their names, the query would be as follows:

```
select * from users order by registered_date desc, first_name asc;
```

Now consider that we have an index defined on both `registered_date` and `first_name`:

```
alter table users add key idx_registered_date_name (registered_date desc,
first_name asc);
```

We will add `explain` to the preceding statement:

```
explain select * from users order by registered_date desc, first_name asc;
```

The output will be as follows:

Id	1
Select type	SIMPLE
table	users
Type	ALL
Possible_keys	NULL
Key	NULL
Key_len	NULL
Ref	NULL
Rows	4
Extra	Using Index

This is an example so we have shown the output of the preceding `explain` statement. In general, MySQL will not use any index on a table if there are very few records.

Here, as we can see, it is mentioned in the **Extra** row that MySQL is using the index for the `order by` clause. This means that our query is using indexing to get the sorted records.

In versions prior to MySQL 8, if there is a different sort order in the index column, MySQL will use `file sort` to sort the data. The `file sort` method uses a full table scan to get the list of sorted records.

Descending indexes are only supported in the InnoDB database engine. Descending indexes cannot be used on full text or spatial index. You also cannot define descending indexes on the `FTS_DOC_ID` column, which is used for FULL TEXT indexing in the InnoDB database engine.

Defining a foreign key in the MySQL table

A foreign key is a reference to the records stored in the primary table. Though a foreign key is not an index, it is important to explicitly define indexes on the table as they can boost the performance when you join the table.

The following is the syntax to add a foreign key while creating a new table:

```
ALTER TABLE tbl_name
ADD [CONSTRAINT [symbol]] FOREIGN KEY
[index_name] (index_col_name, ...)
REFERENCES tbl_name (index_col_name,...)
[ON DELETE reference_option]
[ON UPDATE reference_option]
reference_option: RESTRICT | CASCADE | SET NULL | NO ACTION | SET DEFAULT
```

The following sections are a brief overview of different `reference_option` allowed while defining foreign keys.

RESTRICT

If there is a referring row found in the child table, MySQL will not allow you to delete records from the parent table.

CASCADE

If any records from the parent table are deleted or updated, it will trigger a delete or update action on the child tables as well. So if you remove a record from the parent table, all referencing records from all child tables where the reference option is set to `ON DELETE CASCADE` will also be removed.

SET NULL

When any record from the parent table is updated or deleted, it will set the value of the foreign key column to NULL.

NO ACTION

NO ACTION is similar to the RESTRICT option and will not allow you to remove records from the parent table if any referencing row exists in the child table.

SET DEFAULT

Both InnoDB and NDB database engines do not allow the SET DEFAULT reference option when used in the table syntax.

When defining a foreign key, the data type of the primary key and foreign key must be the same. Additionally, the database engine for both the parent table and child table must be the same. To perform the foreign key checks faster, it is required to define an index on the column where we define foreign keys. MySQL does not allow index prefixing on the columns where a foreign key is defined. In MySQL 8, we can define the primary key and foreign key on the same tables but different columns.

MySQL maintains referential integrity while modifying, deleting, or creating a new table. So when you drop an existing table, if there are any child tables defining foreign keys, MySQL will throw an error. Also, while recreating a table, if there are any existing foreign keys defined on another table, then column names and the order of the columns must be the same as mentioned in the foreign key constraints, otherwise MySQL will show an error while creating the table.

You can set "foreign_key_checks = 0" before dropping or creating a table; when foreign_key_checks is set to zero, MySQL will not verify any references on the SQL commands executed. The default value for foreign_key_checks is set to one.

Dropping foreign keys

The following is the query to remove a foreign key from the table.

```
ALTER TABLE tbl_name DROP FOREIGN KEY fk_symbol;
```

Note that removing a foreign key will not remove any explicitly defined indexes from the table.

Full-text indexing

Fulltext indexing is used for search queries where you need to search for a keyword from a sentence or paragraph stored in MySQL tables.

The following is an example of creating a table with a fulltext index defined:

```
CREATE TABLE blog (
blog_id INT(11) AUTO_INCREMENT NOT NULL PRIMARY KEY,
blog_title VARCHAR(255) NOT NULL,
blog_description TEXT,
FULLTEXT(blog_title,blog_description)
) ENGINE=InnoDB;
```

Now when you want to search for the keyword--let's assume "initial" from the blog table--using fulltext indexing, you can use the following query:

```
SELECT * FROM blog WHERE MATCH (blog_title, blog_description) AGAINST
("initial" IN NATURAL LANGUAGE MODE);
```

This query will return all blogs where the matching "initial" keyword is found in the records. When we use matching keywords in the WHERE condition, MySQL will return rows sorted according to their relevance of the searched keyword. The highest relevant record will be first in the result set and the lowest matching record will be last. To calculate the relevance, MySQL takes the following parameters into consideration:

- Total number of words in a row
- Total number of unique words in a row
- Total number of words in the stored fulltext index
- Number of rows matching the searched keywords

If you want to find out the relevance score of the rows returned by MySQL, you can use MATCH in column names:

```
SELECT MATCH(blog_title, blog_description) AGAINST ("initial" IN NATURAL
LANGUAGE MODE) as relevant_score FROM blog;
```

Now you might have a question--what if we use the MATCH query in the columns as well as the where condition? Will it do index lookup multiple times?

The answer is **no**. When a query is executed, the MySQL optimizer will check whether the same MATCH query is used in the where condition. If it's true, then it will do an index search only once.

As the application of fulltext searching is to search for a keyword in text, fulltext indexes can only be created on CHAR, VARCHAR, or TEXT data types. It is advisable to create a fulltext index after storing the data in the table rather then creating it at the time of table creation. Storing larger data in tables having fulltext indexes defined can create performance issues while doing insert operations.

The following is a simple example or how a fulltext index converts the table-indexed columns to tokenized fulltext indexes:

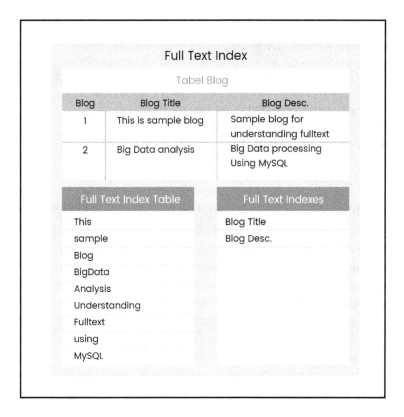

Natural language fulltext search on InnoDB and MyISAM

In natural language fulltext searches, the column used in the match condition must match the columns that were used while creating fulltext indexes. As we have seen in our previous example, to match our keyword, we used `blog_title` and `blog_description` in the match keyword. However, we cannot use `blog_title` or `blog_description` separately. If you want to search your keyword in the title only, then a fulltext index must be created on the `blog_title` field.

There is a certain business logic that is applied when you use natural language fulltext indexes.

Fulltext search has a prebuilt list of keywords that act as stopwords. This means that it will not do indexing on any of these words. For example, the, is, are, and so on are a few stopwords and they are not included in the search index. MySQL maintains a default list of keywords that can be modified. MySQL provides a `ft_stopword_file` parameter where we can specify the name of the file that needs to be used as stopwords instead of using the default stopword list for better customization of your requirement.

MySQL's fulltext parser allows apostrophes or underscores as a part of the word. This means that you can have `mysql_fulltext` or Mysql's featurelist as a valid word list. In this case, we will have three separate words that match, that is, `mysql_fulltext`, Mysql's, and featurelist. If apostrophes are used more than once, then they are skipped and will be considered as two separate keywords. For example, Mysql's will be considered two separate words--Mysql and s. Full text will only consider Mysql a word to look into the index as the default minimum length set for fulltext search is four characters.

If there is a double quote used at the start and end of the searched keywords, MySQL will consider it as a single literal and search for all keywords in the literal.

If searched keywords are present in more than 50% of the records of the table, then fulltext search will return empty results, as MySQL natural language fulltext search has 50% as a threshold. If you are not expecting such behavior and want all results to be displayed, then you should use a Boolean search instead, which does not have the 50% threshold limit.

Fulltext indexing on InnoDB

When a full text index is defined on any char, varchar, or text column of InnoDB, there are a number of index tables created. These tables are referred to as auxiliary tables. Whenever a new record is inserted into the MySQL table, then depending on the fulltext index, its values in the columns are tokenized into multiple words. All these tokenized words are inserted into the auxiliary tables with reference to the table row. There are six such auxiliary tables created where incoming data is partitioned and stored.

As there are multiple auxiliary tables where tokenized words are stored, it can prove to be too expensive to update all these tables every time a new record is inserted, because concurrent requests to these tables will be created multiple times. To avoid this situation, MySQL uses fulltext index caches to cache recently inserted rows. Newly inserted index data is initially stored in the memory cache. There are MySQL parameters that are used to limit or identify the amount of data stored in memory. To configure the fulltext cache size for each of the tables, `innodb_ft_cache_size` can be used. To define the overall cache limit, the `innodb_ft_total_cache_size` parameter can be configured. When the value of the cache size reaches or exceeds the set limit, MySQL will flush the cache and push the cached data into the tables.

Fulltext search in Boolean mode

Using fulltext indexing in Boolean mode allows users to search for multiple words in the index columns using different operators. These operators are used at the beginning or end of the words.

Considering the following blog table lets us understand this better:

blog_id	blog_title	blog_description
1	Introduction to MySQL 8 for big data	This blog will explain importance of MySQL 8 in bigdata lifecycle
2	Querying techniques in MySQL 8	This blog will explain how to query MySQL 8 data
3	Indexing in MySQL 8	This blog will explain how indexing works in MySQL 8

The preceding query will look for all rows containing `Querying` as a keyword, but that do not have indexing.

```
SELECT * FROM blog where MATCH (blog_title, blog_description) AGAINST
('+Querying -Indexing' IN BOOLEAN MODE);
```

This is a list of operators supported `IN BOOLEAN MODE` fulltext queries:

+	This indicates that the words must be present in the rows returned by the query. InnoDB supports only leading + signs, whereas MyISAM can support both leading or trailing + symbols.
-	This indicates that the word must not be there in the rows returned by the query. InnoDB supports only leading - signs, while MyISAM can support leading or trailing - symbols.
@distance	The @distance operator works only for InnoDB and measures the distance between two words mentioned in the search query. You can specify a list of words in double quotes ("") followed by the @distance operator.
~	The tilde sign as a leading operator will consider the score for the rows matching words as negative. Unlike the minus operator, words will be considered in the searched and returned rows.
*	An asterisk is considered a wildcard operator and is always used as a trailing operator. When a keyword is followed by an asterisk, Boolean search will look for the rows matching all records that start with the word specified before the * (asterisk). A word is not considered as a stopword if followed by the * (asterisk).
( )	Parentheses are used to define sub-expressions in the search query. There can be multiple nested parentheses in a query. We will soon see examples of parentheses in a query.
> <	Greater than and less than symbols are used to change the rank of the word in the relevance scores. A greater than symbol increases the weight of the word in the query, while the less than symbol reduces the weight of the word in the search query.
" "	Double quotes are considered literal. When double quotes are used in the search query, fulltext will search for all the words enclosed in double quotes in the rows and exactly in the same order as mentioned. Non-stopping characters are ignored, for example, ',' or '.', while searching for the literals as mentioned in the search query.

The following are a few key properties of MySQL fulltext indexing in Boolean mode:

- Fulltext search in Boolean mode does not hold a 50% threshold like natural language fulltext indexing.
- When using Boolean mode fulltext indexing in InnoDB, it requires all columns used in the MATCH expression to be there in the fulltext index defined. MyISAM can work in Boolean mode without defining a fulltext index, but this can be expensive.
- When using operators, InnoDB accepts single leading operators in fulltext queries. For example, +Querying is supported in InnoDB but ++Querying will throw a syntax error in case of InnoDB, whereas MyISAM will automatically ignore the second Boolean operator.
- Boolean operators as a suffix is not supported in InnoDB. For example, Querying- or Querying+ is not supported in InnoDB and will show a syntax error.
- There is a list of stopwords used by InnoDB and MyISAM that are configurable. innodb_ft_user_stopword_table, innodb_ft_enable_stopword, and innodb_ft_server_stopword_table are tables used by InnoDB for a stopword list, while MyISAM uses ft_stopword_file for the same.

Differentiating full-text indexing and like queries

Like queries are generally used to find exact matches:

```
select * from users where first_name like 'John';
```

Consider the preceding query that is used to find all results with an exact match like John. Now if there is an index defined in the first_name column, then MySQL will use this index to find the results matching John.

Now, consider the following query; there will not be any index used in the query as MySQL does not use indexes that have a wildcard. So there will be a full table scan, which will affect the performance of the query execution.

```
select * from users where first_name like '%John%';
```

Let's consider the following query that does not start with a wildcard but contains a wildcard at the end of the filter:

```
select * from users where first_name like 'John Cena%';
```

This query will return all results that start with the `John Cena` string. However, there will not be any results if any user has the name John or Cena, which might be what we expect in our result.

For fulltext searches, we can define fulltext indexes that use a tokenized-based algorithm to search relevant records, as we have seen in this topic. Using a fulltext search with fulltext indexing is widely used due to its performance and agility.

Spatial indexes

Spatial indexes are different from all other indexes. They cannot be applied on single-dimension data. They can be used to index geographical objects that are normally multidimensional. Spatial indexes use the R-tree data structure to index the data. Since MySQL 5.7, spatial indexes are supported in MyISAM and InnoDB database engines.

The following is a list of spatial data types supported in MySQL:

- POINT
- LINESTRING
- GEOMETRY
- POLYGON
- MULTIPOINT
- MULTILINESTRING
- GEOMETRYCOLLECTION
- MULTIPOLYGON

The following is an example of how to create a spatial index on any spatial column:

```
CREATE TABLE stationary_map (
stationary_id INT(11) NOT NULL AUTO_INCREMENT PRIMARY KEY,
stationary_name varchar(255) NOT NULL,
stationary_location POINT NOT NULL
);
```

To create an index on the `stationary_location` column, the following query can be used:

```
ALTER TABLE stationary_map ADD SPATIAL INDEX(stationary_location);
```

You can drop a spatial index just like any other indexes, as shown in the following code:

```
DROP INDEX stationary_location ON stationary_map;
```

Let's now have a look at indexing JSON data, which plays an important role when we talk about big data and analytics while using it for many use cases.

Indexing JSON data

Big data consists of many documents that are stored in the JSON format, so it is necessary to have proper indexing on JSON data. There is no direct way to define an index on JSON data. We can always create columns from the JSON data and then leverage the generated columns to support indexes.

Let's first understand what generated columns are in MySQL.

Generated columns

Generated columns generally do not have actual information, but they store the information gathered from other columns of the table using some expressions or calculations.

Generated columns can be divided into two types: **virtual generated columns** and **stored generated columns**.

Virtual generated columns

Columns defined as virtual generated columns do not actually store the value but they are calculated on the fly. If there is no column type defined for generated columns, it would use virtual columns by default. InnoDB supports secondary indexes on virtually generated columns. As the value of virtual columns are calculated on the fly, they do not require any additional storage space. However, if an index is created on virtual columns (only for InnoDB), the index will require storage to store the indexed value.

Stored generated columns

The values of stored generated columns are calculated and stored whenever a new row is inserted or an existing row is updated. They store values in the database, hence it requires disk space. Stored generated columns can be indexed as well.

Generated columns can be used for many different scenarios:

- An expression can be stored as a generated column and can be indexed to increase query performance. In this way, a generated column can be used to cache an expression. This expression can also be used as a common stored expression across multiple select queries.
- When a select query is executed with the `where` expression and the expression of the `where` clause matches the generated columns, then the generated columns are indexed. MySQL optimizer will automatically use the generated columns even if they are not explicitly defined in the query.
- Generated columns can be used to calculate or evaluate values. These can be handy, especially for the JSON type of columns.

There are certain rules defined by MySQL to use generated columns:

- Any operators, literals, or built-in functions that are deterministic are allowed. A function is termed deterministic if it can calculate values from the data available in the table and does not require any information from the connected users.
- We cannot use the auto-increment property for a generated column.
- Usage of subqueries, variables, user-defined functions, stored procedures, or variables is not allowed in generated columns.

The following is the syntax for creating generated columns in MySQL 8:

```
Column_name data_type [GENERATED ALWAYS] AS (expression)
[VIRTUAL | STORED]
[UNIQUE [KEY]] [COMMENT comment]
[[NOT] NULL] [[PRIMARY] KEY]
```

The following is an example of how to use generated columns.

Consider the users table where we have `first_name` and `last_name` as columns. Now, if we have high frequency, which would require the combination of `first_name` and `last_name` as `full_name`, then you can create a generated column on the `users` table that will store this concatenated string and return value:

```
CREATE TABLE users (
first_name varchar(100),
last_name varchar(100),
full_name varchar(255) AS (CONCAT(first_name,' ',last_name))
);
```

Now you can use a direct select query to fetch `full_name` from the database:

```
SELECT full_name from users;
```

In InnoDB, we can define a secondary index on the virtual columns. Indexes created on virtual columns are generally referred to as virtual indexes. MySQL InnoDB allows the secondary index to be created on more than one virtual column, or you can define it on a mix of virtual columns and regular columns.

When a secondary index is created on virtual columns, it will need more write operations to create indexes on virtual columns, as the value of the virtual column will be calculated or evaluated at the time of insert and update. If no index is created on virtual columns, it will calculate the value of generated columns at runtime, which can increase the query runtime period.

Defining indexes on JSON

As we discussed earlier, we can create generated columns from the JSON object and then we can create an index on these generated columns, which will make access to JSON data faster.

Consider a JSON object as follows. We need to create a JSON object for the employee details:

```
[
{
'employee_id' : 'emp_0000001',
'employee_first_name' : 'john',
'employee_last_name' : 'carry',
'employee_total_experience_in_years' : '6.5',
'employee_join_date':'2013-03-01',
```

```
'employee_email_address':'john_carry@email.com'
},
{
'employee_id' : 'emp_0000002',
'employee_first_name' : 'bill',
'employee_last_name' : 'watson',
'employee_total_experience_in_years' : '9.5',
'employee_join_date':'2010-05-01',
'employee_email_address':'bill_watson@email.com'
},
{
'employee_id' : 'emp_0000003',
'employee_first_name' : 'sara',
'employee_last_name' : 'perry',
'employee_total_experience_in_years' : '14.5',
'employee_join_date':'2006-07-01',
'employee_email_address':sara_perry@email.com'
}];
```

Let's create a table storing JSON information in the database:

```
CREATE TABLE employee (
employee_detail JSON,
employee_id varchar(255) GENERATED ALWAYS AS
(employee_detail->>'$.employee_id'),
INDEX idx_employee_id(employee_id)
);
```

Now let's insert the JSON objects that we created here:

```
INSERT INTO employee (employee_detail) values
('{"employee_id" : "emp_0000001","employee_first_name" :
"john","employee_last_name" : "carry","employee_total_experience_in_years"
:
"6.5","employee_join_date":"2013-03-01","employee_email_address":"john_carr
y@email.com"}'),
('{"employee_id" : "emp_0000002","employee_first_name" :
"bill","employee_last_name" : "watson","employee_total_experience_in_years"
:
"9.5","employee_join_date":"2010-05-01","employee_email_address":"bill_wats
on@email.com"}'),
('{"employee_id" : "emp_0000003","employee_first_name" :
"sara","employee_last_name" : "perry","employee_total_experience_in_years"
:
"14.5","employee_join_date":"2006-07-01","employee_email_address":"sara_per
ry@email.com"}');
```

Now let's apply the select query using the generated columns:

```
SELECT employee_detail->>'$.employee_join_date' as joining_date FROM
employee WHERE employee_id = 'emp_0000002';
```

It will print 2010-05-01 as the output of the query.

Now let's check the describe sentence to verify whether any index key can be used or not as per following example:

```
DESCRIBE SELECT employee_detail->>'$.employee_join_date' as joining_date
FROM employee WHERE employee_id = 'emp_0000002';
```

id	1
Select_type	SIMPLE
table	employee
partitions	null
type	ref
Possible_keys	idx_employee_id
Key	idx_employee_id
Key_len	103
Ref	Const
Rows	1
Filtered	100
Extra	null

As we can see, the table uses the idx_employee_id index to fetch records. So in this way, we can make searching JSON data much faster than a normal lookup of the JSON records for large datasets.

Summary

You now have good knowledge of the different types of index structures supported by MySQL and now how to create an index in MySQL. You also learned different types of indexes available in MySQL 8 such as clustered index, covering index, descending index, and invisible index. We got a good understanding of fulltext indexing and how natural language fulltext indexes and fulltext indexes on Boolean mode works.

In the next chapter, we will cover some interesting things to boost MySQL performance such as how to set up Memcache, usage of Memcache, Memcache configuration, using Memcache APIs, how to analyze data stored in Memcache, and how to use Memcache APIs in MySQL 8.

4
Using Memcached with MySQL

8

In the previous chapter, we saw how indexing works in MySQL 8 and how it can be useful for better performance. You also learned how to create indexes and saw the different types of indexes available in MySQL 8 such as clustered index, covering index, descending index, and invisible index. We got a good understanding of fulltext indexing and how natural language fulltext indexes and fulltext indexes on Boolean mode works.

In this chapter, we will discuss using Memcached with MySQL 8. The following are the topics that will be covered:

- Setting up Memcached
- Using Memcached
- Analyzing data stored in Memcached
- Memcached replication configuration
- Memcached APIs for different technologies

Let's first start with an overview of Memcached with MySQL 8 followed by other details of Memcached.

Overview of Memcached

While talking about handling Big Data with MySQL, we would have to obviously think about the **performance**--how do we handle the performance when storing and retrieving data frequently? One of the prominent answers is Memcached, which boosts the performance of frequent data retrieval and storage because it skips the query parser, SQL optimizer, and other parts of the engine that are unnecessary and allows us to store or retrieve data directly with InnoDB. Using Memcached, data management is much faster and convenient for handling Big Data.

MySQL 8 provides you with the InnoDB Memcached plugin named `daemon_memcached`, which can help us in managing data easily. It will automatically store and retrieve data from InnoDB tables and provide get, set, and incr operations that remove performance overhead by skipping SQL parsing, which speeds up data operations.

The following diagram will help you understand better how queries are parsed when using Memcache:

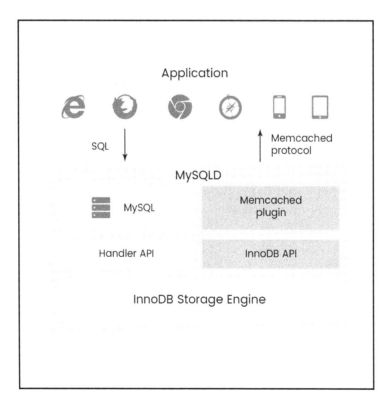

As shown in the previous diagram, the Memcached plugin is directly connected to the **InnoDB Storage Engine**, and SQL parsing layers don't come into its way. This removes the overhead of data retrieval and storing, resulting in faster results than traditional SQL. It transparently writes data into an InnoDB table as well as handling both unstructured and structured data easily. Initially, data will be written on Memcached cache memory and then transferred between the memory and disk automatically. Memcache helps when database transactions are higher, which would take time to store and retrieve data this plugin provides an efficient way to handle Big Data with better scalability and high availability.

The `daemon_memcached` plugin is tied up with the MySQL server process that avoids the network overhead on parsing requests between different processes. This plugin can run with the MySQL instance comfortably as it provides an easy way to control memory and also consumes relatively less CPU.

The Memcached plugin also manages the buffer pool internally, which helps serve subsequent requests for the same data without going into the InnoDB storage engine. It caches the frequent data in the memory and provides data from the memory pool when requested. This basically skips fetching data from the InnoDB tables, which would comparatively have heavy I/O operations; hence, it is faster to retrieve data from the memory of the buffer pool instead of InnoDB.

InnoDB also has capabilities to handle composing and decomposing multiple column values into a single Memcached item value. For instance, if we want to store them data in different columns, we can merge the column values as 1 | 2 | 3 | 4 and store in a Memcached cache. InnoDB will understand this and split the values based on the separator and store them in different columns. This plugin also has the feature of serialization, which converts binary files, code blocks, or any other objects to strings that can be stored, and provides the simplicity to retrieve such objects.

Let's set up Memcached and go through its configuration as we move further.

Setting up Memcached

MySQL has its own Memcached plugin, `daemon_memcached`, which is tightly integrated with the MySQL server. This improves the performance and avoids network traffic over the traditional Memcached approach.

In the traditional way, Memcached was running on a separate port and as a different process; hence, it would have an overhead of network communication between MySQL and Memcached. However, this plugin made it easy to use and lightweight as it is integrated with the MySQL server itself.

Supported environments for this plugin are as follows:

- Linux
- Solaris
- OS X

Let's see to how to set up the `daemon_memcached` plugin in the MySQL server. We would have to install this plugin on each of the MySQL server instances, in case we are using the cluster environment of MySQL.

Installation

To enable the Memcached feature with MySQL, we first need to install the dependency for the Memcached plugin. `libevent` is the dependency that must be installed on the server to enable the Memcached plugin. The following command will help you install the libevent in the Linux server:

```
yum install libevent-dev
```

After installing the required dependency, we need to execute the Memcached configuration script that will create a database and certain tables as part of the Memcached configuration. This configuration script is already available at the following location:

```
<MYSQL_HOME>/share/innodb_memcached_config.sql
```

Here, `<MYSQL_HOME>` is the directory where MySQL has been installed. For Linux, this configuration script file will be available at `/usr/share/mysql/innodb_memcached_config.sql` by default.

To execute this script, use the following command under the MySQL prompt:

```
mysql> source <MYSQL_HOME>/share/innodb_memcached_config.sql
```

The preceding script will create a new database as `innodb_memcache` that will have the following tables:

- `containers`: This is the most important table of the Memcached database. This table contains all the InnoDB table entries that allow you to store Memcached values. An InnoDB table must register in this table in order to use the Memcached plugin. It also describes the mapping with the InnoDB table columns.

- `cache_policies`: A cache policy is defined under this table. It can have different policies for get, set, flush, and delete operations within a single policy. We can specify innodb_only, cache-only, caching, and disable as the policy values against different operations.

- `config_options`: This table has different Memcached settings that can be updated at runtime using SQL. For example, we can configure the separator to identify the different column values from a single string.

Apart from the the preceding databases and tables, Memcached will also create a test database that has only one table named `demo_test`. This table is also mapped in the container table by inserting entries for the table data.

Now it's time to activate the `daemon_memcached` plugin by executing the following command under the MySQL prompt:

```
mysql> INSTALL PLUGIN daemon_memcached soname "libmemcached.so";
```

After successfully activating the Memcached plugin, it will integrate with MySQL and will be automatically activated each time the MySQL server gets restarted.

Verification

Once you have activated the Memcached plugin, it will start listening on port `11211` by default. The Memcached interface can be accessed using the telnet session, as shown in the following screenshot:

```
[root@ip-172-31-22-59 ~]# telnet localhost 11211
Trying 127.0.0.1...
Connected to localhost.
Escape character is '^]'.
```

If you successfully get connected through the telnet command, it means that Memcached has been successfully integrated with MySQL. You can perform certain operations on the Memcached interface to store, retrieve, or delete data.

Here is a list of basic Memcached commands:

Command	Description
get	To retrieve data by key.
set	To store the key/value pair in Memcached. This will also update the value in case a key already exists, hence it is a combination of insert and update.
add	This will insert the new key/value and it will not work if a key already exists.
replace	This is used to update data for the existing key.
append	This will append value at the end of existing value associated with the key.
prepend	This will append value at the beginning of existing value associated with the key.
delete	To delete data by its key.

Using of Memcached

Memcached can be used at various stages in real-world applications. Its integration with MySQL makes it more comfortable for you to handle Big Data. Let's see the importance of using Memcached by understanding the different advantages.

Performance tuner

We always care about the performance while handing Big Data. We may have many questions before we start, such as how MySQL can be optimized from a performance perspective. We assume that managing Big Data with MySQL can impact performance as this is a pure structured database. But no! MySQL has a pretty simple way to handle Big Data by integrating Memcached and using it as a NoSQL database. This way, it will improve the performance latency and provide efficiency while managing Big Data with MySQL.

Memcached is one of the performance tuners for MySQL with Big Data. Memcached removes the SQL layer and directly accesses the InnoDB database tables. Hence, overhead operations like SQL parsing will no longer be executed, which really impacts the performance. Memcached will also serve frequent data requests from memory without going to the database, which makes it faster for data retrieval.

Caching tool

Memcached can be used as a caching tool as it caches the data in memory. A buffer pool is managed by Memcached that caches the InnoDB data and serves to the request rather than going into the InnoDB table. Basically, we do not need to load the data in the cache manually; it will automatically get stored in the cache memory whenever the first request is made from the application. Memcached with MySQL also provides you with a way to make in-memory data persistent so that we can use it significantly for various data types without losing it. Memcached can also start and stop without losing the updates made to the cached data. These data transfers between memory to InnoDB tables get automatically handled by the plugin where we do not need to bother much with consistency of data.

Easy to use

Memcached is quite easy to use with real-world applications and makes it easy for you to handle Big Data by providing greater performance. Now MySQL 8 has the `daemon_memcached` plugin within the MySQL server itself, which makes it lightweight and easy to manage as it does not consume any extra resources and removes the overhead of managing a separate Memcached server.

Analyzing data stored in Memcached

It's time to get our hands dirty by playing with the Memcached interface. An InnoDB table entry should be there in the containers table of the Memcached database to use this table through the Memcached interface. By default, while installing Memcached, a `demo_test` table is automatically created under the `test` database and the same table entry is inserted into the `containers` table. Let's define the new mapping and perform a few operations. I am getting eager to get to the next section!

I have created a `student_result` table to store students' results data with the following query:

```
mysql> CREATE TABLE student_result (
  student_id INT PRIMARY KEY,
  student_name VARCHAR(20),
  maths INT,
  english INT,
  history INT,
  flags INT,
  cas BIGINT UNSIGNED,
  expiry INT);
```

Mapping of the `student_result` table can be done by inserting an entry into the `containers` table as follows:

```
mysql> INSERT INTO innodb_memcache.containers
  (name, db_schema, db_table, key_columns, value_columns, flags, cas_column,
expire_time_column, unique_idx_name_on_key)
  VALUES
  ('default', 'test', 'student_result', 'student_id',
'student_name,maths,english,history','flags','cas','expiry', 'PRIMARY');
```

To make use of this new mapping, it is recommended that you restart Memcached using the following commands:

```
mysql> UNINSTALL PLUGIN daemon_memcached;
  mysql> INSTALL PLUGIN daemon_memcached soname "libmemcached.so";
```

Now we are all set to have some queries executed through Memcached. Let's access the Memcached terminal using `telnet` to store and retrieve student results as follows:

1. Insert a new record:

```
telnet localhost 11211
  Trying 127.0.0.1...
Connected to localhost.
Escape character is '^]'.
set 101 0 0 22
Jaydip|50|60|70
STORED
```

Once you have executed the `set` command with the respective key and data, it will be automatically stored in the `student_result` table, as shown in the following screenshot:

```
mysql> select * from test.student_result;
+------------+--------------+-------+---------+---------+-------+-----+--------+
| student_id | student_name | maths | english | history | flags | cas | expiry |
+------------+--------------+-------+---------+---------+-------+-----+--------+
|        101 | Jaydip       |    50 |      60 |      70 |     0 |   2 |      0 |
+------------+--------------+-------+---------+---------+-------+-----+--------+
1 row in set (0.00 sec)
```

2. Retrieve the record with a key:

```
get 101
VALUE 101 0 15
Jaydip|50|60|70
```

The preceding command will fetch only a single row but it also supports retrieving multiple key/value pairs in a single query, which improves performance by reducing communication traffic. Passing multiple keys with the get command will result in data from each key. The following example shows multiple get support.

3. Retrieve multiple records:

```
get 101 102
VALUE 101 0 15
Jaydip|50|60|70
VALUE 102 0 14
Keyur|45|63|87
END
```

The daemon_memcached plugin also supports ranged queries that can be helpful in finding records with the help of different operators such as <, >, <=, and >=. Conditional-based record finding makes our day easy with range queries. An operator must be preceded by the @ symbol.

4. Range queries:

```
get @>101
VALUE 102 0 14
Keyur|45|63|87
END
```

This will fetch all records that are greater than the 101 key.

Memcached replication configuration

In a simple word, replication is the copying of data from one server to one or more servers. Replication enables the spreading of the load to multiple servers, which improves the performance and decreases the chances of data corruption, as the data is distributed among various servers. MySQL 8 supports different replication methods but the traditional method is to replicate through binary logs of the master server. A binary log is a file that collects all the statements that attempt to change the table data. These statements will be executed on the slave servers to replicate the master data.

The `daemon_memcached` plugin has the capability to manage the binary log on the master server, and the same can be used for replication on slave servers. All Memcached commands are supported by binary logging.

Follow these steps to enable the binary log replication in MySQL 8:

1. During the startup of the server, add the `--innodb_api_enable_binlog=1` and `--log-bin` system variables to enable the binary log on the master server:

```
mysqld ... --log-bin --innodb_api_enable_binlog=1
```

2. Set the replication master by adding the following options to the `my.cnf` or `my.ini` file. A `server-id` should be unique for each of the servers. If you omit server-id (or set it explicitly to its default value of 0), the master refuses any connections from slaves. The MySQL server needs a restart after adding the following properties:

```
[mysqld]
log-bin=mysql-bin
server-id=1
```

3. Set the replication slave by adding the following properties to the `my.cnf` or `my.ini` file. Shut down the server and edit the file by a unique server ID on each slave:

```
[mysqld]
server-id=2
```

4. All servers need to be in sync; hence, take a backup of the master database and restore it in all of the slave servers.
5. Execute the following command to obtain the master binary log coordinates:

```
mysql> SHOW MASTER STATUS;
```

6. Execute the following command on the slave server to set up the slave server using master binary logs:

```
mysql> CHANGE MASTER TO
  MASTER_HOST='localhost',
  MASTER_USER='root',
  MASTER_PASSWORD='',
  MASTER_PORT = 13000,
  MASTER_LOG_FILE='0.000001,
  MASTER_LOG_POS=114;
```

7. Execute the following command to start the slave server:

```
mysql> START SLAVE;
```

Now all the relevant configuration is set to have replication with Memcached. We can verify the configuration by executing queries through Memcached, and the same data will persist to the master and slave servers.

Memcached APIs for different technologies

An application can store and retrieve data through the Memcached interface using various APIs that are available. Memcached APIs are available in different programming languages such as Perl, Python, Java, PHP, C, and Ruby. With the help of a Memcached API, an application can interact with the Memcached interface to store and retrieve information.

Memcached stores information in a cache that can be referred to by a single string as a key. This key is used as a reference for the data retrieval and storage. Memcached always serves data requests based on the key as a reference. The cache therefore operates like a large associative array or hash table.

The Memcached interface has a common method across all the programming languages to store and retrieve information, although the language-specific mechanism might be different. Let's look at a few common methods and their usage:

- get(key): This method is used to fetch information from the cache with respect to the provided key. It returns the data associated with the key, or else returns a null value.

- `set(key, value [, expiry])`: This method is used to store information in the cache with the specified key. It will automatically update the data in case the same key exists, or else it will create a new key/value pair in the cache memory. The third parameter is optional in this method, where we can specify the expiration time of the data. By specifying the expiration time, it will automatically delete cached information when the time matches the provided expiration time. This expiration time should be in seconds format.

- `add(key, value [, expiry])`: This method adds data with reference to the key only if the specified key does not already exist. It is similar to the set method with the only difference being that it will not update the data if the key already exists in the cache. We can specify the expiration time in seconds to clear the data after a stipulated time.

- `replace(key, value [, expiry])`: This method updates existing data with new data, only if the key already exists in Memcached.

- `delete(key [, time])`: This will delete the data associated with the provided key. We can also specify time as an optional parameter to lock the addition of a new item for a stipulated period with the same key.

- `incr(key , value)`: It will increase existing data with the specified value of the associated key.

- `decr(key , value)`: It will decrease existing data with the specified value of the associated key.

- `flush_all`: This will invalidate all the items from the cache. It will not delete them but they are silently destroyed from the cache.

Memcached with Java

Java applications can be easily integrated with the Memcached interface using the client that is already available in Java. This Java client is available in the GitHub repository and you can download it from `https://github.com/gwhalin/Memcached-Java-Client/downloads`.

All the Java classes under the `com.danga.MemCached` package provide a native interface for the Memcached instances. It is preferable to use JSON or non-binary serialization formats for the serialization of data instead of the serialization feature of Java.

You can also obtain the Memcached client for your maven project with the following dependency:

```
<dependency>
 <groupId>com.whalin</groupId>
 <artifactId>Memcached-Java-Client</artifactId>
 <version>3.0.2</version>
</dependency>
```

Let's see how to connect to the Memcached instances using the Java interface.

1. Create a `MemCachedClient` instance:

```
MemCachedClient memCachedClient = new MemCachedClient();
```

2. Configure the list of servers, along with the weightage, with the help of `SockIOPool`:

```
SockIOPool pool = SockIOPool.getInstance();
 pool.setServers( servers );
 pool.setWeights( weights );
```

Here, `servers` contains an array of the Memcached instances that can be used, and `weights` are an individual weight for each of the servers.

3. Different connection properties can also be set in `SockIOPool` such as minimum connection, initial connection, idle timeout, and so on. These properties are optional and based on the requirements.

```
pool.setInitConn( 5 );
 pool.setMinConn( 5 );
 pool.setMaxConn( 250 );
```

4. Initialize the `SockIOPool` pool once you are done with the configuration of the connection parameters:

```
pool.initialize();
```

Let's see the full example that describes integration with the Memcached client:

```
class MemcachedUtil {
private static String[] servers = {"localhost:11211"};
private static Integer[] weights = { 1 };
public MemCachedClient getMemCachedClient() {
SockIOPool pool = SockIOPool.getInstance();
pool.setServers(servers);
pool.setWeights( weights );
```

```
if (!pool.isInitialized()) {
 pool.setInitConn( 5 );pool.setMinConn( 5 );pool.setMaxConn( 250
);pool.initialize();    }MemCachedClient memCachedClient = new
MemCachedClient();memCachedClient.setCompressEnable(false);
memCachedClient.setCompressThreshold(0);
 return memCachedClient;
}
}
```

Memcached with PHP

The Memcached interface can also be integrated with PHP applications through the PECL extension. The following command will help you install the PECL extension for Linux-based systems:

```
yum --install php-pecl-memcache
```

You can also use the the following command:

```
apt-get install php-memcache
```

Once it gets installed, we can specify the global configuration options in the php.ini file. Let's see how to connect Memcached from a PHP application.

Create a Memcached object by connecting to the servers as follows:

```
$memcache = new Memcache;
$memcache->addServer('localhost',11211);
```

We can add multiple servers by calling the addServer method by providing the host name and port number as arguments. This will not immediately open the connection between the Memcached interface and application: it will only open once you try to store or retrieve the value.

Let's see one small example to get data from Memcached:

```php
<?php
 $memcache = new Memcache;
 $memcache->addServer('10.12.4.15',11211);
 $memcache->addServer('10.12.4.16',11211);
$memcache->set('maths','60');
 echo $memcache->get('maths');
?>
```

Memcached with Ruby

There are many modules available to integrate Memcached with the Ruby language. The `Ruby-MemCache` client is one of them, which provides an interface for Memcached. We can install the `Ruby-MemCache` client using `RubyGems` with the help of the following command:

```
gem install Ruby-MemCache
```

This command will automatically install the client and its required libraries. Once we have installed this client, we can then access the Memcached interface as follows:

1. Create a Memcached client:

   ```
   require 'memcache'
   memc = MemCache::new ' 10.12.4.15:11211:1'
   ```

   Here, the one after the port number is the weightage of a particular server. We can also add multiple servers by adding to the same Memcached object, as follows:

   ```
   memc += ["10.12.4.16:11211:2"]
   ```

2. Set data in Memcached:

   ```
   memc["key"] = "value"
   ```

3. Get the data from Memcached:

   ```
   print memc["key"]
   ```

Memcached with Python

To access the Memcached interface with Python applications, a Python Memcached module needs to be installed, which can be downloaded from `https://www.tummy.com/software/python-memcached/`.

After downloading the preceding package, it can be installed using the Python installer as follows:

```
python setup.py install
```

Once we have this module installed, it can be easily accessible by creating a new instance of the `memcache.Client` class:

```
import memcache
memcached = memcache.Client(['localhost:11211'])
```

1. Set data in Memcached:

```
memcached.set('key','value')
```

2. Get the data from Memcached:

```
memc.get('key')
```

All programming languages behave in almost the same way while accessing the Memcached interface. Generic functions are also available in all language interfaces such as get, set, add, replace, delete, and so on. Most of the functionality remains the same across all languages, but it's only a matter of syntax used based on different programming languages.

Summary

In this chapter, we discussed using Memcached with MySQL 8 for Big Data usage and the architecture of the overall system in which Memcached takes a prominent place. You learned how Memcached can be installed on a Linux-based system and we also discussed the usage of Memcached in real-world applications. We also played around with data through the Memcached interface using different query techniques. We covered the Memcached configuration that needs to be done for replication purposes. Finally, we saw the different APIs available for various programming languages including Java, PHP, Ruby, and Python.

In the next chapter, we will see how large data can be distributed using various partitioning techniques to help Big Data, which can be easily managed in MySQL 8.

5
Partitioning High Volume Data

In the previous chapter, you learned the basics of Memcached and its wonderful features. We also went into detail about working in different scenarios and how we can use Memcached APIs to improve the performance of our MySQL query. Let's now learn different partitioning methods and how partitioning can help in case of large data tables in this chapter.

We will cover below topics in this chapter about partitioning in MySQL 8:

- Partitioning in MySQL 8
- Horizontal partitioning in MySQL 8
- Vertical partitioning
- Pruning partitions in MySQL
- Querying on partitioned data

When we talk about big data, it is automatically considered that we need to deal with large data tables where different information is stored. For any organization, it is very important to store data in such a way that the database provides scalability, performance, availability, and security. For instance, in a highly accessed e-commerce store, there are thousands, or more, of orders placed frequently. So to maintain day-wise order delivery showing a dashboard of current orders, what is required is to to query a table showing orders of past five years; the process will take a long time to execute with the current data. Here, historical order data is needed for the analytical purpose of finding user behavior or trends, but this will be required to be performed on limited datasets.

There are various ways to achieve the best suitable solution for high availability, scalability, and highly performing architecture; the key ingredient is partitioning. In a database, data in each table is stored in physical file groups. So by dividing this data table from a single file group to a multiple file group can reduce the file size and help us create a scalable and high performing database.

The following are the key benefits of using partitioning in a database:

- **Scalability**: As data will be shared among more than one partition, servers can be configured to use multiple nodes and partitions can be configured among multiple nodes. Doing so will eliminate any hardware limits and allow the database to scale up to a large extent to accommodate high volume data.
- **High performance**: As data is stored among multiple partitions, each query will be executed on a small portion of the data. For example, in an e-commerce store with order history of more than two years, to get a list of orders placed in the current month will require checking only a single partition and not the entire order history, thus reducing the query execution time. To fetch the query on more than one partition, we can also run this in parallel, thus reducing the overall time to fetch data from the database.
- **High availability**: In partitioning, data is divided across multiple file groups. Each file group is logically connected but can be accessed and worked on independently. So if one of the file groups or partitions gets corrupted or one of the nodes in the server fails, then we will not lose access to the entire table, but only a section of the database will not be available, thus eliminating the chances of system failure and making your system highly available.
- **Security**: It may be that some of the data in tables requires high security measurements for data theft or data leaks. By partitioning, you can provide additional security to one or more partition to avoid any security issues, thus improving data accessibility with data security.

Partitioning in MySQL 8

In general terms, partitioning is logically dividing anything into multiple subgroups so that each subgroup can be identified independently and can be combined into a single partition. Let's understand what partitioning means in terms of **RDBMS**.

What is partitioning?

Partitioning is generally used to divide data into multiple logical file groups for the purpose of performance, availability, and manageability. When dealing with big data, the normal tendency of data is to be in terms of billions of records. So to improve performance of the database, it is better to divide data among multiple file groups. These file groups can be on a single machine or shared across multiple machines and identified by a key. These file groups are known as **partitioned data**.

Partitioning types

Data in the table can be partitioned in two ways:

- Horizontal partitioning
- Vertical partitioning

Horizontal partitioning

When the number of rows in the table is very large, the table can be divided into multiple partitions known as **horizontal partitioning**. When horizontal partitioning is used, each partition of the table contains the same number of columns. It is possible to access all partitions at once, or you can access each partition individually.

Vertical partitioning

In vertical partitioning, the columns of the tables are partitioned to achieve performance and better management of the database. Vertical partitioning can be achieved in two ways. The first one is normalizing tables. Instead of having too many columns in the table, columns can be divided into multiple tables by dividing data. The second one is creating separate physical file groups for defined columns in the table. Vertical partitioning is currently not supported in MySQL 8.

In MySQL, when we do partitioning, all partitions of the table must use a single database engine. In MySQL 8, partitioning is supported only in the InnoDB storage engine. So all partitions of the table and all tables that may need to be partitioned must be using InnoDB as the storage engine. In MySQL 5.7, partitioning was supported in the NDB cluster database engine as well. However, as of now, in MySQL 8, the NDB cluster is not supported so InnoDB remains the only database engine with partitioning support, which is widely used.

Let's look at a few of the benefits associated with partitioning:

- If a table contains historical data, like logs of an application, data older than six months does not provide any significance to the application to be active. If partitioning is created based on months, you can easily remove one of the partitions.
- In the same preceding case of logs, if we want to filter data between two dates, the MySQL optimizer can identify the specific partitions, where it can find the filtered records, which can result in much faster query results, as the number of rows to check is reduced drastically.

- MySQL 8 also supports querying data on particular partitions. It can reduce the number of records to check when you know the partition that needs to be queried for the data required.

Horizontal partitioning in MySQL 8

As mentioned, horizontal partitioning will create more than one partition of the data. Each partition will have the same number of columns. Different partitioning techniques are used to divide the page into multiple partitions. Consider the following figure for horizontal partitioning:

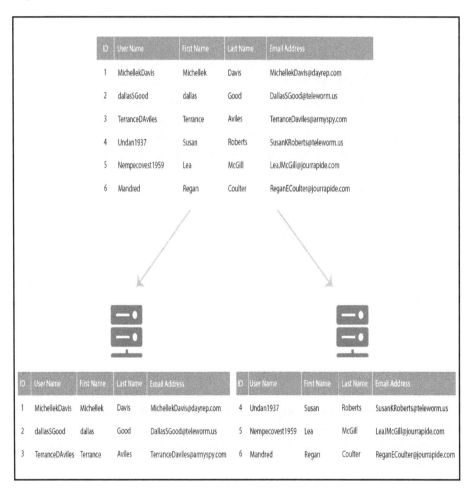

The following is the list of partitioning types supported in MySQL 8:

- Range partitioning
- List partitioning
- Hash partitioning
- Columns partitioning
- Key partitioning
- Sub partitioning

Let's understand each partitioning type in detail.

Range partitioning

When partitioning is done based on expressions that contain contiguous non-repetitive values of ranges, it is known as **range partitioning**. The expression for range partitioning contains the key VALUE LESS THAN operator.

There are multiple data types, based on which we can partition the table:

```
CREATE TABLE access_log (
log_id INT NOT NULL,
type VARCHAR(100),
access_url VARCHAR(100),
access_date TIMESTAMP NOT NULL,
response_time INT NOT NULL,
access_by INT NOT NULL
)
PARTITION BY RANGE (UNIX_TIMESTAMP(access_date)) (
PARTITION p0 VALUES LESS THAN (UNIX_TIMESTAMP('2017-05-01 00:00:00')),
PARTITION p1 VALUES LESS THAN (UNIX_TIMESTAMP('2017-09-01 00:00:00')),
PARTITION p2 VALUES LESS THAN (UNIX_TIMESTAMP('2018-01-01 00:00:00')),
PARTITION p3 VALUES LESS THAN (UNIX_TIMESTAMP('2018-05-01 00:00:00')),
PARTITION p4 VALUES LESS THAN (UNIX_TIMESTAMP('2018-09-01 00:00:00')),
PARTITION p5 VALUES LESS THAN (UNIX_TIMESTAMP('2019-01-01 00:00:00')),
);
```

So as per the preceding query, there will be six partitions created for the access log table. As per the partition, each partition will store access data of four months. So, let's say, when a new access log comes for the date 15th August, it will automatically go to the p2 partition. What will happen if any data comes after 1st January 2019? As there is no partition range defined for any data post 2018, it will throw an error when the data out of range is inserted. So, to overcome this, we should define the upper value of the range. In MySQL 8, we can provide the upper limit using the MAXVALUE keyword. MAXVALUE will always take the maximum possible value for the columns based on the data type. We can do the following partition query to achieve this:

```
PARTITION BY RANGE (UNIX_TIMESTAMP(access_date)) (
PARTITION p0 VALUES LESS THAN (UNIX_TIMESTAMP('2017-05-01 00:00:00')),
PARTITION p1 VALUES LESS THAN (UNIX_TIMESTAMP('2017-09-01 00:00:00')),
PARTITION p2 VALUES LESS THAN (UNIX_TIMESTAMP('2018-01-01 00:00:00')),
PARTITION p3 VALUES LESS THAN (UNIX_TIMESTAMP('2018-05-01 00:00:00')),
PARTITION p4 VALUES LESS THAN (UNIX_TIMESTAMP('2018-09-01 00:00:00')),
PARTITION p5 VALUES LESS THAN (UNIX_TIMESTAMP('2019-01-01 00:00:00')),
PARTITION p6 VALUES LESS THAN MAXVALUE,
);
```

We have created one more partition, p6, with MAXVALUE. So now, if any access log comes on or after 1st January 2019, it will go to partition p6.

This will make it easier for us to perform two tasks:

- It will now allow us to remove data that is stale and of no use. For example, we can delete partition p0 in 2018 as it will have less impact on the data.
- At any point in time, we can change the criteria for the partition using the ALTER table query. So, post 2018, if we want to recreate a partition, it will be an easy task to perform.

When using range partitioning with TIMESTAMP columns, UNIX_TIMESTAMP is the only expression you can use to partition data. When using expressions in range partitioning, it must return a value that can be used by the VALUE LESS THAN expression, otherwise MySQL will give an error.

While inserting data in the database, if the value of the column used for the partitioning is *null*, then MySQL will add the newly inserted row to the lowest partition.

List partitioning

In list partitioning, the partitioning expression contains syntax that checks against a list of values and, based on matching values, partitions are created. The expressions for list partitioning contain the key VALUES IN operator:

```
CREATE TABLE access_log (
log_id INT NOT NULL,
type VARCHAR(100),
access_url VARCHAR(100),
access_date TIMESTAMP NOT NULL,
response_time INT NOT NULL,
access_by INT NOT NULL
website_id INT
)

PARTITION BY LIST(website_id) (
PARTITION PartitionNorth VALUES IN (1,2),
PARTITION PartitionSouth VALUES IN (3,4),
PARTITION PartitionWest VALUES IN (5,6),
PARTITION PartitionEast VALUES IN (7,8)
);
```

If the access log belongs to multiple websites, we can partition the access log table into multiple partitions. Here, we have divided the access log data according to their regions. All access logs from websites belonging to the northern region of the country will reside in a single partition, which can then be useful for analyzing access log data based on the region of the country.

In list partitioning, NULL values in the partition defining keys are accepted only if any of the partition's value lists contains NULL as a permissible value. If we try to insert any record having null value in the key used for a partition, and null is not a permissible value for any of the partitions, it will give an error.

In the preceding example, consider the following list of partitions:

```
PARTITION BY LIST(website_id) (
PARTITION PartitionNorth VALUES IN (1,2),
PARTITION PartitionSouth VALUES IN (3,4),
PARTITION PartitionWest VALUES IN (5,6),
PARTITION PartitionEast VALUES IN (7,8),
PARTITION PartitionNoRegion Values IN (NULL)
);
```

Here, we have defined a new partition, `PartitionNoRegion`. If, in the access log, we are not able to identify the region of the country, and if there is any chance of having `website_id` as a null value, then this data will be stored in the new partition created.

Hash partitioning

Hash partitioning uses user-defined expressions to identify partitions. In hash partitioning, the number of partitions are predefined and, based on expressions applied on the column values, inserted data is partitioned. Hash partitioning distributes data evenly. It is required that the expression must return non-negative integer values:

```
CREATE TABLE access_log (
log_id INT NOT NULL,
type VARCHAR(100),
access_url VARCHAR(100),
access_date TIMESTAMP NOT NULL,
response_time INT NOT NULL,
access_by INT NOT NULL
website_id INT
)
PARTITION BY HASH(website_id)
PARTITIONS 4;
```

As shown in the preceding query, we do not explicitly need to define in which partition a value should be inserted. The only thing that we have defined here is the hashing column, website ID, and number of partitions for the table. The number of partitions is optional and if no number is defined, then it will default to one partition for the table.

In hash partitioning, the partition number is identified using the modulus function:

```
Partition Number = Modulus of (Expression, No of Partition)
In the preceding example, if the newly inserted value has website ID 2:
Partition Number = Modulus of (2,4)
Partition Number = 2
```

So the resulting data will be stored in partition number 2. Based on the output of the preceding formula, the partition number is identified.

In hash partitioning, if `NULL` is used as a value in a partition defining column, `NULL` is considered zero.

Linear hash partitioning is a variant of hash partitioning. Where regular hash partitioning uses modulus to identify partition number, linear hash partitioning uses the power of two algorithms to identify the partition number:

```
CREATE TABLE access_log (
log_id INT NOT NULL,
type VARCHAR(100),
access_url VARCHAR(100),
access_date TIMESTAMP NOT NULL,
response_time INT NOT NULL,
access_by INT NOT NULL
website_id INT
)
PARTITION BY LINEAR HASH(website_id)
PARTITIONS 4;
```

For linear hashing, the calculation of the partition number is done based on the following formula:

```
Resulting Value = POWER OF (2, CEILING (LOG(2, Number of Partition))),
```

The preceding expression will find out a value based on the number of partitions defined in the create table definition:

```
Partition Number = (Expression) & (Resulting Value)
```

MySQL will perform bitwise & operation on the resulting value from expression one to find out the partition number. When the partition number is greater than or equal to the number of partitions, it will use another expression to find out a lower number:

```
While
  Partition Number >= Number of Partition:
  Resulting Value = Resulting Value / 2
  Partition Number = Partition Number & (Resulting Value - 1)
```

So MySQL will loop the code block until it finds the partition number that is lower than the number of partitions defined in the table.

When linear hash partitioning is used, dropping, splitting, adding, or merging of the partitions are much faster compared to regular hash partitioning. However, data is not properly distributed when compared to hash partitioning.

Column partitioning

Column partitioning is actually another variant of range partitioning and list partitioning. Column partitioning supports string columns such as varchar, char, binary, and varbinary in the partitioning expression. Let's check in detail both types of column partitioning.

Range column partitioning

Range column partitioning is different from range partitioning. Range column partitioning only supports the name of the columns in the expression. Also, more than one column can be used for range partitioning. We can use date, datetime, or string as an input for range column partitioning.

```
CREATE TABLE table_name
PARTITION BY RANGE COLUMNS(column_list) (
PARTITION partition_name VALUES LESS THAN (value_list)[,
PARTITION partition_name VALUES LESS THAN (value_list)][, ...]
)
```

As defined in the preceding code, you can define a list of columns, based on which the partitioning of a table can be created:

```
column_list: column_name[, column_name][, ...]
```

There should be an equal number of fields in the value list and column list:

```
value_list: value[, value][, ...]
```

Let's understand this equation by example:

```
CREATE TABLE access_log (
log_id INT NOT NULL,
type VARCHAR(100),
access_url VARCHAR(100),
access_date TIMESTAMP NOT NULL,
response_time INT NOT NULL,
access_by INT NOT NULL
website_id INT
)
PARTITION BY RANGE COLUMNS(website_id,log_id)
PARTITION partition0 VALUE LESS THAN (1,10000)
PARTITION partition1 VALUE LESS THAN (2,10000)
PARTITION partition2 VALUE LESS THAN (1,100000)
PARTITION partition3 VALUE LESS THAN (2,100000)
PARTITION partition4 value LESS THAN (MAXVALUE, MAXVALUE)
```

Here, as you can see, there are five partitions created that store rows partitioned by website ID and log ID. In range column partitioning, a partition is created based on the comparison of combination of columns rather than individual values, as in the case of range partitions. As shown in the example, `partition2` has the value of website ID 1, which is less than `partition1`, having website ID 2. However, this is valid because the combination of website ID and log ID is (`1,100000`), which is greater than (`2,10000`).

In the preceding example, we have used MAXVALUE as the last partition, but it is also possible to have more than one partition having MAXVALUE as a list for one of the columns specified in the partition expression.

Consider the following example to understand MAXVALUE further:

```
PARTITION BY RANGE COLUMNS(website_id,log_id)
PARTITION partition0 VALUE LESS THAN (1,10000)
PARTITION partition1 VALUE LESS THAN (MAXVALUE,100000)
PARTITION partition2 VALUE LESS THAN (MAXVALUE,1000000)
PARTITION partition3 value LESS THAN (MAXVALUE, MAXVALUE)
```

As shown in the preceding example, the column website ID has max value in partitions 1, 2, and 3 while the second parameter log ID of the partition is increasing linearly in each partition, which is a completely valid scenario.

List column partitioning

Like range column partitioning, list column partitioning is also different from list partitioning. You can use multiple columns in list column partitioning. String, datetime, and date are permitted values in list column partitioning.

The following is the syntax used to create list column partitioning:

```
CREATE TABLE table_name
PARTITION BY LIST COLUMNS(column_list) (
PARTITION partition_name VALUES IN [(value_list1),(value_list2)...]
```

As shown in the preceding syntax, we can have multiple lists of values for list column partitioning. For each column, there will be a list of values specified in the partition that has to be used to insert rows into the partition:

```
CREATE TABLE employee (
first_name VARCHAR(25),
last_name VARCHAR(25),
joining_year INT,
designation VARCHAR(100),
)
```

```
PARTITION BY LIST COLUMNS(joining_year,designation) (
PARTITION pRegion_1 VALUES IN((2011,2012),('jr. consultant','sr.
consultant')),
PARTITION pRegion_2 VALUES IN((2013,2014), ('team lead', 'system
architect')),
PARTITION pRegion_3 VALUES IN((2014,2015), ('ui developer', 'ux
developer')),
PARTITION pRegion_4 VALUES IN((2016), ('project manager'))
);
```

As shown here, there are two lists for each of the partitions. So when a new row is inserted, then depending on the value matching the partitioning, it will go to its appropriate partition. Like range column partitioning, a column value in more than one partition can have the same values, but no two partitions can have the same combination of values inserted.

Key partitioning

Key partitioning is very much similar to hash partitioning. Hash partitioning allows a function as part of the partition expression, whereas key partitioning uses the table's key for the partitioning.

The expression for key partitioning uses the `PARTITION BY KEY()` keyword. Here, the key can take the column name as the parameter. If no column is defined in the `KEY`, then MySQL will use the primary key as the default parameter. In the case of no primary key being defined in the table, MySQL will use a unique key to define partitions. Refer to the following example for this:

```
CREATE TABLE sample (
id INT NOT NULL,
name VARCHAR(20),
UNIQUE KEY(id)
)
PARTITION BY KEY()
PARTITIONS 2;
```

If a unique key has to be used by the partitioning and the column is not set as not null, the partitioning syntax will give an error. If there are any primary keys defined on the table, then the key partitioning syntax must use the primary key to generate the partitions. Have a look at the following example:

```
CREATE TABLE sample
(
id INT NOT NULL PRIMARY KEY,
name VARCHAR(20),
email VARCHAR(100),
UNIQUE KEY(email)
)
PARTITION BY KEY(id)
PARTITIONS 2;
```

Here in this example, we have used the primary key for partitioning by the key.

Like hash partitioning, key partitioning also uses the modulus algorithm to generate the partitioning.

We can also define linear key partitioning on a MySQL table. Linear partitioning will use the power of two algorithms to create the mentioned partitions instead of the modulus algorithm used by default:

```
CREATE TABLE sample
(
id INT NOT NULL PRIMARY KEY,
name VARCHAR(20),
email VARCHAR(100),
UNIQUE KEY(email)
)
PARTITION BY LINEAR KEY(id)
PARTITIONS 2;
```

In key partitioning, if NULL is used as a value in the partition defining a column, then NULL is considered zero.

Sub partitioning

As the name suggests, sub partitioning divides the partitioned MySQL table into a second level of partitioning. The following is an example of sub partitioning:

```
CREATE TABLE employee (
id INT NOT NULL PRIMARY KEY,
joining_date DATE,
```

```
)
PARTITION BY RANGE(YEAR(joining_date) )
SUBPARTITION BY HASH(TO_DAYS(joining_date))
SUBPARTITIONS 2 (
PARTITION p0 VALUES LESS THAN (1990),
PARTITION p1 VALUES LESS THAN (2000),
PARTITION p2 VALUES LESS THAN MAXVALUE
);
```

Tables that are partitioned using ranges or lists can be further sub partitioned. In sub partitioning, we can use the hash or key partitioning method.

When using a key as the sub partitioning method, it is required to pass the value of the unique key or primary key as the parameter of the key. This is because when using a key as the sub partitioning method, MySQL will not automatically consider the primary or unique column value as the hashing key.

It is also possible to define the name for each of the sub partitions. When defining sub partitions, the number of sub partitions in each of the partitions must be the same:

```
PARTITION BY RANGE(YEAR(joining_date) )
SUBPARTITION BY HASH(TO_DAYS(joining_date))
SUBPARTITIONS 3 (
PARTITION partition1 VALUES LESS THAN (2005) (
 SUBPARTITION sub1,
 SUBPARTITION sub2,
 SUBPARTITION sub3,

),
PARTITION partition2 VALUES LESS THAN (2015) (
 SUBPARTITION sub4,
 SUBPARTITION sub5,
 SUBPARTITION sub6,
),
PARTITION partition2 VALUES LESS THAN MAXVALUE (
 SUBPARTITION sub7,
 SUBPARTITION sub8,
 SUBPARTITION sub9,
)
);
```

So by now, you have learned the different types of partitioning method in horizontal partitioning. When using any of the partitioning methods, it will be applied to both the table and indexes. It means that it is not possible to partition a table but not the indexes or vice versa. Also, as stated earlier, when a table has a primary or unique key, any column partitioning expression must be part of the primary or unique key. If no primary or unique key is defined for the table, we can use any other columns for the partitioning.

Vertical partitioning

As stated earlier, vertical partitioning divides the columns into multiple file groups.

Vertical partitioning can be achieved by the following:

- Row splitting into multiple file groups that can be stored at multiple locations
- Organizing data into multiple tables by breaking large data tables into smaller database tables

In row splitting, columns from one table are vertically separated into multiple file groups. When there are large datasets stored in a table, it may be difficult to manage large database files on a single location or server. So we can divide some of the columns from the database into a separate file group where can be managed on a separate disk.

Consider the following screenshot for vertical partitioning of the user table. As stated earlier, the database table, users, has been split into two separate partitions stored on different storage.

There can be more than two partitions of the table:

ID	User Name	First Name	Last Name	Email Address	Phone Number	Birth Date
1	MichellekDavis	Michellek	Davis	MichellekDavis@dayrep.com	9412233379	10/10/2086
2	dallasSGood	dallas	Good	DallasSGood@teleworm.us	8329843007	30/03/1972
3	TerranceDAviles	Terrance	Aviles	TerranceDaviles@armyspy.com	7045076659	20/04/1992
4	Undan1937	Susan	Roberts	SusanKRoberts@teleworm.us	4014126825	25/12/1996
5	Nempecovest1959	Lea	McGill	LeaJMcGill@journapide.com	2176567191	3/6/2000
6	Mandred	Regan	Coulter	ReganECoulter@journapide.com	6304832993	9/3/1998
7	Begivaing	Richard	Endres	RichardJEndres@rhyrep.com	3096848793	12/8/1988
8	Biturnight	Gregory	Melton	GregoryMMelton@dayrep.com	6304236158	6/9/1977
9	Stiong	Bernice	Stevenson	BerniceGStevenson@rhyrep.com	7736461308	3/1/2001

ID	User Name	First Name	Last Name	Email Address	Phone Number	Birth Date
1	MichellekDavis	Michellek	Davis	MichellekDavis@dayrep.com	9412233379	10/10/2086
2	dallasSGood	dallas	Good	DallasSGood@teleworm.us	8329843007	30/03/1972
3	TerranceDAviles	Terrance	Aviles	TerranceDaviles@armyspy.com	7045076659	20/04/1992
4	Undan1937	Susan	Roberts	SusanKRoberts@teleworm.us	4014126825	25/12/1996
5	Nempecovest1959	Lea	McGill	LeaJMcGill@journapide.com	2176567191	3/6/2000
6	Mandred	Regan	Coulter	ReganECoulter@journapide.com	6304832993	9/3/1998
7	Begivaing	Richard	Endres	RichardJEndres@rhyrep.com	3096848793	12/8/1988
8	Biturnight	Gregory	Melton	GregoryMMelton@dayrep.com	6304236158	6/9/1977
9	Stiong	Bernice	Stevenson	BerniceGStevenson@rhyrep.com	7736461308	3/1/2001

Vertical partitioning of a single table into multiple file groups is not supported in MySQL. However, we can achieve vertical partitioning by normalizing data. It is always desirable to divide the data into multiple tables if all columns are not required frequently in queries. Integrity constraints can be achieved in MySQL for consistency on normalized data.

Splitting data into multiple tables

Data splitting is the process of organizing columns of a large table into multiple tables that are correlated using primary key--foreign key constraints in a relational database. Large tables can be divided in such a way that columns that are not updated very frequently can be moved to a separate table, and referential integrity can be implemented for this table.

Consider the following tables that have 10 columns in a table.

Table name: users

user_id	first_name	last_name	email_address	profile_image	department	address_line1	address_line2	city	state

Now if we look at these 10 columns, there are certain columns that may be null when data is inserted, as they are optional and may not need to be updated. For example, **profile_image** and address fields frequently updated changes for users. So we can create three different tables out of the users table to store such information.

Table name : users

user_id	first_name	last_name	email_address	department

Table name: user_profile_image

profile_image_id	user_id	profile_image

Table name: user_address

address_id	user_id	address_line1	address_line2	city	state

So now we have three different tables for user information by logically dividing columns of the table. These three tables can be connected by defining foreign keys on the tables. The following syntax is to create three tables of users with foreign key constraints on each of the tables:

```
CREATE TABLE IF NOT EXISTS users (
user_id int(11) NOT NULL,
  first_name varchar(100) NOT NULL,
  last_name varchar(100) NOT NULL,
  email_address varchar(255) NOT NULL,
```

```
    department varchar(100) NOT NULL,
    PRIMARY KEY (user_id),
) ENGINE=InnoDB;
```

As shown here, the user table is created with minimum columns in the table. We have defined the primary key on the `user_id` column, so now we can relate other user-related information using referential integrity.

Now let's create `user_profile_image`:

```
CREATE TABLE IF NOT EXISTS user_profile_image (
    profile_image_id int(11) NOT NULL,
    user_id int(11) NOT NULL,
    profile_image blob NOT NULL,
    PRIMARY KEY (profile_image_id)
) ENGINE=InnoDB;
```

Create the `user_address` table:

```
CREATE TABLE IF NOT EXISTS user_address (
    address_id int(11) NOT NULL,
    user_id int(11) NOT NULL,
    address_line1 VARCHAR(255),
    address_line2 VARCHAR(255),
    city VARCHAR(100),
    state VARCHAR(100),
    PRIMARY KEY (address_id)
) ENGINE=InnoDB;
```

So now we have three different tables to store user information. Each table contains a specific area of a user's information, which are completely independent of each other. So when you want to update information about the user's address, MySQL will not be updating or checking anything in the schema of the users or `user_profile_image` tables.

If you want to delete any user information, then it is desirable to remove all related information from the user. This can be achieved through referential integrity in MySQL. Consider the following syntax to add referential integrity to the `user_profile_image` table:

```
ALTER TABLE user_profile_image
ADD CONSTRAINT fk_user_id FOREIGN KEY (user_id) REFERENCES `users`
(user_id) ON DELETE CASCADE ON UPDATE NO ACTION;
```

What the preceding query will do is add a relation between the `users` and `user_profile_image` tables. MySQL 8 provides some out-of-the-box triggers that can be used while updating or deleting master data. Here, `DELETE CASCADE` means if a record in the users table is removed, then it will automatically remove the related image from the image table, thus providing us with data consistency throughout the database. Similar kinds of constraints can be defined on the address table.

Splitting large tables into multiple tables for partitioning gives us the advantages of scaling the data for any records or documents. For example, we have moved the address data to the `user_address` table. Now, if there is a need to allow multiple addresses for users, then it can be achieved without changing the database design.

When you do vertical partitioning through dividing data into multiple tables, it requires you to add some joins to fetch all the information for a particular record. For example, to fetch all correlated information about the user, the following query needs to be executed:

```
SELECT * FROM
  users
JOIN
  user_profile_image on users.user_id = user_profile_image.user_id
JOIN
  user_address on users.user_id = user_address.user_id
```

So basically, this requires us to join two tables to get all the information about the users. Before vertically splitting data into multiple tables, it is required to normalize your data so that all the existing data is in its most normal form.

Data normalization

Normalization is the process of organizing data in such a way that there is no redundant data in a table. There are multiple levels of normalization available in any relational database system. The following sections give a brief overview of different normalization levels.

First normal form

When there is unique information stored in each column, then data is said to be in its first normal form.

For example, in our preceding example of users, if any user belongs to multiple departments, then there should not be comma-separated values for the department. Instead a new row should be created for such information, for the table to be in first normal form.

Second normal form

To achieve second normal form, a table should already be in its first normal form and all columns in the table should be dependent on a unique identifier of the data.

Third normal form

Data is said to be in third normal form if 2NF is already achieved and data is dependent only on the key of the table.

A database is said to be normalized if 3NF is achieved.

Boyce-Codd normal form

A table is said to be **BCNF** (**Boyce-Codd normal form**) if all relational tables can be identified using a single primary key from the master table.

Fourth normal form

If there is no multi-valued dependency of the primary key, the table is in its fourth normal form.

Fifth normal form

A table is in its fifth normal form if data cannot be further divided into more tables without losing data.

A detailed explanation of the normalization forms is out of the scope of this book.

When you split your data columns into multiple tables, the joining of two or more tables may require you to add proper columns to the joining criteria, and also proper indexing is required on the columns. More details on defining indexes on columns can be found in Chapter 3, *Indexing your data for high performing queries*. To implement best practices on joining techniques, you can refer to Chapter 8, *MySQL 8 best practices*.

Pruning partitions in MySQL

Pruning is the selective extraction of data. As we have multiple partitions of big data, it will go through each partition during retrieval, which is time consuming and impacts performance. Some of the partitions will also be included in search while the requested data is not available inside that partition, which is an overhead process. Pruning helps here to search for only those partitions that have the relevant data, which will avoid the unnecessary inclusion of those partitions during retrieval.

This optimization that avoids the scanning of partitions where there can be no matching values is known as the pruning of partitions. In partition pruning, the optimizer analyzes FROM and WHERE clauses in SQL statements to eliminate unneeded partitions, and scans those database partitions that are relevant to the SQL statement. Let's see an example.

Suppose that we have a table with the following structure:

```
CREATE TABLE student (
rollNo INT NOT NULL,
name VARCHAR(50) NOT NULL,
class CHAR NOT NULL,
marks INT NOT NULL,
)
PARTITION BY RANGE(marks) (
PARTITION p0 VALUES LESS THAN (35),
PARTITION p1 VALUES LESS THAN (65),
PARTITION p2 VALUES LESS THAN (85),
PARTITION p3 VALUES LESS THAN MAXVALUE
);
```

Now, if we want to search students who all have marks of less than 35, then the query would look like this:

```
SELECT * FROM student WHERE marks < 35;
```

It is clear that we need to search from the partition p0 only, and none of the other partitions need to be included for the scanning of the result. This is because students who obtain marks of less than 35 are placed inside the p0 partition. This way, it will limit the search of the other partitions, which takes less time and improves the performance as compared to searching all of the partitions.

The following query will only search the partitions p1 and p2, while the rest of them will be ignored:

```
SELECT * FROM student WHERE marks > 50 AND marks < 80;
```

Such a way of removing partitions that are not required during scanning is called **pruning**. Partition pruning will always be faster than a normal query as it will scan from the required partitions rather than searching all of the data.

Pruning can be performed with the help of the WHERE condition. You can use different arithmetic operators like <, >, <=, >=, <>, and =. If we use = (equal operator), then it will identify which partition contains this value and only that partition will be scanned for the respective results. We can also use BETWEEN and IN clauses as follows:

```
SELECT * FROM student WHERE marks IN (30,50);
SELECT * FROM student WHERE marks BETWEEN 50 AND 80;
```

The optimizer will evaluate the expression and determine the partition in which it needs to searched from. In the first statement, the optimizer will get to know that the first value will be contained in the p0 partition, while the second value will be contained in the p1 partition. As p2 and p3 does not contain any relevant values, it will skip these partitions for further scanning. In the second statement, it will search only p1 and p2 partitions.

Pruning can also work with a table that is partitioned by DATE, TIMESTAMP, or DATETIME. Let's understand this by looking at an example.

Suppose we have a table partitioned by DATE as follows:

```
CREATE TABLE access_log (
 log_id INT NOT NULL,
 type VARCHAR(100),
 access_url VARCHAR(100),
 access_date TIMESTAMP NOT NULL,
 response_time INT NOT NULL,
 access_by INT NOT NULL
 )
PARTITION BY RANGE (UNIX_TIMESTAMP(access_date)) (
PARTITION p0 VALUES LESS THAN (UNIX_TIMESTAMP('2017-05-01 00:00:00')),
PARTITION p1 VALUES LESS THAN (UNIX_TIMESTAMP('2017-09-01 00:00:00')),
PARTITION p2 VALUES LESS THAN (UNIX_TIMESTAMP('2018-01-01 00:00:00')),
PARTITION p3 VALUES LESS THAN (UNIX_TIMESTAMP('2018-05-01 00:00:00')),
PARTITION p4 VALUES LESS THAN (UNIX_TIMESTAMP('2018-09-01 00:00:00')),
PARTITION p5 VALUES LESS THAN (UNIX_TIMESTAMP('2019-01-01 00:00:00')),
);
```

Now let's apply pruning by executing the following queries:

```
SELECT * FROM access_log WHERE access_date = UNIX_TIMESTAMP('2017-08-01 00:00:00');
```

In this case, it will only scan the partition p1 as the data of the respective date is included only under this partition, and the other partitions are ignored. We need to ensure the format of the date because it will cause NULL if we have passed an invalid date format.

Partition pruning will work with SELECT, DELETE, and UPDATE statements, while the INSERT query does not support partition pruning:

```
UPDATE access_log SET access_by = 10 WHERE access_date =
UNIX_TIMESTAMP('2017-08-01 00:00:00');

SELECT * FROM access_log WHERE UNIX_TIMESTAMP(access_date) =
UNIX_TIMESTAMP('2017-08-01 00:00:00');

DELETE FROM access_log WHERE UNIX_TIMESTAMP(access_date) =
UNIX_TIMESTAMP('2017-08-01 00:00:00');
```

So far we have seen an example of range partitions only. You might be wondering if it can be applied to other partitioning or not! Yes, it can be applied to all other partitions as well. Let's see a basic example of pruning different partitions.

Pruning with list partitioning

Pruning can easily work with list partitioning to determine the respective partitions and check against the limited partitions only. Suppose we have a table with different employee information as follows:

```
CREATE TABLE employees (
 id INT NOT NULL,
 fname VARCHAR(30),
 lname VARCHAR(30),
 hired DATE NOT NULL DEFAULT '1970-01-01',
 separated DATE NOT NULL DEFAULT '9999-12-31',
 job_code INT,
 store_id INT
 )
PARTITION BY LIST(store_id) (
PARTITION pNorth VALUES IN (3,5,6,9,17),
PARTITION pEast VALUES IN (1,2,10,11,19,20),
PARTITION pWest VALUES IN (4,12,13,14,18),
PARTITION pCentral VALUES IN (7,8,15,16)
 );
```

Now let's fetch the employees by their stores with the IDs of (5, 6, 8):

```
SELECT * FROM employees WHERE store_id IN (5,6,8);
```

The optimizer can easily determine in which partition the values (5, 6, 8) are contained. These values are found under pNorth and pCentral and the rest of the partitions are cut down for scanning.

Pruning with key partitioning

A key-based partition can also take benefit from pruning to improve performance. Suppose we have a student table with the following information:

```
CREATE TABLE student (
 id INT NOT NULL PRIMARY KEY,
 name VARCHAR(20)
 )
 PARTITION BY KEY()
 PARTITIONS 4;
```

Now let's fetch the student information whose ID is contained between one to three:

```
SELECT * FROM student WHERE id > 1 AND id <3;
```

This will transform the where clause into the range of WHERE id (*1,2,3*) and apply the pruning. With the HASH and KEY partition, pruning can be applied only to the integer columns. The pruning will not work if we have partitioned the DATE column with HASH or KEY partitioning.

Querying on partitioned data

When big data is stored in MySQL, it is recommended to make partitions of the data so that it can be easily retrieved whenever it's needed. This is because it will take too much time to execute queries for the unpartitioned data. Partitioning can be useful to execute queries on the selected partitions only instead of the whole table's data. It is always faster to execute queries on some chunks of data instead of the whole bulk. There are two ways to execute queries to make this faster using partitioning:

- **Partition pruning**: As we have seen in the previous topic, pruning can be used to retrieve data from specific partitions only. This pruning work automatically determines the partition in which it needs to query data from.

- **Providing partition selections with the query**: We can provide the partition name explicitly, along with the query being executed only on that particular partition. This way, partition selection can be specified within the queries. The following SQL statements support explicitly specifying a partition name:
    - SELECT
    - INSERT
    - UPDATE
    - REPLACE
    - DELETE
    - LOAD DATA
    - LOAD XML

Here is the syntax used with the preceding query to specify the partition name explicitly:

```
PARTITION (partition_names)
```

Here, `partition_names` is the collection of partitions separated by a comma. This option always comes after the table name in which the partition belongs in the query. We can specify the name of the partition or the sub partition of the specified table, and in case the partition does not exist, then it will throw an error saying, `"partition 'partition-name' does not exist"`.

Executing a query with this option will only check the mentioned partition, while the rest of the partitions will be ignored. Let's see an example of using this partition option.

Suppose we have student results details as per the following table structure:

```
CREATE TABLE student (
 rollNo INT NOT NULL,
 name VARCHAR(50) NOT NULL,
 class CHAR NOT NULL,
 marks INT NOT NULL
 )
PARTITION BY RANGE(marks) (
PARTITION p0 VALUES LESS THAN (35),
PARTITION p1 VALUES LESS THAN (65),
PARTITION p2 VALUES LESS THAN (85),
PARTITION p3 VALUES LESS THAN MAXVALUE
);
```

Let us now insert data into student table as per following example:

```
INSERT INTO student VALUES
(1, "Jaydip", "A", 80),
(2,"Keyur","B", 30),
(3,"Palak","A", 45),
(4,"Malav","B", 84),
(5,"Parth","C", 25),
(6,"Kandarp","B",60),
(7,"Chintan","C", 90);
```

Let's use the partition option to fetch the records from partition p3 only:

```
SELECT * FROM student PARTITION (p2);
```

```
mysql> SELECT * FROM student PARTITION (p2);
+--------+--------+-------+-------+
| rollNo | name   | class | marks |
+--------+--------+-------+-------+
|      1 | Jaydip | A     |    80 |
|      4 | Malav  | B     |    84 |
+--------+--------+-------+-------+
2 rows in set (0.00 sec)
```

As you can see in the preceding output, it will only show the records from partition **p2**, while the rest of the records are not displayed. You can also specify multiple partitions in the same query as follows:

```
SELECT * FROM student PARTITION (p1,p2);
```

```
mysql> SELECT * FROM student PARTITION (p1,p2);
+--------+---------+-------+-------+
| rollNo | name    | class | marks |
+--------+---------+-------+-------+
|      3 | Palak   | A     |    45 |
|      6 | Kandarp | B     |    60 |
|      1 | Jaydip  | A     |    80 |
|      4 | Malav   | B     |    84 |
+--------+---------+-------+-------+
4 rows in set (0.00 sec)
```

Multiple partitions can be specified with a comma separator, and it will fetch the records from all mentioned partitions. This partition option can work with any partition type. You might have a question: how do we get the name of the partition in KEY or HASH partitioning as we are not specifying any partition name? In the case of KEY and HASH partitioning, MySQL gives the name of each partition automatically, starting from *p0,p1,p3,p4... pN-1*, where *N* is the number of partitions. For sub partitions, it assigns names such as *pXsp0*, *pXsp1, pXsp2... pXspN-1*, where *X* is the parent partition name and *N* is the total sub partitions. Let's see an example of KEY partitioning.

Suppose we have a table that is partitioned by the key:

```
CREATE TABLE student1 (
  id INT NOT NULL PRIMARY KEY,
  name VARCHAR(20)
)
PARTITION BY KEY()
PARTITIONS 4;
```

Let us now insert data into **student1** table as per following example where we would populate data:

```
INSERT INTO student1 VALUES
  (1,"Jaydip"),
  (2,"Keyur"),
  (11,"Parth"),
  (12,"Palak"),
  (3,"Kandarp");
```

Here, we have not explicitly specified any partition name; hence, it will automatically assign *p0,p1,p2* and *p3* as the name of each partition. Let's test this by fetching records from the first partition:

```
SELECT * FROM student1 PARTITION(p0);
```

```
mysql> SELECT * FROM student1 PARTITION(p0);
+----+--------+
| id | name   |
+----+--------+
|  1 | Jaydip |
+----+--------+
1 row in set (0.00 sec)
```

As shown in the preceding output, it will display all the records from partition p0, which will be automatically assigned in the case of key partitioning.

So far, we have used partitioning with the SELECT query, but as we discussed previously, it can work with other queries as well. Let's use this option with other queries.

DELETE query with the partition option

When we use the partition option with the delete statement, it will only delete rows from partitions or sub partitions that are mentioned in the query.

Suppose we have the following students available with class **A**:

```
mysql> SELECT * FROM student WHERE class = "A";
+--------+--------+-------+-------+
| rollNo | name   | class | marks |
+--------+--------+-------+-------+
|      3 | Palak  | A     |    45 |
|      1 | Jaydip | A     |    80 |
+--------+--------+-------+-------+
2 rows in set (0.00 sec)
```

Execute the following query to delete students with class 'A' from partition p2:

```
DELETE FROM student PARTITION(p2) WHERE class = 'A';
```

```
mysql> SELECT * FROM student WHERE class = "A";
+--------+--------+-------+-------+
| rollNo | name   | class | marks |
+--------+--------+-------+-------+
|      3 | Palak  | A     |    45 |
|      1 | Jaydip | A     |    80 |
+--------+--------+-------+-------+
2 rows in set (0.00 sec)

mysql> DELETE FROM student PARTITION(p2) WHERE class = "A";
Query OK, 1 row affected (0.01 sec)

mysql> SELECT * FROM student WHERE class = "A";
+--------+--------+-------+-------+
| rollNo | name   | class | marks |
+--------+--------+-------+-------+
|      3 | Palak  | A     |    45 |
+--------+--------+-------+-------+
1 row in set (0.00 sec)
```

As shown in the preceding output, it has deleted respective records from partition **p2** and the rest of the partitions are untouched by this query. Other data with class "**A**" still exists, which belongs to the other partitions.

UPDATE query with the partition option

An Update statement behaves the sameway as the others with the partition option. It will only update the records of the selected partition. Let's update the class column with 'A' in the student table if they have marks of more than 50 for partition P1 only:

```
UPDATE student PARTITION(P1) SET class = 'A' WHERE marks > 50;
```

See the following output that shows the record before executing the Update query and the after-effects of the Update query:

```
mysql> SELECT * FROM student PARTITION(p1);
+--------+---------+-------+-------+
| rollNo | name    | class | marks |
+--------+---------+-------+-------+
|      3 | Palak   | A     |    45 |
|      6 | Kandarp | C     |    60 |
+--------+---------+-------+-------+
2 rows in set (0.00 sec)

mysql> UPDATE student PARTITION(P1) SET class = 'A' WHERE marks > 50;
Query OK, 1 row affected (0.00 sec)
Rows matched: 1  Changed: 1  Warnings: 0

mysql> SELECT * FROM student PARTITION(p1);
+--------+---------+-------+-------+
| rollNo | name    | class | marks |
+--------+---------+-------+-------+
|      3 | Palak   | A     |    45 |
|      6 | Kandarp | A     |    60 |
+--------+---------+-------+-------+
2 rows in set (0.01 sec)
```

INSERT query with the partition option

The partition option with the insert statement behaves a bit differently when inserting records into the specific partition. It will validate it if the respective record is suitable for the partition. If the record is not suitable for the partition, then it will cause an error saying, *Not matching the given partition set.* Let's insert a record into partition P2 of the student table:

```
INSERT INTO student PARTITION(P2) VALUES(7,'Jaydip','A',70);
```

As shown in the following output, for the first time, it has thrown an error because we have tried to store 30 marks in **p2** partition while this partition contains marks between 65 to 85 only. After that, when we tried to store 70 marks, it has inserted successfully. Hence, it always checks whether the partition can hold the specific record or not before inserting it.

```
mysql> SELECT * FROM student PARTITION(p2);
+--------+-------+-------+-------+
| rollNo | name  | class | marks |
+--------+-------+-------+-------+
|      4 | Malav | B     |    84 |
+--------+-------+-------+-------+
1 row in set (0.00 sec)

mysql> INSERT INTO student PARTITION(P2) VALUES(7,'Jaydip','A',30);
ERROR 1748 (HY000): Found a row not matching the given partition set
mysql> INSERT INTO student PARTITION(P2) VALUES(7,'Jaydip','A',70);
Query OK, 1 row affected (0.01 sec)

mysql> SELECT * FROM student PARTITION(p2);
+--------+--------+-------+-------+
| rollNo | name   | class | marks |
+--------+--------+-------+-------+
|      4 | Malav  | B     |    84 |
|      7 | Jaydip | A     |    70 |
+--------+--------+-------+-------+
2 rows in set (0.00 sec)
```

In the scenario of using multiple partitions with the insert statement, it will insert the record into the respective partition that is matched with the partition criteria. Also, if none of the partitions match any single record, then the whole insertion will fail and throw an error.

Summary

In this chapter, you learned horizontal partitioning and vertical partitioning. Different types of horizontal partitioning were discussed. Then we understood how to achieve the best available advantages of vertical partitioning in MySQL. You also learned pruning methods and queries to fetch values from more than one partition. We discussed deleting or altering partitions in MySQL. In the next chapter, we have some exciting topics to be cover. You will learn how we can improve MySQLs performance using replications and the different replication methods available in MySQL 8.

6

Replication for building highly available solutions

In the previous chapter, you learned what partitioning is, the types of partitioning, and querying on partitioned data, which helps in bettering performance.

We are going to discuss below topics in details:

- High availability
- Replication
- Group Replication

High availability

Today, data is the most important part of any web, mobile, social, enterprise, and cloud application. Ensuring that data is always available is the top priority for any application. A small amount of downtime can result in significant loss of revenue and reputation for an organization.

Continuous availability of the data has become very critical in current time. And as the size of the data increases with time, it can become tricky to maintain huge amount of data available at any point of time. Losing a connection with the application for the fraction of a time can also make a huge impact on the organization and it can put the reputation of the organization at a stake.

To avoid any impact of inconsistency in application access because of the database, it is the demand of time to build up a highly available architecture. To build a highly available application infrastructure, many things are required to be considered, such as the capabilities of the technologies used for building application, need of the business to build such infrastructure etc. This will definitely impact hence we should need to consider those things before making any conclusion for building a highly available architecture.

MySQL 8 has capabilities to provide back end for the application for achieving high availability and preparing a fully scalable system. An ability of the system to keep the connection persistent, in case a part of infrastructure fails and ability of the system to recover from such failure is considered as high availability. A failure of the system can be caused by either the maintenance activity on one part of the system like hardware or software upgrade, failure of the software installed.

If we considered scalability in terms of MySQL 8, MySQL 8 supports scalability to replicate the database across multiple MySQL server for sharing the load of queries from the application.

Requirement for achieving HA and scalability may vary from system to system. Each system requires different configuration in order to achieve these abilities. MySQL 8 also supports different approaches such as replication of data across multiple MySQL servers or preparing multiple data centers based on geographical locations and serving the client requests from the data centers closer to the location of the client. Such solutions can be used to achieve the highest up time of MySQL.

Attributes which matter on choosing the right solution for high availability, depends upto which extent the system can be called as highly available, as such requirement varies from system to system. For smaller applications, where user load is not expected to be very high, setting up the replication or cluster environment can result in very high cost. In such cases providing the correct configuration of the MySQL can also be enough to reduce application load. We will learn more about setting up correct configuration of MySQL in Chapter 7, MySQL 8 Best Practices.

Following sections are primary solutions supported by MySQL 8 for high availability and their brief details.

MySQL replication

MySQL Replication allows data from one server to be replicated onto the multiple MySQL servers. MySQL Replication provides master-slave design, so that one of the server from the group acts as a master where write operations are performed from the application and then master server copies data to the multiple slave servers. Replication is a well established solution for high availability and is used by the social giants like Facebook, Twitter, and so on.

MySQL cluster

This is another popular high availability solution for MySQL. Clustering enables data to be replicated to multiple MySQL servers with automated sharing. It is designed for better availability and throughput.

Oracle MySQL cloud service

Oracle MySQL cloud service delivers a MySQL database service which enables organizations to rapidly, securely and cost-effectively deploy modern applications powered by the world's most popular open source database.

MySQL with the Solaris cluster

The Sun Solaris Cluster HA for the MySQL data service provides a mechanism for orderly startup and shutdown, fault monitoring, and automatic failover of the MySQL service. The following MySQL components are protected by the Sun Cluster HA for the MySQL data service.

There are some further options available using third-party solutions. Each architecture that is used to achieve highly available database services is differentiated by the levels of up-time that each offers. These architectures can be grouped into three main categories. The following diagram explains the architecture for each category:

- Data replication
- Clustered and virtualized systems
- Geographically-replicated clusters

Following is the figure to illustrate three different techniques and level of system up-time that can be achieved by implementing it.

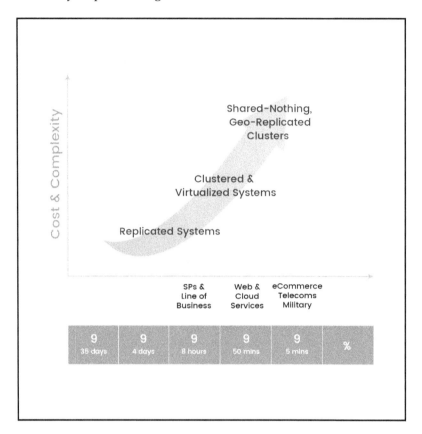

As per the figure these three techniques are:

- Data replication to multiple MySQL server through MySQL 8 group replication
- Setting up MySQL on virtual servers and building clustered virtual environment
- Geographical based data replication, where each server in different geographical location serves separate group of clients and does not share any common data among them

System complexity as well as cost can play big part in choosing any of the three techniques. So before choosing any of the three techniques as mentioned in previous figure, certain question has to be asked to yourself:

- What data is important to you and how much it is important
- What will be impact on the application if you lose some of the data
- What will be impact on the application if all data is lost. Does the restoring any historical backup can serve your purpose or not
- What would be the impact if you couldn't access the database for a minute, an hour, a day, or a week?

Based on the best answer of the question, you can select right option for your application with optimal cost and highly available solution. This discussion gives us a fair overview of MySQL 8's high availability. Now let's discuss replication and how we can configure different types of replication in detail.

Replication with MySQL

MySQL replication works based on master-slave architecture. From group of MySQL servers, one server acts as a master and other servers work as slave server. All write operations are performed on the master server while read operations are performed on any of the slave servers. Connection between master and slave servers is done based on the configuration. In coming topics we will learn different configuration for synchronizing master and slave databases.

Benefits of replication in MySQL 8

Let's quickly look at a few benefits of MySQL 8 replication.

Scalable applications

As we said earlier, replication shares load between master and slave databases. So, now amount of activity for the database has been reduced. Master will only perform write operation and will not be worried about the read operations, while slaves will only be taking care of read operation without worrying about write operations. This mechanism actually makes the MySQL to perform faster. Also, it is easy to add more MySQL server to the replication group to scale out the architecture in case of heavy server load.

Secure architecture

One of the advantage we can get because of this replication is, one of the slave server can be used for backup rather than performing backup activity on master MySQL server. This makes backup process independent of application using MySQL 8. There won't be any impact on Master's write operation. In simple terms, it eliminates chances of any data corruption during backup.

Large data analysis

As read operations are performed on the slave servers, we can make one of the slave server to perform complex read queries, which makes it possible to generate reports for doing data analysis on MySQL 8 as performing complex read queries will not impact the overall application performance.

Geographical data sharing

Group replication makes it possible to copy the Master's data to the slave server to be residing at remote location and performing the read operations for separate group of client without impacting masters' operations.

Methods of replication in MySQL 8

Let's have a quick glance at different methods of replication provided in MySQL 8.

Replication using binary logs

Based on replicating events from the master server generated binary logs, which will be synchronized with master and slave. This method is supported by MySQL 5.1; however, in MySQL 8, it has plenty of new and exciting functionalities which will be covered in `Chapter 7`, *MySQL 8 Best Practices*, for performance improvement.

Replication using global transaction identifiers

Global transaction identifiers (GTID) uses transaction based replication of data instead of binary log file based replication. Until and unless, transactions that has been operated and committed on the master servers are present on all the slave servers, GTID will not consider replication is in consistent state.

In MySQL 8 Replication can be done either in asynchronous mode or in semi-synchronous mode. In asynchronous mode, write operations are performed on the master server immediately, while replication in slaves is done periodically as per the configuration.

In semi-synchronous mode of replication, if semi-synchronous configuration is enabled on master and at least one slave server, a transaction on master node waits before getting transaction time out until the semi-synchronous enabled node confirms that required data or update has been received. And on time-out, master node again looks for the semi-synchronous slave and performs the replication.

Replication configuration

Now let's understand different replication methods' configuration available in MySQL 8 in details.

1. Replication with binary log file
2. Replication with GTIDs
3. Multiple source replication in MySQL 8

In addition to this, we will check on different configuration available for setting up replication on the servers.

Replication with binary log file

Binary log file contains logs of all MySQL operations done in MySQL. Each operation is stored in different format. So for replication based on binary file, master server performs insert and updates operations which are reflected in the binary log file. Now, slaves nodes are configured to read these binary files and same events are executed in the binary file of the slave servers to replicate the data onto the slave servers..

A copy of the entire binary log is shared by the master server with all the slave servers. By default, all events from the master are executed on the slave. We can configure slaves to process events that belongs to any particular database or table only. We can also configure on slave server to process specific events from the master to be executed on the slave server.

While executing events on the slave server from the binary log shared by the master, it is responsibility of the slave to remember the position in the file where it has performed last execution. Slave server can be configured to read the binary log periodically. So, if there are more than one slaves, each slave will have it's own track of number of operations it has to perform on the next execution scheduled.

All servers used in replication, either master or slave server, contains their own unique ID, termed as `server-id`. To read the binary log from the master node, slave severs contains the information related to master such as host name, log filename, and position inside the file.

Let's discuss how to set up the replication. We are assuming that you already have two MySQL servers to perform the replication. This example will use the following IP addresses of the MySQL server:

- 12.34.56.789: Master database
- 12.23.34.456: Slave database

Replication master configuration

Open the MySQL configuration file on the master server:

```
sudo vim /etc/mysql/my.cnf
```

Inside this file, we have to make the following changes. The first step is to find the section that looks like this, binding the server to the localhost:

```
bind-address= 127.0.0.1
```

Replace the standard IP address with the IP address of the master server:

```
bind-address= 12.34.56.789
```

This change allows the slave MySQL server to access databases using the IP address.

Now we have to configure the unique `server-id` for the master and provide the path for the binary log on the master server. Make sure that the following line is uncommented:

```
server-id= 1
log-bin= /var/log/mysql/mysql-bin.log
```

Here, `mysql-bin.log` is the filename where all logs are stored.

Finally, we need to configure the database that will be replicated on the slave server. You can include more than one database by repeating this line for all of the databases you need:

```
binlog_do_db= shabbirdb
```

shabbirdb is name of the database. After making the changes, restart the server:

```
sudo service mysql restart
```

Now the next steps grant privileges to the slave. Open the MySQL command prompt:

```
mysql -u root -p
```

Create a MySQL user to be used by the slave and use the GRANT SQL statement to provide access to the user, which is going to be a user from the slave server:

```
CREATE USER 'shabbirslave'@'%' IDENTIFIED BY 'password';
GRANT REPLICATION SLAVE ON *.* TO 'dbslave'@'%' IDENTIFIED BY 'password';
```

Flush the privileges cache using the following command:

```
FLUSH PRIVILEGES;
```

Now switch to the database that you want to replicate:

```
USE shabbirdb;
```

Take your database backup using the `mysqldump` command that we will use to create the slave server. Before back up, lock your database and check the current position of the database, which you will use later when you create the slave server:

```
FLUSH TABLES WITH READ LOCK;
```

Following is command to check master server status:

```
SHOW MASTER STATUS;
```

Output of the command will display name of the binary file and the position from where it will start reading.

```
mysql> SHOW MASTER STATUS;
+-------------------+----------+--------------+------------------+
| File              | Position | Binlog_Do_DB | Binlog_Ignore_DB |
+-------------------+----------+--------------+------------------+
| mysql-bin.000001  |      102 | shabbirdb    |                  |
+-------------------+----------+--------------+------------------+
1 row in set (0.00 sec)
```

As shown in the output, output of the command will display the location inside the log file, from where slave server will start replicating. `mysql-bin.000001` is the name of the log file to be read by slaves. We will use this log file name and position as reference in the further examples.

For doing further configuration, we will use database in the lock mode itself. Any further command in single session will unlock the existing locks. So, it is necessary that upcoming command should be applied in the separate MySQL session.

Now, we will need to export the database using the MySQL's `mysqldump` command with the lock mode enabled.

```
mysqldump -u root -p shabbirdb > shabbirdb.sql
```

Once database is exported, we can unlock the database:

```
UNLOCK TABLES;
QUIT;
```

So by performing all previous steps, we are done with configuring the master server for the replication. Now, next step would be to configure slave server.

Replication slave configuration

So as master server is configured, let's connect with the slave MySQL server and create database that we will use for replication as slave.

```
CREATE DATABASE shabbirdb;
quit;
```

Database that we had exported in the lock mode need to be imported here in the slave servers.

```
mysql -u root -p shabbirdb < /path/to/shabbirdb.sql
```

Now, we need to configure the slave configuration. Open the `my.cnf` file of the slave server:

```
sudo vim /etc/mysql/my.cnf
```

Now we have to provide a unique `server-id` to the slave server:

```
server-id = 2
```

Then, we have to configure `relay-log`, `log_bin`, and `binlog_do_db` in the `my.cnf` file:

```
relay-log = /var/log/mysql/mysql-relay-bin.log
log_bin = /var/log/mysql/mysql-bin.log
binlog_do_db = newdatabase
```

Restart MySQL:

```
sudo service mysql restart
```

The next step is to enable the replication from within the MySQL shell.

Open the MySQL shell and type in the following details, replacing the values to match your information that has been recorded from the master server:

```
CHANGE MASTER TO MASTER_HOST='12.34.56.789',MASTER_USER='shabbirslave',
MASTER_PASSWORD='password', MASTER_LOG_FILE='mysql-bin.000001',
MASTER_LOG_POS=  103;
```

This command accomplishes several things at the same time:

- It designates the current server as the slave of our master server
- It provides the server with the correct login credentials
- It lets the slave server know where to start replicating from the master log file, and the log position (103) comes from the numbers that we wrote down previously

Now activate the slave server:

```
START SLAVE;
```

Replication with GTIDs

Using this method, each transaction can be identified and tracked as it is committed on the master server and applied on the slave server. This method is not referring to log files or positions within those files when starting a new slave or failing over to a new master. GTID-based replication is completely transaction-based; it is simple to determine whether master and slave servers are consistent. As long as all transactions committed on a master are also committed on a slave, consistency between the two is guaranteed.

Using a global transaction ID provides two main benefits:

- **It's easy to change a master server to connect with a slave server during failover**: GTID is unique out of all servers in the replication group. The slave server remembers the global transaction ID of the last event from the old master. This makes it easy to know where to resume replication on the new master, as the global transaction IDs are known throughout the entire replication hierarchy.

- **The state of the slave is recorded in a crash-safe way**: The slave keeps track of its current position in the `mysql.gtid_slave_pos` system table. If this table is using a transactional storage engine (such as InnoDB, which is the default), then updates to the state are done in the same transaction as updates to the data. This makes the state crash-safe; if the slave server crashes, crash recovery on restart will make sure that the recorded replication position matches the changes that were replicated. This is not the case for old-style replication, where the state is recorded in a file, `relay-log.info`, which is updated independently of the actual data changes and can easily get out of sync if the slave server crashes.

Before we jump into the configuration part, let's understand GTID better.

Global transaction identifiers

A GTIDs is a unique key created and associated with each transaction (Insert and Update operations) committed on the master server. The key is not only unique to the master server, but it's unique across all servers in replication. There is one-to-one mapping between all transactions and all GTIDs.

A GTID is represented as a pair of source IDs and transaction IDs, separated by a colon character (`:`):

```
GTID = source_id:transaction_id
```

`source_id` is the `server_uuid` of the master server. The `transaction_id` is a sequence number determined by the order in which the transaction was committed on the server. For instance, the 23rd transaction to be committed originally on the server with the UUID `17ede83a-8b22-11e7-8d2e-d0bf9c10f6c8` has this GTID:

```
17ede83a-8b22-11e7-8d2e-d0bf9c10f6c8:23
```

This format is used with `START SLAVE` as an argument for slave database configuration. This format is used to represent GTIDs in the output of statements such as `SHOW SLAVE STATUS` as well as in the binary log.

GTID important variables are as follows:

- **gtid-mode**: ON | OFF
- **enforce-gtid-consistency**: Prevents execution of the non-transactional safe statements
- **gtid-purged**: Transactions have been purged from the binary logs
- **gtid-executed**: Transactions already executed on the server
- **gtid-next**: GTID for the next transaction

The generation of GTID consists of the following steps:

1. When a transaction is executed and committed on the master server, this transaction is assigned to GTID. This GTID is written to the master's binary log.
2. After the binary log data is transmitted to the slave and stored in the slave's relay log, the slave reads the GTID and sets the value of its `gtid_next` system variable as this GTID. This tells the slave server that the next transaction must be logged using this GTID.
3. The slave verifies that this GTID has not already been used to log a transaction in its own binary log. If this GTID has not been used, the slave then writes the GTID, applies the transaction, and writes the transaction to its binary log. By reading and checking the transaction's GTID first, before processing the transaction itself, the slave guarantees not only that no previous transaction having this GTID has been applied on the slave, but also that no other session has already read this GTID but has not yet committed the associated transaction. In other words, multiple clients are not permitted to apply the same transaction concurrently.
4. As `gtid_next` is not empty, the slave does not attempt to generate a GTID for this transaction but instead writes the GTID stored in this variable, that is, the GTID obtained from the master immediately preceding the transaction in its binary log.

The gtid_executed table

This is the default table of MySQL. This table contains an interval of several GTIDs. This table has the following columns:

- `source_uuid CHAR(36) NOT NULL`: The uuid of the master server where the transaction was originally executed
- `interval_start BIGINT NOT NULL`: First number of interval
- `interval_end BIGINT NOT NULL`: Last number of interval

If `gtid_mode` is enabled, it stores the GTIDs in the `gtid_executed` table, and if `binlog` is disabled, it stores transaction owned GTIDs.

GTID master's side configurations

Open MySQL configuration file on the master server:

```
sudo vim /etc/mysql/my.cnf
```

Inside this file, we have to make the following changes:

```
[mysqld]
server-id       = 1
log-bin         = mysql-bin
binlog_format   = ROW
gtid_mode       = on
enforce_gtid_consistency
log_slave_updates
```

Restart MySQL to apply the configuration changes:

```
sudo service mysql restart
```

Create a MySQL user to be used by the slave and use the GRANT SQL statement to provide access for a user that will be used by the slave server:

```
CREATE USER 'shabbirslave'@'%' IDENTIFIED BY 'password';
GRANT REPLICATION SLAVE ON *.* TO 'shabbirslave'@'%' IDENTIFIED BY
'password';
```

Take your database backup using the `mysqldump` command, which is used to create the slave server:

```
mysqldump -u root -p shabbirdb > shabbirdb.sql
```

GTID slave's side configurations

So, as we have configured master server, now let's configure slave server. We will need to create database on the slave server that we exported from the master.

Import the database that you previously exported from the master database:

```
mysql -u root -p shabbirdb < /path/to/shabbirdb.sql
```

Add the following variables to `my.cnf`:

```
[mysqld]
server_id        = 2
log_bin          = mysql-bin
binlog_format    = ROW
skip_slave_start
gtid_mode        = on
enforce_gtid_consistency
log_slave_updates
```

Restart MySQL to apply the configuration changes:

```
sudo service mysql restart
```

Execute the `CHANGE MASTER TO` command:

```
CHANGE MASTER TO
MASTER_HOST='12.34.56.789',
MASTER_PORT=3306,
MASTER_USER='shabbirslave',
MASTER_PASSWORD='password',
MASTER_AUTO_POSITION=1;
```

Start the replication:

```
START SLAVE;
```

It is important to specify position from where slave server will start sync process. . This is because `mysqldump` has information above the GTID. This variable is copied into the slave server during the importing of the dump and is used for the syncing of the database:

```
-- -- GTID state at the beginning of the backup --
SET @@GLOBAL.GTID_PURGED='b9b4712a-df64-11e3-b391-60672090eb04:1-7';
```

MySQL multi-source replication

MySQL multi-source server is the reverse of traditional master to slave replication. in one master multiple slave mechanism, multiple slave servers are connected to single master for the read operation. in MySQL multi-source replication, there are more than one master databases where write operations are being performed. And one single slave server connects with multiple master databases and replicate data from all masters in parallel.

As we learnt MySQL multi-source replication can connect to more than one Master server and perform the replication operation in parallel it has many benefits, While master slave replication is considered for high availability and scalability, multi-source replication can be considered backup activity or collecting information from more than one server to generate a consolidated reports. Any conflict in transactions arise during the replicating from multiple source servers cannot be detected or resolved by the MySQL 8. Any such conflicts in transactions must be taken care by the application itself. For replications Slave server creates one separate channel for each of the source server it is connected to perform replication operation

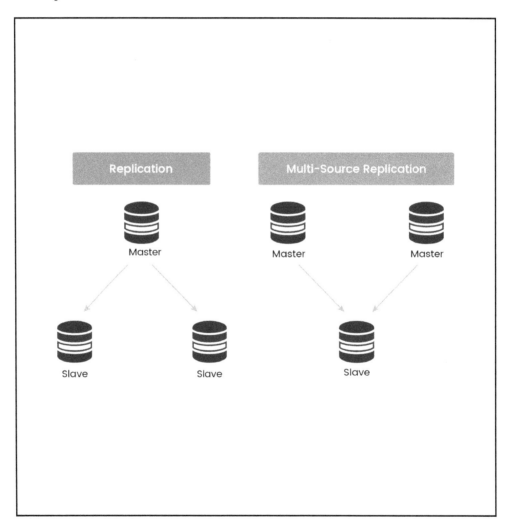

Multi-source replication configuration

Master servers can be configured using Global transaction IDs. we will come to configuring Master node later in the chapter when we will discuss on--*Replication with global transaction identifiers* . Slave servers in multi-source replication cannot work on file-base repositories. MySQL supports either file based or table based repositories to be configured. so we need to make sure that our slave MySQL server is configured using the table-based repositories.

```
sudo vim /etc/mysql/my.cnf
```

Add the following lines to the `my.cnf` file:

```
[mysqld]
master-info-repository    = TABLE
relay-log-info-repository = TABLE
```

You can check whether the table-based repository is enabled via the MySQL command shell:

```
mysql> SHOW VARIABLES LIKE '%repository%';
+---------------------------+-------+
| Variable_name             | Value |
+---------------------------+-------+
| master_info_repository    | TABLE |
| relay_log_info_repository | TABLE |
+---------------------------+-------+
```

Now you need to modify your configuration files for server-id to make sure that all servers will have a unique server-id used in replication.

Let's consider that we are using three servers for multi-source replication, as follows:

- 12.34.56.789: Master #1 database
- 12.34.56.790: Master #2 database
- 12.23.34.456: Slave database

The base setup of GTID-based transactions will be on Master #1 and Master #2 servers with the help of `gtid_mode= ON` as we have discussed earlier in *Replication with Global Transaction Identifiers* topic.

To ensure slave servers are using table-bases repositories for replication, we can create slave users on master servers. Once configurations are verified we can add master servers to the slave using the CHANGE MASTER TO command.

For example, add a new master with the host name Master #1 using port 3451 to a channel called master-1:

```
CHANGE MASTER TO MASTER_HOST='12.34.56.789', MASTER_USER='shabbirslave',
MASTER_PORT=3451,
MASTER_PASSWORD='password',
MASTER_AUTO_POSITION = 1 FOR CHANNEL 'master-1';
```

In the same way, you can add another server, master-2, to the replication channel:

```
CHANGE MASTER TO MASTER_HOST='12.34.56.790', MASTER_USER='shabbirslave',
MASTER_PORT=3451,
MASTER_PASSWORD='password',
MASTER_AUTO_POSITION = 1 FOR CHANNEL 'master-2';
```

Let's take a small example to understand how data is replicated from both master servers to slave servers:

```
CREATE DATABASE `hrms`;
use hrms;
CREATE TABLE `employee` (
`emp_id` int(9) NOT NULL AUTO_INCREMENT,
`emp_name` varchar(60) NOT NULL,
`emp_job_title` varchar(60) NOT NULL,
`emp_joining_date` date NOT NULL,
PRIMARY KEY (`emp_id`)
) ENGINE=InnoDB AUTO_INCREMENT=1;
```

The key to make multi-source replication work is to ensure that you don't have the same primary keys on both masters. If both masters have the same primary key for two different records, the data could be corrupted once it reaches the slave. Let's create the same database with different auto increment keys.

You can alternate values for our primary key column, employee_id. You could have your application do this, but an easy way is to use the `auto_increment` variable. In your configuration file, you will want to add this for both master databases:

```
[mysqld]
auto_increment_increment = 2
```

Master #1- Create new database as *hrms* with the auto increment 100000 as shown in the following code:

```
CREATE DATABASE `hrms`;
use hrms;
CREATE TABLE `employee` (
`emp_id` int(9) NOT NULL AUTO_INCREMENT,
`emp_name` varchar(60) NOT NULL,
`emp_job_title` varchar(60) NOT NULL,
`emp_joining_date` date NOT NULL,
PRIMARY KEY (`emp_id`)
) ENGINE=InnoDB AUTO_INCREMENT=100000;
```

Master #2- Same database we will create in Master 2 with the auto increment 100001.

```
CREATE DATABASE `hrms`;
use hrms;
CREATE TABLE `employee` (
`emp_id` int(9) NOT NULL AUTO_INCREMENT,
`emp_name` varchar(60) NOT NULL,
`emp_job_title` varchar(60) NOT NULL,
`emp_joining_date` date NOT NULL,
PRIMARY KEY (`employee_id`)
) ENGINE=InnoDB AUTO_INCREMENT=100001;
```

Let's assume that both master servers are already set up with the GTID master configuration. Now take a look at each of the master servers for the master status:

```
mysql> SHOW MASTER STATUS\G
*************************** 1. row ***************************
File: mysql-bin.000001
Position: 154
Binlog_Do_DB:
Binlog_Ignore_DB:
Executed_Gtid_Set:1
row in set (0.00 sec)
```

Now let's add some data to the Master #1 server and see what happens to the master status:

```
mysql> INSERT INTO employee (emp_name, emp_job_title,
emp_joining_date,emp_joining_date) VALUES('Shabbir','Lead
Consultant','2015-09-29');
Query OK, 1 row affected (0.02 sec)

mysql> SHOW MASTER STATUS\G
*************************** 1. row ***************************
File: mysql-bin.000001
Position: 574
Binlog_Do_DB:
Binlog_Ignore_DB:
Executed_Gtid_Set: 63a7971c-b48c-11e5-87cf-f7b6a723ba3d:1
1 row in set (0.00 sec)

mysql> INSERT INTO employee (emp_name, emp_job_title,
emp_joining_date,emp_joining_date) VALUES('Jaydip','Sr
Consultant','2014-10-12');
Query OK, 1 row affected (0.02 sec)

mysql> show master status\G
*************************** 1. row ***************************
File: mysql-bin.000001
Position: 994
Binlog_Do_DB:
Binlog_Ignore_DB:
Executed_Gtid_Set: 63a7971c-b48c-11e5-87cf-f7b6a723ba3d:1-2
1 row in set (0.00 sec)

mysql> select * from employee;
+-----------+---------------+----------------+-----------+------------+
| employee_id | employee_name | job_title| joining_year  |
+-----------+---------------+----------------+-----------+------------+
| 100001 | Jaydip  | Sr Consultant   | 2014-10-12 |
| 100003 | Shabbir | Lead Consultant | 2015-09-29 |
+-----------+---------------+----------------+-----------+------------+
2 rows in set (0.00 sec)
```

You can see how the values for the `employee_id` column are now incremented by two. Now we can insert two lines of data into Master #2:

```
mysql> INSERT INTO employee (employee_name, job_title,
joining_date,joining_date) VALUES('Kandarp','Lead
Consultant','2014-12-11');
mysql> INSERT INTO employee (employee_name, job_title,
joining_date,joining_date) VALUES('Chintan','Director','2013-01-01');

mysql> show master status\G
*************************** 1. row ***************************
File: mysql-bin.000005
Position: 974
Binlog_Do_DB:
Binlog_Ignore_DB:
Executed_Gtid_Set: 75e2e1dc-b48e-11e5-83bb-1438deb0d51e:1-2
1 row in set (0.00 sec)

mysql> select * from employee;
+----------+-------------+-----------------+------------+-----------+
| emp_id   | emp_name| emp_job_title    | emp_joining_year  |
+----------+-------------+-----------------+------------+-----------+
| 100002   | Kandarp | Lead consultant  | 2014-12-11        |
| 100004   | Chintan | Director         | 2013-01-01        |
+----------+-------------+-----------------+------------+-----------+
2 rows in set (0.00 sec)
```

Now you have two sets of GTIDs to replicate over to the slave.

Master #1 and Master #2 GTID sets:

```
63a7971c-b48c-11e5-87cf-f7b6a723ba3d:1-2
75e2e1dc-b48e-11e5-83bb-1438deb0d51e:1-2
```

Now let's see how data is replicated from both servers. Before we start the replication, let's check the status of the slave server:

```
mysql> show slave status\G
Empty set (0.00 sec)
```

Now let's add the master database to the slave using CHANGE MASTER:

```
CHANGE MASTER TO MASTER_HOST='12.34.56.789', MASTER_USER='shabbirslave',
MASTER_PORT=3451,
MASTER_PASSWORD='password',
MASTER_AUTO_POSITION = 1 FOR CHANNEL 'master-1';
```

Now we can start the slave for the channel master-1:

```
mysql> START SLAVE FOR CHANNEL 'master-1';
```

This command, at the same time, will start SQL_THREAD and IO_THREAD. Now if you check the slave status, you can see that you GTIDs from Master #1 have already been retrieved and applied to the database:

```
mysql> SHOW SLAVE STATUS FOR CHANNEL 'master-1'\G
*************************** 1. row ***************************
Slave_IO_State: Waiting for master to send event
Master_Host: 192.168.1.142
...
Master_UUID: 63a7971c-b48c-11e5-87cf-f7b6a723ba3d
...
Slave_SQL_Running_State: Slave has read all relay log; waiting for more
updates
...
Retrieved_Gtid_Set: 63a7971c-b48c-11e5-87cf-f7b6a723ba3d:1-2
Executed_Gtid_Set: 63a7971c-b48c-11e5-87cf-f7b6a723ba3d:1-2
Auto_Position: 1
...
Channel_Name: master-1
```

Now if you look at the employee table in the slave server, you will be able to find both entries from the Master #1 server.

Now let's start replication for the second master:

```
CHANGE MASTER TO MASTER_HOST='12.34.56.790', MASTER_USER='shabbirslave',
MASTER_PORT=3451,
MASTER_PASSWORD='password',
MASTER_AUTO_POSITION = 1 FOR CHANNEL 'master-2';
```

Now if we check the slave status again, all GTIDs from both master servers will have been retrieved and applied to the slave database.

Statement-based versus row-based replication

In **statement-based replication**, the MySQL master records the events as SQL statements in the binlog file. These statements are picked up by the MySQL slaves and replayed in the same way as they were played at the master.

In **row-based replication**, the MySQL master records the events as actual rows that indicate how the rows are changed at the master.

Group replication

A traditional MySQL replication implies to the master-slave architecture when write operations are performed by one server acting as master and other servers acting as slave are configured to periodically execute the replication to fetch data from the master and store locally. Each slaves in the master-slave replication has their own copy of the data and slaves do not share any information between them, basically we can term it as shared-nothing mechanism.

MySQL 8 has built in support for the Group replication. Group replication consists of more than one server each of which can act as master server. Servers in the group co-ordinate with message passing mechanism. For example, if any transaction commit operations is requested, it is relayed to the server group. Server group then approves a transaction and one of the server commits the write operation which then replicated to the group. For any read operation, no approval is needed from the server group and all such read requests are performed immediately. This architecture is bit complex then the general master slave architecture but it provides better atomicity and consistency.

The upcoming figure describes how group replication works and how it's different from traditional replication:

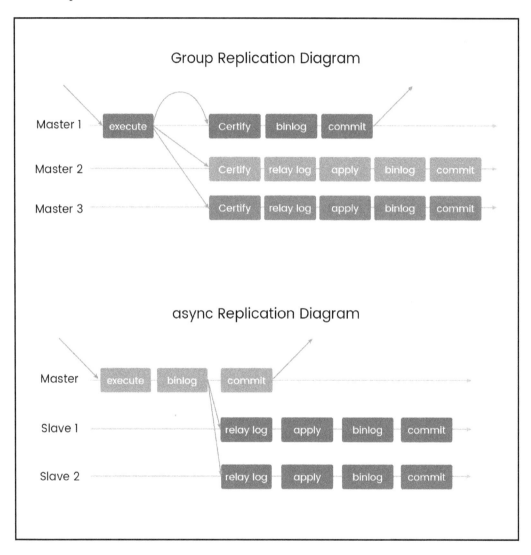

Requirements for group replication

There are certain requirements which needs to take care while performing group replication. Here are those common requirements.

Data must be stored in the InnoDB storage engine:

As MySQL group replication is completely transactions driven. there may be possibility of running concurrent transactions on multiple servers. So if any conflict arise during the execution, MySQL will rollback to previous safe state. So a database engine which can support transaction commit and rollback feature only can be used for the group replication. So right now in MySQL 8 only InnoDB supports Transactions.

Every table must have a primary key: As MySQL uses primary key for resolution of any conflict which arise during the parallel transaction executing in more than one server in group, Each table in the database which we are using for replicaiton, must have primary key defined explicitely.

IPv4 network: The group communication engine used by MySQL group replication only supports IPv4.

Low latency, high bandwidth network: If servers participating in group replications are far from each other, then transaction commit or rollback latency will be high so it is desirable that servers are close enough to each other in group replication.

Up to nine servers in the group: The group size is limited by design to support maximum of nine servers.

Group replication configuration

Open the main MySQL configuration file on each MySQL server in the group:

```
sudo vim /etc/mysql/my.cnf
```

Navigate to the [mysqld] section of the my.cnf file and add the configuration step by step:

```
[mysqld]
gtid_mode = ON
enforce_gtid_consistency = ON
master_info_repository = TABLE
relay_log_info_repository = TABLE
binlog_checksum = NONE
log_slave_updates = ON
log_bin = binlog
```

```
binlog_format = ROW
transaction_write_set_extraction = XXHASH64
loose-group_replication_bootstrap_group = OFF
loose-group_replication_start_on_boot = OFF
loose-group_replication_ssl_mode = REQUIRED
loose-group_replication_recovery_use_ssl = 1# General replication settings
```

This section contains general settings related to the global transaction IDs and binary logging that is required for group replication, and configures SSL for the group.

Group replication settings

To configure group replication on all the group members, we need to configure few parameters. We need to setup the group unique id using `loose-group_replication_group_name` .it will be unique identifier of the group. We nee to whitelist all the group members using the `loose-group_replication_ip_whitelist` parameter. We also need to provide seed parameter loose-group_replication_group_seeds which is identical to whitelist parameter, only difference seed has it contains the port number with the server IP addresses. Below is the configuration parameter that need to be setup.

```
loose-group_replication_group_name = "959cf631-538c-415d-8164-ca00181be227"
loose-group_replication_ip_whitelist =
"213.121.111.112,213.121.123.2,213.121.121.324"
loose-group_replication_group_seeds =
"213.121.111.112:33061,213.121.123.2:33061,213.121.121.324:33061"
```

Choosing a single master or multi-master

A Single Master configuration has only one group member which performs write operations, while multi-master group replication allows all group members to perform write operations. Below are the configuration that need to be enabled for allowing mult-master group replication.

```
loose-group_replication_single_primary_mode = OFF
loose-group_replication_enforce_update_everywhere_checks = ON
```

These settings must be the same on each of your MySQL servers.

It is possible to change the configuration of group replication from multi-master to single master configuration or vice versa without loosing any data. For changing configuration of the group, configuration of each of the server in the group has to be changed. After changing configuration, a restart of MySQL service is required on each of the group member. A downtime is required to configure the group replication with the new settings.

Host-specific configuration settings

Certain configurations are specific to each server in the group that also need to be configured.

- Server ID
- Server Local Address
- Remote address to be shared with other member
- server's local address and port number

The `server_id` is a unique number for each member of group replication.It is possible to setup any unique value for each of the group member. For our example, for the first member, just set this to 1 and increment the number each additional host. `bind-address` and `report_host` are server's IP address that will be used for external clients to connect with. The `loose-group_replication_local_address` is also server's IP address with the port (`33061`) number appended to the IP address:

```
server_id = 1
bind-address = "213.121.111.112"
report_host = "213.121.111.112"
loose-group_replication_local_address = "213.121.111.112:33061"
```

Apply this configuration to each of the MySQL servers and save the `my.cnf` file.

By this step, we are ready for enabling the group replication. all configuration bootstrap has been done. we can now restart the MySQL service on each of the group member

```
sudo service mysql restart
```

By Default, MySQL uses port 3306 for any connection request coming to MySQL server. So if any firewall installed on your server, apply below commands to add them to allow list.

```
sudo ufw allow 33061
sudo ufw allow 3306
```

With access to the MySQL ports open, we can create a replication user and enable the group replication plugin.

Configuring a Replication User and enabling the Group Replication Plugin

Now, our servers are ready for the group replication. So, before we setup group replication plugin, we need to create a separate user for the replication purpose. Please keep in mind that while creating replication user, binary log should be turned off to avoid any conflict if the replication process begins and servers starts reading binary logs for the replication.

We will grant replication user replication privileges, then flush the privileges to implement the changes. Now, we can re-enable binary logs to resume normal operations.

Make sure to use a secure password when creating the replication user:

```
SET SQL_LOG_BIN=0;
CREATE USER 'shabbir_user'@'%' IDENTIFIED BY 'password' REQUIRE SSL;
GRANT REPLICATION SLAVE ON *.* TO 'shabbir_user'@'%';
FLUSH PRIVILEGES;
SET SQL_LOG_BIN=1;
```

Use the CHANGE MASTER TO statement to configure the server to use the given credentials for the group_replication_recovery replication channels, the next time it needs to recover its state from another member:

```
CHANGE MASTER TO MASTER_USER='shabbir_user',
MASTER_PASSWORD='password' FOR CHANNEL 'group_replication_recovery';
```

A `Group` replication plugin is required in MySQL 8 to start the group replication, this plugin can be installed using following command:

```
INSTALL PLUGIN group_replication SONAME 'group_replication.so';
```

Following command will show whether the required plugin is enabled or not:

```
SHOW PLUGINS;
```

Starting group replication

We have done configuration on different group members.We have created separate replication users and we have enabled the group replication plugin. Now, we can setup database to start the replication.

Bootstrap node

Following steps are required to perform on **a single member of the group**:

```
SET GLOBAL group_replication_bootstrap_group=ON;
START GROUP_REPLICATION;
SET GLOBAL group_replication_bootstrap_group=OFF;
```

Next, create a test database and table to test our replication:

```
CREATE DATABASE `hrms`;
use hrms;
CREATE TABLE `employee` (
`emp_id` int(9) NOT NULL AUTO_INCREMENT,
`emp_name` varchar(60) NOT NULL,
`emp_job_title` varchar(60) NOT NULL,
`emp_joining_date` date NOT NULL,
PRIMARY KEY (`emp_id`)
) ENGINE=InnoDB AUTO_INCREMENT=1;

INSERT INTO employee (emp_name, emp_job_title,
emp_joining_date,emp_joining_date) VALUES('Shabbir','Lead
Consultant','2015-09-30');
```

Now start group replication in the **second server.** As we already have an active member, we don't need to bootstrap the group and can just join it:

```
START GROUP_REPLICATION;
```

In the same way, you can start in another server. To check the membership list from the `replication_group_members`, perform the following:

```
SELECT * FROM performance_schema.replication_group_members;

Output:
+--------------------------+------------------------------------------+--------
--------+-------------+---------------+
| CHANNEL_NAME | MEMBER_ID | MEMBER_HOST | MEMBER_PORT | MEMBER_STATE |
+--------------------------+------------------------------------------+--------
--------+-------------+---------------+
| group_replication_applier | 13324ab7-1b01-11e7-9dd1-22b78adaa992 |
213.121.111.112 | 3306 | ONLINE |
| group_replication_applier | 1ae4b211-1b01-11e7-9d89-ceb93e1d5494 |
213.121.123.2 | 3306 | ONLINE |
| group_replication_applier | 157b597a-1b01-11e7-9d83-566a6de6dfef |
213.121.121.324 | 3306 | ONLINE |
+--------------------------+------------------------------------------+--------
--------+-------------+---------------+
3 rows in set (0.01 sec)
```

So this way, you can add multiple MySQL instances when you want.

Summary

In this chapter, you learned about high availability and why high availability is required. Then, we covered various replication methods to achieve high availability in MySQL 8 architectures and approaches. We understood different types of replication methods in MySQL 8 and the usability for each method. We also explored how to configure each type of replication with a few real-time examples.

Now it's time to move on to the next chapter, where we will see wonderful practices to achieve performance, scalability, security, and availability using MySQL 8.

7
MySQL 8 Best Practices

In the previous chapter, you learned how to use replication to build highly available solutions. It covered a lot of interesting aspects such as failovers, group replications, clustering, and so on. In this chapter, we will go through the best practices of MySQL 8, which is a much-awaited version that promises to address many of the shortfalls of the prior versions and has exciting new features. MySQL 8 promises not to be just a standalone database, but also will play a significant role in various areas including big data solutions.

Topics that we will be covering in this chapters are mentioned below:

- MySQL benchmarks and configurations
- Best practices for MySQL queries
- Best practices for the Memcached configuration
- Best practices for replication

Due to prominent optimizations and changes, MySQL 8 advanced its version directly from the release of MySQL 5.7. MySQL 8 will not have the limitation of files that was previously restricting the number of databases that you can have. There are many more such exciting features, which we have covered in Chapter 1, *Introduction to Big Data and MySQL 8*. MySQL 8 can now store millions of tables in a database. It will also make modifications to tables swiftly.

I am excited to go through this chapter as MySQL 8 best practices not only impacts your database performance, scalability, security, and availability, but also overall exposes how your system performs for the end user. This is our end goal, isn't it? Let's look at benchmarks that have been derived in our test lab, which would raise your eyebrows for sure!

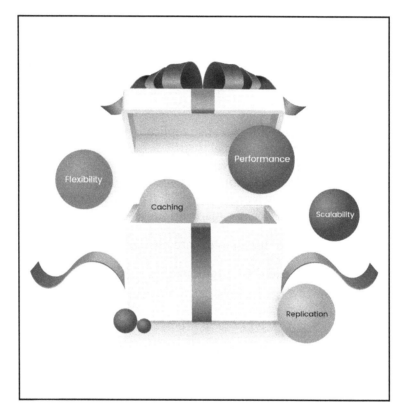

The following topics will be covered in this chapter:

- MySQL benchmarks and configurations
- Best practices for MySQL queries
- Best practices for the Memcached configuration
- Best practices for replication

MySQL benchmarks and configurations

We have gone through various new features and improvements MySQL 8 is coming up with. It makes us more excited as performance is always what we crave for. MySQL 8 not being generally available yet, Oracle hasn't published its benchmark results. We didn't wait for it and did analysis on our own in a few areas.

Configuration best practices of MySQL is the cherry on the cake; without the cherry, the cake seems incomplete. In addition to configurations, benchmarking helps us validate and find bottlenecks and address them. Let's look at a few specific areas that would help us understand best practices for configuration and performance benchmarking.

Resource utilization

IO activity, CPU, and memory usage is something that you should not miss out. These metrics help us know how the system is performing while doing benchmarking and at the time of scaling. It also helps us derive impact per transaction.

Stretch your timelines of benchmarks

We often would like to have a quick glance at performance metrics; however, ensuring that MySQL behaves in the same way for a longer duration of testing is also a key element. There is some basic stuff that might impact performance when you stretch your benchmark timelines like memory fragmentation, degradation of IO, impact after data accumulation, cache management, and so on. We don't want our database to get restarted just to clean up junk items, correct? Hence, it is suggested to run benchmarking for a long duration for stability and performance validation.

Replicating production settings

Let's benchmark in a production-replicated environment; wait. Let's disable database replication in a replica environment until we are done with benchmarking. Gotcha, we have got some good numbers!

It often happens that we don't simulate completely what we are going to configure in the production environment. It can prove to be costly as we unintentionally would be benchmarking in an environment that might have an adverse impact when it's in production. Replicate production settings, data, workload, and so on in your replicated environment while you do benchmarking.

Consistency of throughput and latency

Throughput and latency go hand in hand. It is important to keep your eyes primarily focused on throughput; however, latency over time might be something to be looked out for. Performance dips, slowness, or stalls were noticed in InnoDB in its earlier days. It has improved a lot by now, but as there might be other cases depending on your workload, it is always good to keep an eye on throughput along with latency.

Sysbench can do more

Sysbench is a wonderful tool to simulate your workloads, whether it be thousands of tables, transaction intensive, data in-memory, and so on. It is a splendid tool to simulate and give you nice representation.

Virtualization world

I would like to keep this simple; bare metal as compared to virtualization isn't the same. Hence, while doing benchmarking, measure your resources according to your environment. You might be surprised to see the difference in results if you compare both.

Concurrency

Big data is seated on heavy data workload; high concurrency is important. MySQL 8 is extending its maximum CPU core support in every new release. Optimizing concurrency based on your requirement and hardware resources should be taken care of.

Hidden workloads

Do not miss out factors that run in the background like reporting for big data analytics, backups, and on-the-fly operations while you are benchmarking. The impact of such hidden workloads or obsolete benchmarking workloads can make your days (and nights) miserable.

Nerves of your query

Oops, did we miss the optimizer? Not yet. An **optimizer** is a powerful tool that will read the nerves of your query and provide recommendations. It's a tool that I use before making changes to a query in production. It's a savior when you have complex queries to be optimized.

These are a few areas that we should look out for. Let's now look at a few benchmarks that we did on MySQL 8 compared to MySQL 5.7.

Benchmarks

To start with, let's fetch all the column names from all the InnoDB tables. The following is the query that we executed:

```
SELECT t.table_schema, t.table_name, c.column_name
FROM information_schema.tables t,
information_schema.columns c
WHERE t.table_schema = c.table_schema
AND t.table_name = c.table_name
AND t.engine='InnoDB';
```

The following figure shows how MySQL 8 performed a thousand times faster when having four instances:

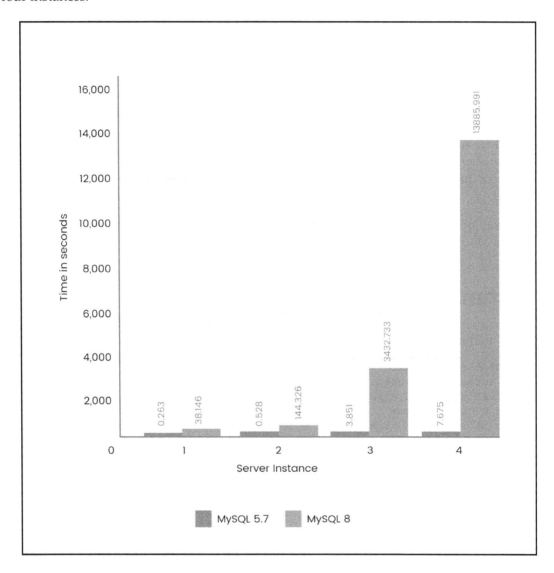

Following this, we also performed a benchmark to find static table metadata. The following is the query that we executed:

```
SELECT TABLE_SCHEMA, TABLE_NAME, TABLE_TYPE, ENGINE, ROW_FORMAT
FROM INFORMATION_SCHEMA.TABLES
WHERE TABLE_SCHEMA LIKE 'chintan%';
```

The following figure shows how MySQL 8 performed around 30 times faster than MySQL 5.7:

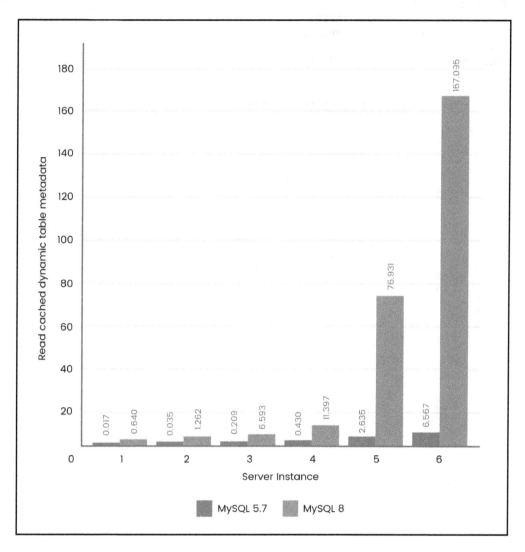

It made us eager to go a bit more in detail. So, we thought of doing one last test to find dynamic table metadata.

The following is the query that we executed:

```
SELECT TABLE_ROWS
FROM INFORMATION_SCHEMA.TABLES
WHERE TABLE_SCHEMA LIKE 'chintan%';
```

The following figure shows how MySQL 8 performed around 30 times faster than MySQL 5.7:

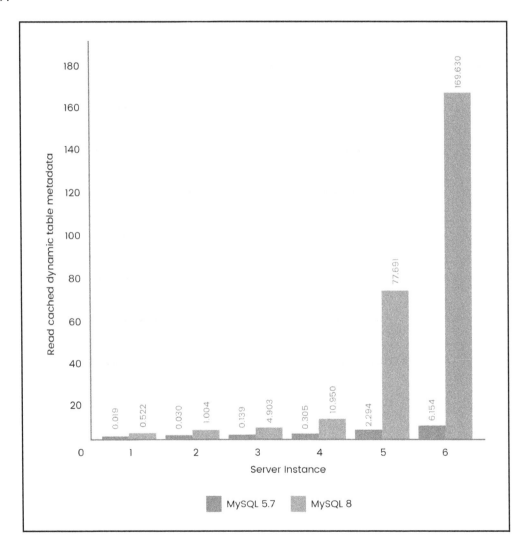

MySQL 8.0 brings enormous performance improvement to the table. Scaling to one million tables, which is a need for many big data requirements, is now achievable. We look forward to many more benchmarks officially released once MySQL 8 is available for general purposes.

Let's now look at our next topic that would make your life easy. It's all about taking things into consideration for query formation.

Best practices for MySQL queries

It would be difficult to write the best queries for reference and reuse. It will always vary based on the nature of your application, architecture, design, table structure, and so on. However, precautions can be taken while writing MySQL queries for better performance, scalability, and integrity.

Let's go through a few of the best practices that we should keep in mind while designing or writing MySQL queries.

Data types

A database table would consist multiple columns having data types such as numeric or string. MySQL 8 provides various data types than just limiting to numeric or string.

- Small is good. As MySQL loads data in memory, a large data size would adversely impact performance. Smaller sets can accommodate more data in memory and reduce overheads of resource utilization.
- Fix your length. If you don't fix the data type length, it would have to go and fetch the required information each time it needs. So, wherever it's possible, you can limit data length by using the char data type.

Not null

Not null data is something that MySQL doesn't like much. Not null columns use more storage, impact the performance, and require additional processing within MySQL. Optimizing such queries referring to null data is difficult as well. When a null data column is indexed, it uses additional bytes for each entry.

Indexing

Indexing is important as it can improve the performance of your badly designed query and table structure or it can become even a good designed query into a bad one which can impact performance too.

Search fields index

Generally, we do indexing on fields that are used as filters in MySQL queries. It obviously helps reading faster but can adversely impact writes/updates so indexing only what you need would be a smart decision.

Data types and joins

MySQL can do joins for data types that are different but the performance can be impacted if MySQL is asked to use different data types for join fields as it would have to convert from one to another for each row.

Compound index

If a query is supposed to refer multiple columns of a table, a composite index for such columns might be helpful. Compound index refers the columns from the results set by the first column, second column, and so on.

Order of columns plays a significant role in the performance of the query, so while designing the table structure and index, you need to use it effectively.

Shorten up primary keys

Small is good for primary keys too. Shortening up primary keys would benefit analogously to how we discussed datatypes. Due to smaller primary keys, your index size would be smaller and hence the usage of cache would be less, so it can accommodate more data in memory. It is preferred to use numeric types as it would be much smaller than characters to achieve the goal of shortening up primary keys. It can be helpful while doing joins as generally, primary keys are referred for the joining.

Index everything

Indexing everything is a good thought, MySQL wouldn't use it. Do you know that MySQL will do a full table scan if it is supposed to scan an index higher than 30%? Do not index values that don't need to be indexed.

We need to keep in mind that indexing helps--if done correctly--in fetching data; however, while writing/updating data, it is an overhead.

Fetch all data

`select *...` - Arrghh! Do not use this unless it is really needed. So far, my experience hasn't needed this. Fetching all data will slow down the execution time and impact heavily on resource utilization of the MySQL server. You need to provide a specific column name or appropriate conditions.

Application does the job

Let the application also do the job for MySQL. You can avoid having clauses like `order by` to let applications do ordering. Doing ordering in MySQL is much slower than in applications. You can identify queries that should be planned to be taken care of by the application.

Existence of data

Checking the existence of data with the help of the `EXISTS` clause is much faster. The `EXISTS` clause will return the output as soon as it fetches the first row from the fetched data.

Limit yourself

Limit yourself to the data that you need to fetch. Always ensure that you use appropriate limits while fetching the data as unwanted data being fetched wouldn't be useful and would impact performance. Use the `LIMIT` clause in your SQL queries.

Analyze slow queries

This is a good practice to follow. We might miss out queries to either optimize or realize having adverse impact as data grows. You might have changes in the requirement of data to be fetched where we might miss seeing the impact of the queries. It is good to always keep a watch on slow queries that can be configured in MySQL and optimize them.

Query cost

What is the cost of your query? Explain is the right answer to this. Use the explain query parameter to know what is impacting your query--whether it is a full table scan, index scans, range access, and so on. Use the information provided by **Explain** wisely, to optimize the query further. It is a wonderful, quick handy tool of MySQL. If you know that you have done your best, indexing comes as a savior to optimize it further based on your needs.

Best practices while writing a query start with requirements, designs, implements, and ongoing maintenance. It's a complete life cycle that we can't diversify. Understanding schemas, indexes, and analyses plays a significant role. What matters to us is the response time and optimum resource utilization.

I personally love to deep dive into this much more than what we can mention here--it's a world of relations! Your query will meet a row or column of a table or get joined with another table. On top of this, if you haven't done it right, you are trying to find a relation from a subset that is not required. How do we forget indexes who are saviors if used appropriately? All these together would show our relations and would promptly respond to a query requested.

Let's move forward and look toward the best practices for the Memcached configuration in detail.

Best practices for the Memcached configuration

We have already gone through Memcached setup and configuration along with using it with different APIs in `Chapter 4`, *Using Memcached with MySQL 8*. The key takeaways that you would like to consider for Memcached configuration best practices are what we will be going through now.

Resource allocation

Memory allocation for Memcached shouldn't be allocated over the available physical memory or without considering other resources that would be utilizing memory. If we overallocate memory, there are high chances that Memcached would have memory allocated from swapspace. This may lead to delay while inserting or fetching values because swap space is stored on disk, which is slower than in-memory.

Operating system architecture

With operating system architecture having 32 bits, one needs to be cautious. As we know, there are limitations to provision resources in 32-bit operating system architecture. Similarly, Memcached having 4GB RAM with 32-bit operating system architecture shouldn't be set more than 3.5GB RAM as it can behave strangely for performance and can also result in crashes.

Default configurations

Some key default configuration parameters should always be fine-tuned based on your needs:

- **Memory allocation**: By default, it is 64MB; instead it should be reconfigured based on needs and testing
- **Connections**: By default it is 1,024 concurrent connections; instead it should be reconfigured based on needs and testing
- **Port**: By default it listens on port `11211`; instead it should listen to another port for security purposes
- **Network Interface**: By default it accepts connections from all network interfaces; instead it should be limited for security purposes

Max object size

You should look at configuring maximum object size, which, by default, is 1 MB. However, it can be bumped up to 128 MB. It is purely based on what type of data you are going to store and accordingly, its maximum object size should be allowed. Allowing overhead data to be stored in Memcached can adversely impact as it would have much more data supposed to be retrieved.

Backlog queue limit

Backlog queue limit is all about the number of connections to Memcached it should keep in queue if it reaches the limit of allowed connections. Ideally, your number of connections allowed should be configured in a way that should suffice for most of your needs. Backlog queue limit can be helpful when there is an unexpected peak load on Memcached. Ideally, it should not go beyond 20% of total connections or it can impact the experience of system fetching information from Memcached because of heavy delays.

Large pages support

On systems that support large memory pages support, you should enable Memcached to leverage it. Large pages support helps allocate a large data chunk to store data and also reduces the number of caches missed calls using this.

Sensitive data

Storing sensitive data in Memcached would be open for threat as somebody having access to Memcached can view the sensitive information. One should obviously take precautions to limit the exposure of Memcached. You can also have sensitive information encrypted before storing it on Memcached.

Restrict exposure

Memcached doesn't have many security features inbuilt. One of the things is exposing Memcached access within required boundaries. If your application server needs to talk to Memcached, only allow Memcached being accessed from that server with the help of system firewall rules like IP Tables or similar techniques.

Failover

Memcached doesn't have good failover techniques. It is suggested to have your application configured in a way to failover to an unavailable node and regenerate data into another instance. It is good to have at least two Memcached configured to avoid failure due to unavailability of the instance.

Namespaces

You can leverage namespaces provided by Memcached, which basically adds prefixes to the data before storing in Memcached. It can help when you have multiple applications talking to Memcached. It is helpful and, using some basic principles of naming conventions, you can derive the solution. If there is data that is storing data of First Name and Last Name, you can use prefixes such as FN and LN respectively. This would help you easily identify and retrieve data from the application.

Caching mechanism

One of the easiest ways to start leveraging caching in Memcached is to use a two-column table; you can leverage namespaces provided by Memcached, which basically adds prefixes. First columns would be a primary key, and database schema should be the address requirement of a unique identifier with the help of primary key mapping along with unique constraints. In case you want to have a single item value by combining multiple column values, you should take care of choosing appropriate data types.

Queries having a single WHERE clause can be mapped easily into Memcached lookups while using = or IN operators in the queries itself. In cases where multiple WHERE clauses are used or complex operations are parsed such as <,>. LIKE, BETWEEN, Memcached would get you through challenges. It is suggested to have such complex operations using traditional SQL queries to your database.

It would be beneficial to cache entire objects in Memcached instead of opting to cache individual rows from MySQL 8. For instance, for a blogging website, you should cache the entire object of blog port in Memcached.

Memcached general statistics

To help you understand the statistics of Memcached better, we will provide an overview of health and performance. Statistics returned by Memcached and their meaning is shown in the following table.

Terms used to define the value for each of the statistics:

- **32u**: 32-bit unsigned integer
- **64u**: 64-bit unsigned integer
- **32u:32u**: Two 32-bit unsigned integers separated by a colon

- **String**: Character string

Statistic	Data type	Description
pid	32u	Process ID of the Memcached instance
uptime	32u	Uptime (in seconds) for this Memcached instance
time	32u	Current time (as epoch)
version	string	Version string of this instance
pointer_size	string	Size of pointers for this host specified in bits (32 or 64)
rusage_user	32u:32u	Total user time for this instance (seconds:microseconds)
rusage_system	32u:32u	Total system time for this instance (seconds:microseconds)
curr_items	32u	Current number of items stored by this instance
total_items	32u	Total number of items stored during the life of this instance
bytes	64u	Current number of bytes used by this server to store items
curr_connections	32u	Current number of open connections
total_connections	32u	Total number of connections opened since the server started running
connection_structures	32u	Number of connection structures allocated by the server
cmd_get	64u	Total number of retrieval requests (get operations)
cmd_set	64u	Total number of storage requests (set operations)
get_hits	64u	Number of keys that have been requested and found present
get_misses	64u	Number of items that have been requested and not found

Statistic	Data type	Description
delete_hits	64u	Number of keys that have been deleted and found present
delete_misses	64u	Number of items that have been deleted and not found
incr_hits	64u	Number of keys that have been incremented and found present
incr_misses	64u	Number of items that have been incremented and not found
decr_hits	64u	Number of keys that have been decremented and found present
decr_misses	64u	Number of items that have been decremented and not found
cas_hits	64u	Number of keys that have been compared and swapped and found present
cas_misses	64u	Number of items that have been compared and swapped and not found
cas_badvalue	64u	Number of keys that have been compared and swapped, but the comparison (original) value did not match the supplied value
evictions	64u	Number of valid items removed from cache to free memory for new items
bytes_read	64u	Total number of bytes read by this server from network
bytes_written	64u	Total number of bytes sent by this server to network
limit_maxbytes	32u	Number of bytes this server is permitted to use for storage
threads	32u	Number of worker threads requested
conn_yields	64u	Number of yields for connections (related to the -R option)

Reference: `https://dev.mysql.com/doc/refman/8.0/en/ha-memcached-stats-general.html`

These are a few handy items that should be kept handy for best practices of Memcached; it's time for us to move ahead and look at best practices for replication.

Best practices for replication

MySQL 8 has done some great improvements in the replication part. The purpose of MySQL 8 is all about scalability, performance, and security with utmost integrity of data, which is expected to be a game-changer in big data too.

Throughput in group replication

Group replication basically takes care of committing transactions once most of the members in group replication have acknowledged the transaction received concurrently. This helps in a better throughput if the overall number of writes is not exceeding the capacity of the members in group replication. If there is a case where capacity is not planned appropriately, you would notice lags on affected members as compared to other members in the group.

Infrastructure sizing

`Infrastructure sizing` is a common success factor for performance and the best practices checklist. If infrastructure sizing is not proper or uneven across the nodes in group replication, it might adversely impact replication fundamentals topology. Each component should be considered while considering throughput required from them.

Constant throughput

To achieve constant throughput is a good success factor. What if you start experiencing workload that starts affecting the rest of the members in group replication? It might be a case where your master keeps on accepting additional workload and would be lagging for some time, after which it might return to an acceptable level before burning out all the resources. Additionally, you can implement queuing methodology that can prevent you from burning down resources and only allow to pass on workloads to the members that are predefined based on capacity.

While considering queuing methodology, one needs to keep in mind about not letting queues grow exponentially. This would impact the end user as there would be lag in data being updated. However, one needs to decide based on needs and the business requirement to achieve constant throughput across the system.

Contradictory workloads

Fundamentally, group replication is designed to allow updates from any of the members in the group. Rollback of transactions based on overlap of rows is checked for each of the transactions; the rest are committed and sent to be updated to other members in the group. If several updates on the same row happen frequently, it can result in multiple rollbacks. You might come across cyclic situations wherein one server updates, requests others to update, in parallel another has already updated for the same row--it would result in rollback.

To prevent such a scenario, you can have the last member of the group apply the update after which you proceed to another one. You can have similar updates routed only from the same node where the earlier one had been executed to prevent chances of cyclic rollback conditions.

Write scalability

Distribute your write workload by sharing out write operations, which might result in better throughput and better scalability on write performance. It would be dependent on contradictory workloads that you would be expecting in the system. This is helpful when your peak workload is being executed is one that can share the load. In common cases, if you have good capacity planning done with write scalability, you would see trivial improvement.

Refer to the following diagram that depicts this:

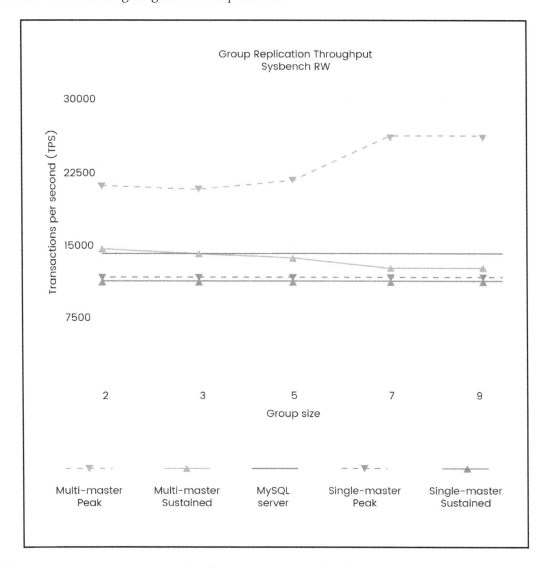

You can notice that with the help of multi-masters to distribute, your load has better throughput. It also considers the group size in multi-master configuration.

Summary

I am sure that while reading the chapter, you would be keeping in mind the things to be taken care of or recollecting if there's anything missing in your MySQL 8 implementation. In these chapter we discussed about best practices for MySQL 8 which would be helpful at various stages like implementation, usage, management, and troubleshooting and would act as pointers for Best Practices of MySQL 8; it might vary based in different use-cases. Proper testing and verification would help affirm on the benefits of having best practices implemented.

We have broadly covered some exciting topics about MySQL 8 benchmarks and a few configuration parameters. MySQL queries pointers were also discussed with caching using Memcached best practices. Lastly, we discussed MySQL replication best practices in which we went through a few critical pointers. Anything written in this chapter would be less, but pointers provided are necessary.

By now, we have a good implementation completed for MySQL 8; it's time to integrate with other systems. Let's now move on to look at how API integration of NoSQL with big data solutions can be achieved in the next chapter. We will go through different APIs to get MySQL and NoSQL to talk to each other.

8

NoSQL API for Integrating with Big Data Solutions

In the previous chapter, we looked at best practices for MySQL 8 that we should follow in various aspects such as performance, implementation, security, and so on. Best practices always align the product with the industry standard and also give a good output. We have seen different best practices for different phases like Benchmark and Configuration, which detail configuration parameters to provide better benchmark results. Best practices for queries helps in designing complex queries and providing better performance. Best practices for Memcached need to be maintained while implementing caching mechanisms. The valid replication configuration will always result in better scalability and can provide better performance with low latency.

This chapter talks about integrating MySQL 8 to work like NoSQL with the different APIs available. We will see how MySQL, an RDBMS, will work as NoSQL to handle big data. MySQL provides various APIs in different programming languages that we can easily integrate with applications and manage big data. Let's explore some of the APIs with basic examples in different programming languages.

Below are the topics highlighted that we are going to discuss in this chapter:

- NoSQL overview
- NoSQL versus SQL
- Implementing NoSQL APIs

NoSQL overview

The word NoSQL means **No SQL**, which means that it will skip the SQL layer and use the database directly. As data is rapidly growing everyday and big data enters the picture to make the data scalable and faster, then NoSQL helps in managing massive volumes of data with the evolution of the **Relational Database Management System** (**RDBMS**).

Many have also interpreted NoSQL as **Not Only SQL**, because this is not a complete replacement of the SQL layer but, we can say, a complementary addition to the Relational Database. NoSQL does not follow the rules of a relational database and can access data with the traditional database easily.

MySQL has already maintained its popularity in the structured world, but as per the current scenario, data has been pushing the boundaries, which takes storage and analysis to an entirely new level. This push of data has raised the need for NoSQL under big data to make stronger analysis and provide effective performance. This way, MySQL has unlocked its pure structured world and moved forward to NoSQL along with the high performance, high availability, and extending limits of being a traditional RDBMS.

Let's see the major advantages of having a NoSQL database.

Changing rapidly over time

The main problem with RDBMS is the change management. As data is growing day by day, we might need to change the structure of data models in RDBMS ,which is quite risky and needs to be done carefully by considering downtime and without affecting the existing data.

NoSQL can help us mange this rapid change without affecting anything because NoSQL allows applications to store and manage data with any structure that it wants with different kinds of storage like key/value store or document store.

Scaling

When scaling enters the picture in RDBMS due to heavy loads of data, then we might need to worry because it requires expensive servers and hardware to scale up the RDBMS. However, the new breed of NoSQL provides solutions to scale out and distribute the load across multiple hosts with very low cost as compared to the RDBMS. It also has the capability to transparently perform horizontal scaling as the transaction rates increases without affecting the system.

Less management

No more database administration required! With the RDBMS, we might require a Database Administrator to manage the database, which is really an overhead cost. NoSQL is generally designed to require less management and provides auto repair, data distribution, and simpler data models, which allows the user to manage less as compared to the RDBMS. However, someone should always be there for the performance, availability, and critical data stores.

Best for big data

As we have discussed, increasing transaction rates and volume of data have given birth to the term big data. The capacity of RDBMS to handle such a need is quite limited and also affects performance. NoSQL is basically designed to handle big data that has many capabilities, and its simpler approach to storing and retrieving data really boosts the performance.

Nowadays, data analytics is one of the common requirements for most enterprises and NoSQL makes it easy to do analytics on big data. Extracting meaningful business intelligence from very high volumes of data might be a tedious task to achieve with traditional relational database systems. Keeping in mind all the factors on continuously increasing data and the dynamic structure of data, we can say that NoSQL is the best way to handle big data.

NoSQL versus SQL

Let's see the major differences between NoSQL and SQL databases:

NoSQL	SQL
NoSQL is referred to as a non-relational and distributed database system.	SQL is referred to as relational database system.
NoSQL is horizontally scalable.	SQL is vertically scalable.
NoSQL does not use a structured query language. It has an unstructured query language, which varies from database to database.	SQL uses the structured query language to manipulate the data.
NoSQL does not have a fixed or predefined schema.	SQL has a predefined static database.
NoSQL stores data in key/value pairs.	SQL stores data in tabular format.
For complex relational queries, NoSQL is not suitable.	SQL is best suited for complex relational queries.
Preferable to handle big data.	Preferable to handle relational data.
NoSQL stores data in the form of collections where data can be duplicated and stored in a single entity. Hence, reading/writing on a single entity is easier and faster.	SQL stores data in a normalized way and breaks down with the separate tables, which avoids data redundancy and duplication. However, reading/writing needs to be performed on a different entity, hence complex queries may take place in the processing of data.

Implementing NoSQL APIs

So far, we have seen how NoSQL databases can help in various ways and also walked through the differences between SQL and NoSQL. Now you might be wondering how we can store/retrieve data to MySQL? MySQL 8 is already providing many APIs in different languages to access MySQL, which works like NoSQL. MySQL has implemented NoSQL interfaces on the top of InnoDB and MySQL Cluster engines, which bypass the SQL layer completely.

Hence, it will store key/value data directly to the MySQL tables with higher speed without doing SQL parsing and optimization. MySQL still maintains all the advantages of its existing relational database infrastructure and the user can continue executing complex queries with SQL on the same datasets.

There are mainly two types of NoSQL APIs used with MySQL 8 in various programming languages.

- NoSQL API with the Memcached layer
    - NoSQL API with Java
    - NoSQL API with PHP
    - NoSQL API with Python
    - NoSQL API with Perl
- NoSQL API with NDB Cluster
    - NDB API for NodeJS
    - NDB API for Java
    - NDB API with C++

Let's see each API in detail.

NoSQL with the Memcached API layer

As we have seen in Chapter 4, *Using Memcached with MySQL 8*, a native Memcached API is part of MySQL 8 and MySQL Cluster. You can use this API to read and write data with the help of the Memcached client. Nowadays, many enterprises require SQL RDBMS with NoSQL techniques to access the data and MySQL 8 provides a solution of Not Only SQL with the help of the Memcached interface.

Memcached APIs directly access the InnoDB and MySQL Cluster engines without transformation to SQL along with ensuring low latency and high throughput for read/write queries. The daemon_memcached plugin runs on the same process space so that the user gets very low latency access to their data while also leveraging the scalability enhancements delivered with the InnoDB. Make sure that you have installed and configured Memcached as described in Chapter 4, *Using Memcached with MySQL 8*. Now let's start developing the Memcached client with different programming languages.

Let's assume that we have a contact list that has simple information as follows:

Contact Person Name	Company Name	Email Address	Mobile Number
Jaydip Lakhatariya	KNOWARTH	`jaydip.lakhatariya@knowarth.com`	9111111111
Chintan Mehta	KNOWARTH	`chintan.mehta@knowarth.com`	9222222222
Kandarp Patel	KNOWARTH	`kandarp.patel@knowarth.com`	9333333333
Shabbir Challawala	KNOWARTH	`shabiir.challawala@knowarth.com`	9444444444

We will store this information in MySQL RDBMS and access through the NoSQL API. Let's first perform the prerequisites to build an application of the contact list and then we will see NoSQL APIs in different languages.

Prerequisites

The first step in developing the application is the database design. We need to create a table in MySQL with all the required fields. Here is the query that will create a table for the contact information:

```
CREATE TABLE Contacts (
  id INT PRIMARY KEY,
  firstName VARCHAR(20),
  lastName VARCHAR(20),
  emailAddress VARCHAR(100),
  mobileNumber VARCHAR(10),
  companyName VARCHAR(100)
);
```

Once the table has been created successfully, we need to add a table entry to Memcached tables (as explained in `Chapter 4`, *Using Memcached with MySQL 8*):

```
INSERT INTO innodb_memcache.containers
SET
 name = "contacts_table",
 db_schema = "demo",
 db_table = "Contacts",
 key_columns = "id",
 value_columns = "firstName,lastName,emailAddress,mobileNumber,companyName"
 unique_idx_name_on_key = "PRIMARY";
```

That's all as part of the prerequisites. Now we are all set to learn the NoSQL API with different programming languages.

NoSQL API with Java

Java is the most used programming language and Memcached provides a built-in library with the `com.whalin.MemCached` package, which is easily integrated with the Java-based application. It becomes very easy to create instances and perform various operations such as set, get, delete, and many more. The following example of a Java class has first initialized the connection with the Memcached server in the constructor and has a different method for the various operations:

```java
import com.whalin.MemCached.MemCachedClient;
import com.whalin.MemCached.SockIOPool;
import java.util.Map;

public class ContactMemcachedClient {

    private static String[] servers = {"localhost:11211"};
    private static Integer[] weights = { 1 };
    private MemCachedClient memcachedClient;
    public static final String NAMESPACE = "@@contacts_table";

    /**
     * Initialize connection
     */
    public ContactMemcachedClient() {
        SockIOPool pool = SockIOPool.getInstance();
        pool.setServers(servers);
        pool.setWeights( weights );
        if (!pool.isInitialized()) {
            pool.setInitConn(5);
            pool.setMinConn(5);
            pool.setMaxConn(250);
            pool.initialize();
        }
        MemCachedClient memCachedClient = new MemCachedClient();
        this.memcachedClient = memCachedClient;
    }
    /**
     * Add/Update value of specified key
     * @param key
     * @param value
     */
    public void set(String key, Object value) {
            memcachedClient.set(key, value);
```

```
    }
  /**
   * Fetch value by key
   * @param key
   * @return
   */
  public Object get(String key) {
    return memcachedClient.get(key);
  }
  /**
   * Delete value by key
   * @param key
   * @return
   */
  public Object delete(String key) {
    return memcachedClient.delete(key);
  }
  /**
   * Fetch values as map from the multiple keys
   * @param keys
   * @return
   */
  public Map<String, Object> getAllByKey(String[] keys) {
    return memcachedClient.getMulti(keys);
  }
  /**
   * Check weather value exists against key or not
   * @param key
   * @return
   */
  public boolean isKeyExists(String key) {
    return memcachedClient.keyExists(key);
  }
}
```

Now, let's create an instance of the preceding class and execute the methods for the various operations:

```
ContactMemcachedClient contactMemcachedClient = new
ContactMemcachedClient();

// Store contact details
String valueTobeStored =
"jaydip,lakhatariya,jaydip@knowarth.com,9111111111,knowarth";
contactMemcachedClient.set(ContactMemcachedClient.NAMESPACE + "101",
valueTobeStored);

// Fetch contact detail
```

```
contactMemcachedClient.get(ContactMemcachedClient.NAMESPACE + "101");

// Delete contact detail
contactMemcachedClient.delete(ContactMemcachedClient.NAMESPACE + "101");
```

NoSQL API with PHP

With PHP, we can access the Memcached interface and manage the data as NoSQL uses APIs provided for MySQL 8. It is required to install the PECL extension to use Memcached in PHP-based applications. Here is a sample PHP program that displays the list of contacts and has a form that will store new contact information using the NoSQL API. A simple example in the PHP program illustrates basic operations such as storing new contacts and deleting contacts.

Let's create a init.php file with the following content to connect to the Memcached instance:

```php
<?php
  $memcache = new Memcache;
  $memcache->addServer('10.12.4.15',11211);
?>
```

Now let's create another file addContact.php to add data to the database:

```php
<?php require "init.php"; ?>
<?php
  if (isset($_POST['submit'])) {
    $key = $_POST['contactId'];
    $value = $_POST['firstName'];
    $value .= ",". $_POST['lastName'];
    $value .= ",". $_POST['emailAddress'];
    $value .= ",". $_POST['mobileNumber'];
    $value .= ",". $_POST['companyName'];
    $memcache->set($key,$value);
  }
?>

<html xmlns="http://www.w3.org/1999/xhtml" xml:lang="en" lang="en">
  <head>
    <meta http-equiv="Content-Type" content="text/html; charset=utf-8" />
    <title>Add Contact</title>
  </head>
  <body>
  <form method="post">
```

```
        <p><b>Contact Id</b>: <input type="text" size="20"
name="contactId"></p>
        <p><b>First Name</b>: <input type="text" size="20"
name="firstName"></p>
        <p><b>Last Name</b>: <input type="text" size="20"
name="lastName"></p>
        <p><b>Email Address</b>: <input type="text" size="20"
name="emailAddress"></p>
        <p><b>Mobile Number</b>: <input type="text" size="20"
name="mobileNumber"></p>
        <p><b>Company Name</b>: <input type="text" size="20"
name="companyName"></p>
        <input type="submit" name="submit" value="submit">
      </form>
    </body>
</html>
```

We can create `deleteContact.php` that can help delete data:

```
<?php
    if (isset($_POST['contactId'])) {
        $contact = $memcache->get($_POST['contactId']);
        if(isset($_POST['contactId'])) {
            $memcache->delete($_POST['contactId']);
        }
    }
?>
```

NoSQL API with Python

Python is a fully functional high-level programming language and is widely used in data analysis, artificial intelligence, scientific computing, and big data applications. MySQL 8 has Memcached API support for the Python language, which can accomplish different use cases related to big data. We need to install the Python Memcached module in order to use the Memcached API with the Python language. Let's try some of the Memcached APIs with the Python language to manage contacts.

Retrieve contact information from the command line and store it through the Memcached API with the help of the following code:

```
import sys
import memcache
memcached = memcache.Client(['127.0.0.1:11211'], debug=1);

# Insert Contact Detail
def addContact(contactId, firstName, lastName, emailAddress, mobileNumber,
companyName):
   valueTobeStore = firstName + ","
   valueTobeStore = lastName + ","
   valueTobeStore = emailAddress + ","
   valueTobeStore = mobileNumber + ","
   valueTobeStore = companyName
   memcached.set(contactId,valueTobeStore)
   print "Contact information has stored successfully"

# Get contact information pass from the command line
contactId= sys.argv[0]
firstName= sys.argv[1]
lastName= sys.argv[2]
emailAddress = sys.argv[3]
mobileNumber = sys.argv[4]
companyName = sys.argv[5]

# Call addContact method to store contact information
addContact(contactId, firstName, lastName, emailAddress, mobileNumber,
companyName)
```

Fetch contact information by ID passed through command-line arguments, as stated in the following example:

```
import sys
import memcache
memcached = memcache.Client(['127.0.0.1:11211'], debug=1);

# Fetch contact information by id
def getContactById(contactId):

   contact = memcached.get(contactId)
   print(contact)

# Get contact id from the command line
contactId= sys.argv[0]
getContactById(contactId)
```

Delete contacts by their IDs, which is passed by the command-line argument, as stated in the following example:

```
import sys
import memcache
memcached = memcache.Client(['127.0.0.1:11211'], debug=1);

def deleteContact(contactId)
    memcached.delete(contactId)
    print "Contact information has been deleted successfully"

# Get contact information pass from the command line
contactId= sys.argv[0]
deleteContact(contactId)
```

NoSQL API with Perl

Perl-based applications should have the `Cache::Memcached` module in order to access the Memcached interface. It can be installed using the following command:

```
perl -MCPAN -e 'install Cache::Memcached'
```

Once this module has been installed successfully, we can make use of the Memcached protocol through the native interface.

Let's look at an example, which accepts contact information from the command line and stores the information in Memcached, after which we will verify the stored information by fetching it by key:

```
#!/usr/bin/perl
use Cache::Memcached;
use Data::Dumper;

# Configure the memcached server
my $memcache = new Cache::Memcached {
    'servers' => [ 'localhost:11211']
};

my $contactId=$ARGV[0];
my $firstName=$ARGV[1];
my $lastName=$ARGV[2];
my $emailAddress=$ARGV[3];
my $mobileNumber=$ARGV[4];
my $companyName=$ARGV[5];

#Store contact Information
```

```
$contactData = $firstName . ",". $lastName . "," . $emailAddress . "," .
$mobileNumber . "," . $companyName;
$memcache->set($contactId,$contactData))

#Fetch contact information to check if it stored or not
my $contact = $cache->get($contactId);
if (defined($contact))
{
  print "$contact\n";
}
else
{
  print STDERR "Contact Information does not stored";
}
```

NDB Cluster API

Clustering is a mechanism to distribute the load between multiple servers. Enterprises always need to think about high availability, performance, and scalability while working with big data. A single-node architecture might not fulfill this requirement about availability, scalability, and performance. There are certain questions that might arise with single-node architecture like the following:

- What if the single node goes down?
- Will a single node provide good performance as all the requests need to be served by a single server only?
- How can we make it scalable if the request load increases?

NDB Cluster, which stands for the **Network Database**, enables clustering of an in-memory database with the shared-nothing system. This can easily handle scenarios of high availability and scalability, and increase the performance as it distributes loads against multiple servers. A shared-nothing system means multiple nodes are interconnected for the purpose of distributed computing with their own memory and own storage.

MySQL Cluster is built on the NDB or NDB CLUSTER storage engine, which provides low latency, high throughput, scalability, and high availability. This adopts horizontal scaling and auto sharding to serve heavy load read/write operations through the different NoSQL queries. An NDB Cluster is a set of different nodes where each task is running on its own processor.

Node is just part of the cluster that can be categorized with the Management Node, Data Node, and SQL Node:

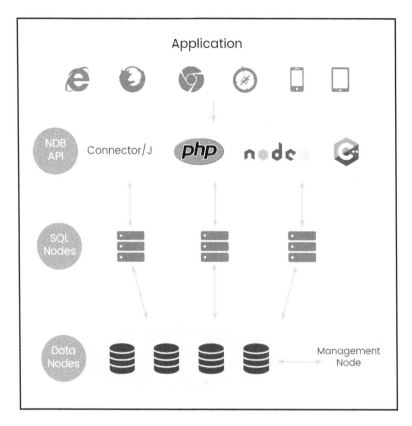

As described in the NDB Cluster architecture diagram, data nodes are responsible for the storage of data. This data can be accessed using different NoSQL APIs with various programming languages such as NodeJS, Java, C++, and HTTP/REST, also knows as **NDP API**. Let's make our hands dirty by exploring the NDP API with different languages.

NDB API for NodeJS

NDB Cluster 7.3 has introduced the API for applications written in JavaScript using NodeJS. The MySQL connector for JavaScript includes an adaptor that can directly access the NDB storage engine. This interface is asynchronous with a built-in NodeJS event model. NodeJS is a platform that has really good performance as it has been built on Google Chrome's V8 JavaScript Engine.

An NDB Cluster JavaScript driver for NodeJS makes it very easy to directly access data from JavaScript. Hence, extra latency of parsing objects to SQL operations is removed and it can directly read/write data from the data nodes of the NDB Cluster. It is required to install the `mysql-js` adapter and `node-mysql` driver in order to run a NodeJS application with the NDP API.

Let's build a simple application of NodeJS to perform some of the operations on contact management with the help of the following example.

First of all, we need to import the `mysql-js` module, create a class as `Contact` with its attributes, and map it with the table, as shown in the following code:

```
var nosql = require('mysql-js');

var Contact = function(contactId, firstName, lastName, emailAddress,
mobileNumber, companyName) {
    if (contactId) this.contactId = contactId;
    if (firstName) this.firstName = firstName;
  if (lastName) this.lastName = lastName;
  if (emailAddress) this.emailAddress = emailAddress;
  if (mobileNumber) this.mobileNumber = mobileNumber;
  if (companyName) this.companyName = companyName;
};

// Map class with the Table
var annotations = new nosql.TableMapping('Contacts').applyToClass(Contact);
```

Create a callback function that will be invoked after it tries to establish a connection with the MySQL Cluster:

```
var onOpenSession = function(err, session) {
  if (err) {
    console.log('Error while opening session');
        console.log(err);
        process.exit(0);
    } else {
    console.log('Connection established successfully');
    // Store contact information
    var contact = new Contact(123, 'Jaydip', 'Lakhatariya',
'jaydip.lakh@gmail.com', '9111111111', 'Knowarth Tech');
        session.persist(contact, onInsert, contact, session);
    }
};
```

As shown in the preceding code, if a successful connection gets established, then it will insert the new contact information and call the following callback method:

```
var onInsert = function(err, object, session) {
    if (err) {
    console.log("Error occurred while inserting new contact")
        console.log(err);
    } else {
        console.log('Contact Inserted Successfully');

        // Find the contact from the database
        session.find(Contact, 123, onFindContact);
    }
};
```

Create a callback function that will be invoked whenever the Find operation gets executed:

```
var onFindContact = function(err, contact) {
    if (err) {
    console.log("Error while fetching contact")
        console.log(err);
    } else {
        console.log('Found Contact information is: ' +
JSON.stringify(contact));
    // Delete the respective contact
    session.remove(contact, onDeleteContact, contact.contactId);
    }
};
```

If the preceding method achieves success in retrieving contact information, then it will try to remove the same contact and the following callback function will be executed:

```
var onDeleteContact = function(err, object) {
  if (err) {
    console.log("Error while deleting contact");
    console.log(err);
  } else {
    console.log('Successfully deleted contact id: ' + object.contactId);
  }
  process.exit(0);
};
```

At the end, we need to initialize and open a connection for `ndb` with the help of the following code:

```
// Initialize the database properties
var dbProperties = nosql.ConnectionProperties('ndb');

// Connect to the database
nosql.openSession(dbProperties, Contact, onOpenSession);
```

JavaScript can easily work with the objects, hence it provides an easy way to map the table data directly with the object. We can access the table information in the form of an object. In our example, we have the `Contact` class defined with the various attributes that have been mapped with the `Contacts` table of MySQL using the `TableMapping` class.

We should define `ndb` as connection properties to directly access the data nodes rather than going into the MySQL Server. An `openSession` method creates a bridge between the API and data nodes. We can also specify a callback function with the `openSession` method as JavaScript is an event-driven programming language.

Let's execute the program that we created and see the output:

```
[root@ip-172-31-22-59 ~]$ node my-test.js
Connection established successfully
Contact Inserted Successfully:
Found Contact information is:
{"contactId":"123","firstName":"Jaydip","lastName":"Lakhatariya","emailAddr
ess":"jaydip.lakh@gmail.com","phoneNumber":"9724371151","companyName":"KNOW
ARTH"}
Successfully deleted contact id: 123
>
```

NDB API for Java

Java-based enterprise applications can easily access MySQL Cluster using the NoSQL API with the help of the ClusterJ interface. This interface is designed to provide high performance while storing and retrieving information directly from the MySQL Cluster database. It is very easy to use for developers using the native Java interface and JPA plugin because it automatically provides the mapping of table-oriented views of the data stored in MySQL Cluster to the Java objects used by the application.

To do mapping between tables and Java objects, it is required to annotate interfaces representing the Java objects where each interface is mapped with the table while each property of that interface is mapped with the columns of the table, the same as the JPA/Hibernate interface.

This `clusterj` connector comes along with the MySQL Cluster. Once you have installed MySQL cluster, then the required `jar` libraries are available under the `/share/java` folder of MySQL. Navigate to this folder and copy `clusterj.jar` and `clusterj-api.jar` files and place them in your application. Let's try to integrate `clusterj` for the contact information.

First of all, we need to provide certain properties that describe how clusterJ needs to connect with the MySQL Cluster, such as the connection URL, port number, which database to use, authentication details, and other attributes like timeout and max transaction.

Here is the sample file with the name `clusterj.properties` available under the application source code:

```
com.mysql.clusterj.connectstring=localhost:1186
com.mysql.clusterj.database=demodb
com.mysql.clusterj.connect.retries=4
com.mysql.clusterj.connect.delay=5
com.mysql.clusterj.connect.timeout.before=30
com.mysql.clusterj.connect.timeout.after=20
com.mysql.clusterj.max.transactions=1024
```

Create a model interface to map with the table, as per the following code. The name of the table can be automatically mapped with the model interface using the `@PersistenceCapable` annotation. Also, the column name can be mapped with the `@Column` annotation of the clusterJ library.

```
import com.mysql.clusterj.annotation.Column;
import com.mysql.clusterj.annotation.PersistenceCapable;
import com.mysql.clusterj.annotation.PrimaryKey;

@PersistenceCapable(table="Contacts")
public interface Contact {
  @PrimaryKey
  public int getId();
  public void setId(int id);

  @Column(name="firstName")
  public String getFirstName();
  public String setFirstName(String firstName);
  @Column(name="lastName")
  public String getLastName();
```

```
    public String setLastName(String lastName);
    @Column(name="emailAddress")
    public String getEmailAddress();
    public String setEmailAddress(String emailAddress);
    @Column(name="mobileNumber")
    public String getMobileNumber();
    public String setMobileNumber(String mobileNumber);
    @Column(name="companyName")
    public String getCompanyName();
    public String setCompanyName(String companyName);
}
```

Now, we are all set to take a glance at basic operations with the help of the following example:

```
import com.mysql.clusterj.ClusterJHelper;
import com.mysql.clusterj.SessionFactory;
import com.mysql.clusterj.Session;
import com.mysql.clusterj.Query;
import com.mysql.clusterj.query.QueryBuilder;
import com.mysql.clusterj.query.QueryDomainType;
import java.io.File;
import java.io.InputStream;
import java.io.FileInputStream;
import java.io.*;
import java.util.Properties;
import java.util.List;

public class clusterJ {

  private static Session session;
  public static void main (String[] args) {
    // Load the properties from the clusterj.properties file
    File propsFile = null;
    InputStream inStream = null;
    Properties props = null;
    props.load(inStream);
    try {
      propsFile = new File("clusterj.properties");
      inStream = new FileInputStream(propsFile);
      props = new Properties();
      props.load(inStream);
    } catch(Exception e) {
      System.err.println(e);
      return;
    }
    // Connect to database and create session
    SessionFactory factory = ClusterJHelper.getSessionFactory(props);
```

```
      session = factory.getSession();
      if(session != null) {
        System.out.println("Connection Established Successfully");
      }
      saveContact(123, "Jaydip", "Lakhatariya", "jaydip.lakh@gmail.com",
  "9724371151", "Knowarth");
      findByContactId(123);
      deleteContactById(123);
    }
  }
```

Here is the method to save contact information:

```
  private static void saveContact(int contactId, String firstName, String
  lastName, String emailAddress, String mobileNumber, String companyName) {
    // Create and initialise Contact information
    Contact newContact = session.newInstance(Contact.class);
    newContact.setId(contactId);
    newContact.setFirstName(firstName);
    newContact.setLastName(lastName);
    newContact.setEmailAddress(emailAddress);
    newContact.setMobileNumber(mobileNumber);
    newContact.setCompanyName(companyName);
    // Store contact information to the database
    session.persist(newContact);
    System.out.println("Contact information has been saved successfully");
  }
```

This method is responsible for finding the contact information based on its ID:

```
  private static void findByContactId(int contactId) {
    Contact contact = session.find(Contact.class, contactId);
    if(contact != null) {
      System.out.println("Contact found with name: " + contact.getFirstName()
  + " " + contact.getLastName());
    } else {
      System.out.println("No contact found with the ID " + contactId);
    }
  }
```

This method will be responsible for deleting contact information by its ID:

```
  private static void deleteContactById(int contactId) {
    session.deletePersistent(Contact.class, contactId);
    System.out.prinln("Deleted contact detail of id: " + contactId);
  }
```

Let's execute the preceding program and see the output:

```
Connection Established Successfully
Contact information has been saved successfully
Contact found with name: Jaydip Lakhatariya
Deleted contact detail of id: 123
```

Here is a short description of the clusterJ classes used in the preceding program:

- **SessionFactory**: One instance per MySQL Cluster and is used to hold the sessions. All clusterJ configuration properties are associated with this class.
- **ClusterJHelper**: Provides helper methods to bridge between the API and the implementation.
- **Session**: One instance per user and represents the cluster connection. All operations can be performed using this class only.

This clusterJ provides a good interface for developers but it also has some limitations that makes developers using OpenJPA with the ClusterJPA plugin more appropriate. Here are the limitations of clusterJ:

- We must have to declare interfaces for the entities rather than classes. The Developer needs to provide signatures of the getter/setter methods rather than the properties; we also cannot add any extra methods to the interface.
- We cannot make relationships between properties and objects.
- Only a single table operation is supported where we cannot make multi-table inheritance.
- As queries are limited to a single table, we cannot perform joins.
- It does not support lazy loading, hence it will load the entire record set one time including large objects.

NDB API with C++

The NDB API for C++ can be achieved using the `NdbApi.hpp` library, which provides a number of classes for various purposes, as described in the following points:

- `Ndb`: A primary class of the NDB API and represented as NDB Kernel
- `Ndb_cluster_connection`: Handles the connection to a cluster of data nodes
- `NdbTransaction`: Manages database transactions
- `NdbOperation`: Handles different operations such as delete tuple, insert tuple, read tuple, update tuple, and so on

Let's see an example of using the NDP API in the C++ language, where we will define required libraries, functions, and macros:

```cpp
#include <NdbApi.hpp>
#include <stdio.h>
#include <iostream>

static void run_application(Ndb_cluster_connection &);
static void create_table(MYSQL &);
static void do_insert(Ndb &);
static void do_update(Ndb &);
static void do_delete(Ndb &);
static void do_read(Ndb &);

#define PRINT_ERROR(code,msg) \
  std::cout << "Error occurred: " << code << ", Message: " << message << std::endl

#define APIERROR(error) { \
  PRINT_ERROR(error.code,error.message); \
  exit(-1); \
}
```

Let's set the main method that will create a connection with MySQL Cluster and call the `run_application` method:

```cpp
int main(int argc, char** argv)
{
  // Initialize ndb
  ndb_init();

  // Connect MySQL Cluster
  {
    const char *connection_string = "localhost:1186";
    Ndb_cluster_connection cluster_connection(connection_string);

    // Connect to cluster management server (ndb_mgmd)
    if (cluster_connection.connect(4, 5, 1))
    {
      std::cout << "A management server is not ready yet.\n";
      exit(-1);
    }

    // Connects to the storage nodes (ndbd's)
    if (cluster_connection.wait_until_ready(30,0) < 0)
    {
      std::cout << "Data nodes are not ready yet.\n";
      exit(-1);
```

```
    }

    // Run the application code
    run_application(cluster_connection);
  }
  ndb_end(0);
  return 0;
}
```

Define the `run_application` method that will initialize the connection with the database and execute different operations:

```
static void run_application(Ndb_cluster_connection &cluster_connection)
{
  // Connect to database via NDB API
  Ndb myNdb( &cluster_connection, "demodb" );
  if (myNdb.init()) APIERROR(myNdb.getNdbError());

  //Do different operations on database
  do_insert(myNdb);
  do_update(myNdb);
  do_delete(myNdb);
  do_read(myNdb);
}
```

A `do_insert` method will add new contact information:

```
static void do_insert(Ndb &myNdb)
{
  const NdbDictionary::Dictionary* myDict= myNdb.getDictionary();
  const NdbDictionary::Table *myTable= myDict->getTable("Contacts");
  if (myTable == NULL) APIERROR(myDict->getNdbError());

  NdbTransaction *myTransaction= myNdb.startTransaction();
  if (myTransaction == NULL) APIERROR(myNdb.getNdbError());
  NdbOperation *myOperation= myTransaction->getNdbOperation(myTable);
  if (myOperation == NULL) APIERROR(myTransaction->getNdbError());
  myOperation->insertTuple();
  myOperation->equal("id", 123);
  myOperation->setValue("firstName", "Jaydip");
  myOperation->setValue("lastName", "Lakhatariya");
  myOperation->setValue("emailAddress", "jaydip.lakh@gmail.com");
  myOperation->setValue("mobileNumber", "9724371151");
  myOperation->setValue("companyName", "KNOWARTH");

  if (myTransaction->execute( NdbTransaction::Commit ) == -1)
    APIERROR(myTransaction->getNdbError());
  myNdb.closeTransaction(myTransaction);
```

```
    }
```

A `do_update` method will update the existing record with the new contact information:

```
static void do_update(Ndb &myNdb)
{
    const NdbDictionary::Dictionary* myDict= myNdb.getDictionary();
    const NdbDictionary::Table *myTable= myDict->getTable("Contacts");
    if (myTable == NULL) APIERROR(myDict->getNdbError());

    NdbTransaction *myTransaction= myNdb.startTransaction();
    if (myTransaction == NULL) APIERROR(myNdb.getNdbError());

    NdbOperation *myOperation= myTransaction->getNdbOperation(myTable);
    if (myOperation == NULL) APIERROR(myTransaction->getNdbError());

    myOperation->updateTuple();
    myOperation->equal( "id", 123);
    myOperation->setValue("firstName", "Keyur");
    myOperation->setValue("lastName", "Lakhatariya");
    myOperation->setValue("emailAddress", "Keyur.lakh@gmail.com");
    myOperation->setValue("mobileNumber", "9998887771");
    myOperation->setValue("companyName", "KNOWARTH");

    if( myTransaction->execute( NdbTransaction::Commit ) == -1 )
    APIERROR(myTransaction->getNdbError());

    myNdb.closeTransaction(myTransaction);
}
```

A `do_delete` method will delete the contact information with ID 123:

```
static void do_delete(Ndb &myNdb)
{
    const NdbDictionary::Dictionary* myDict= myNdb.getDictionary();
    const NdbDictionary::Table *myTable= myDict->getTable("Contacts");

    if (myTable == NULL)
        APIERROR(myDict->getNdbError());

    NdbTransaction *myTransaction= myNdb.startTransaction();
    if (myTransaction == NULL) APIERROR(myNdb.getNdbError());

    NdbOperation *myOperation= myTransaction->getNdbOperation(myTable);
    if (myOperation == NULL) APIERROR(myTransaction->getNdbError());

    myOperation->deleteTuple();
    myOperation->equal( "id", 123);
```

```
    if (myTransaction->execute(NdbTransaction::Commit) == -1)
      APIERROR(myTransaction->getNdbError());

  myNdb.closeTransaction(myTransaction);
}
```

A `read` method will fetch the record with contact id `123` and display the email address and mobile number:

```
static void do_read(Ndb &myNdb)
{
  const NdbDictionary::Dictionary* myDict= myNdb.getDictionary();
  const NdbDictionary::Table *myTable= myDict->getTable("Contacts");

  if (myTable == NULL)
    APIERROR(myDict->getNdbError());

    NdbTransaction *myTransaction= myNdb.startTransaction();
    if (myTransaction == NULL) APIERROR(myNdb.getNdbError());

    NdbOperation *myOperation= myTransaction->getNdbOperation(myTable);
    if (myOperation == NULL) APIERROR(myTransaction->getNdbError());

    myOperation->readTuple(NdbOperation::LM_Read);
    myOperation->equal("id", 123);

    NdbRecAttr *emailRecAttr= myOperation->getValue("emailAddress", NULL);
  NdbRecAttr *mobileRecAttr= myOperation->getValue("mobileNumber", NULL);
    if (emailRecAttr == NULL) APIERROR(myTransaction->getNdbError());
  if (mobileRecAttr == NULL) APIERROR(myTransaction->getNdbError());

    if(myTransaction->execute( NdbTransaction::Commit ) == -1)
      APIERROR(myTransaction->getNdbError());

  printf("FirstName is: \n", emailRecAttr->aRef());
  printf("Mobile Number is: \n", mobileRecAttr->aRef());
  myNdb.closeTransaction(myTransaction);
}
```

Hence, enterprises running on different programming languages can integrate APIs with their applications to work like NoSQL. It can be easily integrated with a single-server node or cluster environment with the help of the Memcached interface or NDB API. Developers can choose APIs based on their preferred language to handle big data easily. It really provides better performance as it bypasses the SQL layer and directly uses the data. With the help of these APIs, we can use MySQL as a NoSQL database.

Summary

At the end of this chapter, we can now be sure about how we can use MySQL as a NoSQL database with our application that is built on different programming languages. At the start of this chapter, we discussed about the NoSQL database and its major advantages to use for use in our applications. Later, we have seen the differences between SQL and NoSQL and then we started looking into the different APIs with basic examples. We have understood the Memcached API with basic examples in different programming languages such as Java, PHP, Python, and Perl, which provide access to MySQL as a NoSQL database. Then, we have seen different NoSQL APIs used to manage the database for a clustered environment. We have discussed the NDB API and how it can be used with different programming languages such as NodeJS, Java, and C++. These different, supporting NoSQL APIs make it convenient for the developers and enterprises to handle big data within MySQL.

In the next chapter, we will understand how we can make use of Hadoop to help MySQL in handling big data and Apache Sqoop to transfer data between Hadoop and MySQL. We will see this with a real-world scenario use case.

9

Case study: Part I - Apache Sqoop for exchanging data between MySQL and Hadoop

In the previous chapter, we learnt about different techniques of using NoSQL API for MySQL. We went through examples of PHP, JSON, and Java to connect and consume data using NoSQL API. In this chapter, we will learn how we can use Apache Sqoop and Hadoop in Big Data life cycle for processing unstructured data to structured data which can be easily manipulated by relational databases such as MySQL.

Below are the topics we are going to cover in this chapter:

- Case study for log analysis
- Apache Sqoop overview
- Integrating Apache Sqoop with MySQL and Hadoop
- Importing unstructured data to Hadoop HDFS from MySQL
- Loading structured data to MySQL using Apache Sqoop

In Chapter 1, *Introduction to Big Data and MySQL 8*, we learnt how MySQL fits into the life cycle of Big Data. Let's say we are creating a people sentiment analysis system based on tweets and Facebook posts made by the users. As we already know, there are millions of tweets and Facebook posts made by the users every second, so our first task is to capture all this information and store it somewhere in the database. Then the next step is to categorize the unstructured information properly, based on the tag keywords used by the users in their posts. The third step is to store this data back into the structured database, where we can create appropriate relations and referential integrity among data.

Apache Sqoop is used in step 1 for transferring unstructured data from MySQL to Hadoop for fast processing of data.

Case study for log analysis

Another example of analyzing large data set for commercial use would be log analysis. Consider an e-commerce application where thousands of users visit the sites daily. Not 100 percent of the users visiting the application are going to purchase the product. People visiting the e-commerce applications tend to do the following activities most of the time:

- Purchase a product
- View products purchased by their friends and/or relatives
- Read reviews by other people on product they are looking to purchase
- Look for the products with best offers

So, in case a person who has not bought products yet, is considered to be a potential buyer. It is very important to attract such potential buyers and convert their visit to the application into a sale. So in this case, if the application can identify which are the products being visited by the potential buyers and on which particular product or category they have spent the maximum time, the application can highlight similar products with best offers or popular and best selling products in similar categories to them, based on their page visits. Users will find it very interesting when they will see products variations they are looking for and it will provide seamless user experience on the application.

One more case of analyzing user's activity log for an e-commerce application is to reduce abandoned carts on the application. Abandoned cart means when a user has added few items in his/her cart but has not gone through the order confirmation step and has left the cart unattended at some stage. It is important to identify at which stage of shopping the users are facing difficulties in confirming their order. Such log analysis can help an e-commerce store to identify which are the pages where most of the users have left the cart or even identify which are the pages taking most of the time. On an average, a user spends between 5 to 10 minutes of time on e-commerce applications, so it is very important that they hit right pages during this period.

Based on the analysis of activity log, following are the things we can identify for the application:

- Average time a visitor spends on the application
- Average number of pages visited by visitors per session
- Average number of daily visitors
- Day of a week or month of the year when traffic is most on the application
- User's browsing flow to identify up to find out drop out ratio at different stage of browsing

Using MySQL 8 and Hadoop for analyzing log

As we learnt earlier how a log analysis can turn a user's activity log into generation of revenue, it is very important to find out how such information can be stored in a database. Activity log information is generated when user's are browsing the application, so the information we get from the activity log are in their raw format. It requires some additional calculation on the activity log to identify the information we require. There are millions of hits we get daily on an application, so doing such analytical calculation in relational database like MySQL can be tricky, as it may put additional load on it. Best approach here would be to leave MySQL 8 serve the application front end and gather all activity log information in their raw format using other technologies available which are developed for processing large data set. There are Big Data technologies available, like Hadoop, which can compute large amount of data within seconds.

So what we can do here is that we can store all the raw data we received from the activity log into the MySQL 8. This log information will be unstructured and will not provide any useful information. Then we can transfer this unstructured activity log to the Apache Hadoop. Apache Hadoop is an open source Big Data platform that restructures data into a format that can be presented to the users. Once the data is converted into a presentable format, using Hadoop algorithms like map reduce, we can transfer a well structured data back to MySQL 8. Then based on this structured data in MySQL 8, different reports can be prepared to extract various information. To transfer large amount of data from MySQL 8 to Hadoop, we can use Apache Sqoop. Apache Sqoop is again an open source technology to exchange data between relational databases and non relational databases. We will learn more about Apache Sqoop, Hadoop, and how to exchange data between Hadoop and MySQL 8 using Sqoop.

Apache Sqoop overview

Relational databases like MySQL are most popular when dealing with most of the business applications. As MySQL is open source, it is a default choice for many of the applications. Applications built using MySQL as database can belong to different domains, such as e-commerce, e-learning, medicine or health information sites, and social media applications, as mentioned in Chapter 1, *Introduction to Big Data and MySQL 8*. Each of these domains has the capacity to generate large number of data which has to be stored in MySQL. Some of this data is structured, like a user's registration information or a user's cart information, which can be maintained well by MySQL. On the other hand, some of the data is unstructured, like a user's last accessed page information, likes, shares, or tweets. This user's access information can be utilized very well to enhance user's experience while using application by analyzing user's behaviour or set up a recommendation engine based on the predictive analysis of generated data.

As we stated earlier, analytical data generated by the application need to be stored in MySQL in raw or unstructured format. This unstructured data stored in MySQL has to be transferred to Big Data technologies like Hadoop in order to analyze and restructure them quickly using different algorithm available in Big Data technologies. Transfer of this large data can be done either by building custom programs or through other ready to use tools that are available. Apache Sqoop is one such tool that can be used for transferring data from MySQL.

Apache Sqoop is used for effectively transferring bulk of data between Apache Hadoop and relational databases like MySQL, Oracle, and Postgres. Sqoop can import or export data in parallel to speed up data transmission between the source and destination database. Output generated by Sqoop import process can be either stored in delimited text files or binary Avro or SequenceFiles. SequenceFiles contains data in serialized format.

Following is a simple figure that briefly explains relation between MySQL, Sqoop, and Hadoop:

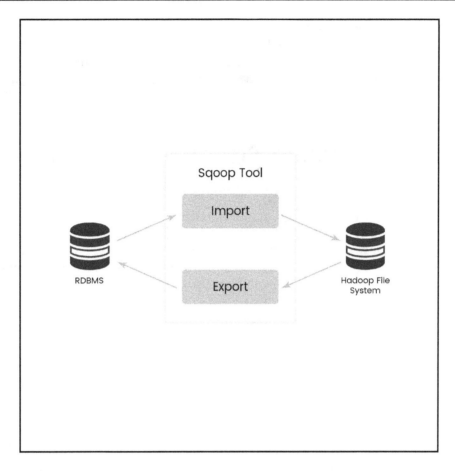

Sqoop provides command line interface to the user for performing different actions for importing or exporting data between Hadoop and MySQL. Sqoop provides multiple features, such as:

- Parallel data transmission
- Incremental imports
- Imports based on SQL Select queries
- Different connection string supports for different relational databases

Import process of Sqoop runs in parallel, because of which the output of the Sqoop import process is multiple generated files. These generated files can be used by Hadoop distributed file system to manipulate data copied from MySQL. Import process also generates a `java` class. This `java` class has the ability to serialize or deserialize data, and read the delimited text.

Once processing of the imported data is done in Hadoop distributed file system, the data can be imported back to MySQL. Like the import process, the export process also runs multiple files in parallel to insert data back to MySQL. Data inserted into MySQL is now well structured and can be used by respective front end applications for creating different analytical reports easily.

Integrating Apache Sqoop with MySQL and Hadoop

Apache Sqoop can only work if Hadoop is installed on the server. Apache Sqoop requires Linux based operating system to work . For Hadoop and Sqoop to work on the Linux server, Java must be installed on the server. Once Sqoop is installed on the server, we will need to download Sqoop's MySQL connector which will allow JDBC driver to connect with MySQL database for transferring data with Hadoop.

Hadoop

is an open source, Big Data framework to process and analyze large amount of data sets quickly by using a cluster of environment. Because of Hadoop's multiple slave nodes environment, it's easy to avoid system failure or data loss if one or more nodes go off. Hadoop basically works with multiple modules such as **Yet Another Resource Negotiator (YARN)**, **Hadoop distributed file system (HDFS)**, and MapReduce. Hadoop's MapReduce algorithm is used for parallel processing of the data. MapReduce is used to convert unstructured data to a structured format using different MapReduce algorithms.

MapReduce

MapReduce algorithm of Hadoop is used for processing large amount of data in parallel on a clustered environment, where data is laid down in more than one node. It provides great scalability to the Hadoop cluster. MapReduce algorithm performs two separate tasks: Map and reduce. In the Map task, the algorithm takes unstructured data as an input, processes the data, and converts it to key pair values.

Following image shows task of MapReduce. It shows how a task from a client is divided into multiple maps that do computational work on the input and then reduce algorithm reduces the number of the process to be minimal to share in the output.

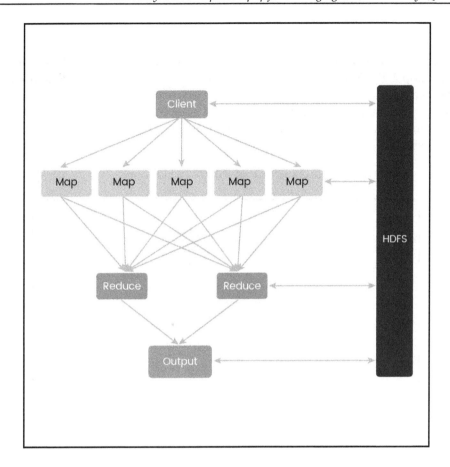

Hadoop distributed file system

Hadoop distributed file system (HDFS), is a data storing system used by Hadoop. HDFS consists of clusters of nodes for storing billions of records on the system. Data information is broken into multiple chunks and these chunks are processed parallel to faster data transfer. Also, each data chunk is copied onto multiple nodes, so that in case of failure of one node, the data can be read from the other nodes till the failed node gets repaired. HDFS uses master slave architecture.

The master node is called **name node** and the slaves are called data nodes. Name node does not consist of any data but it contains information of data file tree and it's block structure is copied into the HDFS. Actual data is stored in the multiple slaves or data nodes.

YARN

Yet Another Resource Negotiator or **YARN** is used for cluster resource management. As of Apache Hadoop 2, the YARN service can be divided into two categories: Resource manager and Node manager. Resource manager manages the resources that need to be assigned to various applications and it also keeps track of live node managers. Node manager provides required resources in the form of container. The following image will demonstrate on how YARN processes the requests made by multiple client.

Following image explains the architecture of YARN in Hadoop:

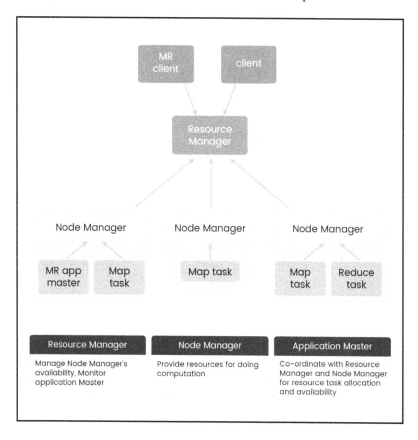

Setting up Hadoop on Linux

For setting up Hadoop, we need to download it from `apache.org` and configure different configurations for Hadoop. We need to set up different configurations, such as name node, data node, and yarn, in order to start Hadoop services.

1. First we need to download Hadoop from `apache.org`:

```
[root@ip-172-31-22-59 local]# wget http://www-us.apache.org/dist/hadoop/common/h
adoop-2.6.5/hadoop-2.6.5.tar.gz
--2017-10-02 07:25:51--  http://www-us.apache.org/dist/hadoop/common/hadoop-2.6.
5/hadoop-2.6.5.tar.gz
Resolving www-us.apache.org (www-us.apache.org)... 140.211.11.105
Connecting to www-us.apache.org (www-us.apache.org)|140.211.11.105|:80... connec
ted.
HTTP request sent, awaiting response... 200 OK
Length: 199635269 (190M) [application/x-gzip]
Saving to: 'hadoop-2.6.5.tar.gz'

hadoop-2.6.5.tar.gz 100%[===================>] 190.39M  7.93MB/s    in 14s

2017-10-02 07:26:06 (13.3 MB/s) - 'hadoop-2.6.5.tar.gz' saved [199635269/1996352
69]

[root@ip-172-31-22-59 local]#
```

2. After installing Hadoop, we can configure the path variables on the system. Also, we need to configure YARN on the server. YARN is a sub part of Hadoop which distinct MapReduce's data processing and scheduling and resource management part so that data processing of MapReduce can be done faster. Going in detail of YARN is out of scope of this book. Let's go through the following steps to configure Apache Hadoop:

```
[root@ip-172-31-22-59 local]# mv hadoop-2.6.5 hadoop
[root@ip-172-31-22-59 local]# export HADOOP_HOME=/usr/local/hadoop
[root@ip-172-31-22-59 local]# export HADOOP_MAPRED_HOME=$HADOOP_HOME
[root@ip-172-31-22-59 local]# export HADOOP_COMMON_HOME=$HADOOP_HOME
[root@ip-172-31-22-59 local]# export HADOOP_HDFS_HOME=$HADOOP_HOME
[root@ip-172-31-22-59 local]# export YARN_HOME=$HADOOP_HOME
[root@ip-172-31-22-59 local]# export HADOOP_COMMON_LIB_NATIVE_DIR=$HADOOP_HOME/lib/native
[root@ip-172-31-22-59 local]# export PATH=$PATH:$HADOOP_HOME/sbin:$HADOOP_HOME/bin
[root@ip-172-31-22-59 local]# source ~/.bashrc
[root@ip-172-31-22-59 local]# cd $HADOOP_HOME/etc/hadoop
```

We nee to to set Java path into Hadoop's configuration as demonstrated below:

```
cd $HADOOP_HOME/etc/hadoop
export JAVA_HOME=/usr/local/java
```

3. Once the configuration variables are set, we need to update Hadoop's configuration files in order to start Hadoop.

4. In `core-site.xml` file, update the property as shown in the following screenshot; the `core-site.xml` file tells Hadoop where name node will run on the server:

```
<configuration>
    <property>
        <name>fs.default.name</name>
        <value>hdfs://localhost:9000</value>
    </property>
</configuration>
```

5. Once `core-site.xml` is set, we need to set name node and data node in Hadoop HDFS. Following is configuration required in `hdfs-site.xml` file for setting up name node and data node:

```
<configuration>
<property>
        <name>dfs.replication</name>
        <value>1</value>
    </property>

    <property>
        <name>dfs.name.dir</name>
        <value>file:///home/hadoop/hadoopinfra/hdfs/namenode</value>
    </property>

    <property>
        <name>dfs.data.dir</name>
        <value>file:///home/hadoop/hadoopinfra/hdfs/datanode</value>
    </property>
</configuration>
```

6. We need to set YARN's configuration on the server, as shown next:

```
<configuration>

<property>
        <name>yarn.nodemanager.aux-services</name>
        <value>mapreduce_shuffle</value>
    </property>
</configuration>
```

7. Then we need to set the mapred configuration file. The `mapred-site.xml` file comes by default with Hadoop with suffix `.template`. First we need to rename the existing file from `mapred-site.xml.template` to `mapred-site.xml`, and then configure it as shown next:

```
cp mapred-site.xml.template mapred-
site.xml</strong></strong></strong>
```

Following is the content of the `mapred-site.xml` file:

```
<configuration>
<property>
     <name>mapreduce.framework.name</name>
     <value>yarn</value>
 </property>
</configuration>
```

8. Now we are done with the configuration of Hadoop. Start Hadoop services as shown in the following commands:

```
$ start-dfs.sh
$ start-yarn.sh
```

Once Hadoop services are started, we can verify the Hadoop cluster application interface from the browser by accessing it with `8088` port. For example, `http://localhost:80888` will show the list of applications running on the Hadoop cluster:

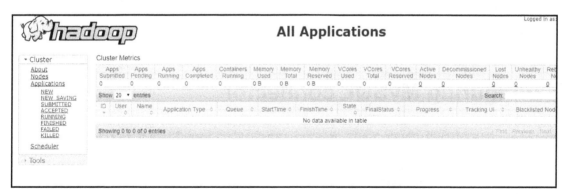

Installing Apache Sqoop

Now that we are done with Apache Hadoop, we can configure Sqoop on the server. Following are the commands to configure Sqoop on the server:

```
[root@ip-172-31-22-59 local]# wget http://www-us.apache.org/dist/sqoop/1.4.6/sqoop-1.4.6.bin__hadoop-2.0.4-alpha.tar.gz
--2017-10-08 13:26:33--  http://www-us.apache.org/dist/sqoop/1.4.6/sqoop-1.4.6.bin__hadoop-2.0.4-alpha.tar.gz
Resolving www-us.apache.org (www-us.apache.org)... 140.211.11.105
Connecting to www-us.apache.org (www-us.apache.org)|140.211.11.105|:80... connected.
HTTP request sent, awaiting response... 200 OK
Length: 16870735 (16M) [application/x-gzip]
Saving to: 'sqoop-1.4.6.bin__hadoop-2.0.4-alpha.tar.gz'

sqoop-1.4.6.bin__hadoop-2.0.4-alpha.tar.g 100%[=====================================================================================>]  16.09M  13.6MB/s    in 1.2s

2017-10-08 13:26:34 (13.6 MB/s) - 'sqoop-1.4.6.bin__hadoop-2.0.4-alpha.tar.gz' saved [16870735/16870735]

[root@ip-172-31-22-59 local]# tar xf sqoop-1.4.6.bin__hadoop-2.0.4-alpha.tar.gz
[root@ip-172-31-22-59 local]# mv sqoop-1.4.6.bin__hadoop-2.0.4-alpha sqoop
[root@ip-172-31-22-59 local]#
```

Once Sqoop is downloaded, we need to enable its configuration from the `conf` directory:

```
cd $SQOOP_HOME/conf
mv sqoop-env-template.sh sqoop-env.sh
```

Now we need to configure Sqoop with the installation path of Hadoop. The following screenshot shows to configure those in Sqoop:

```
[root@ip-172-31-22-55 bin]# export HADOOP_COMMON_HOME=/usr/local/hadoop
[root@ip-172-31-22-55 bin]# export HADOOP_MAPRED_HOME=/usr/local/hadoop
```

Apache Sqoop is now configured on our server. We can now setup MySQL connector for Sqoop, which will be one of our last step in configuring Apache Sqoop with Hadoop and MySQL 8.

Configuring MySQL connector

Now that Hadoop is downloaded on the server and Sqoop is also configured, we need to install Sqoop's MySQL connector in order to transfer data from MySQL to Hadoop.

MySQL connector can be downloaded `https://dev.mysql.com/downloads/connector/j/8.0.html`. Once MySQL connector is downloaded apply below commands to copy the MySQL connector's executable jar to Sqoop:

```
unzip mysql-connector-java-5.1.19.zip
cd mysql-connector-java-5.1.19
mv mysql-connector-java-5.1.19-bin.jar /usr/local/sqoop/lib
```

We are done with all the configurations required for Apache Sqoop to import/export data between Hadoop and MySQL 8. In the next topic, we will learn how to import data to Hadoop HDFS using Apache Sqoop.

Importing unstructured data to Hadoop HDFS from MySQL

Using Sqoop, we can transfer data from relational database to Hadoop HDFS. As Sqoop uses **Java Database Connectivity (JDBC)** driver for connecting with the source, it can be used with any relational database having support of JDBC connection strings. In the previous section, we downloaded and configured Sqoop's MySQL connector, so now let's see how to connect with MySQL databases from Sqoop and transfer the data to HDFS.

Sqoop import for fetching data from MySQL 8

To understand Sqoop's import process, let's create a database and table in MySQL 8, which we will use throughout the chapter for demonstrating examples:

```
mysql> create database hadoop_bigdata;
Query OK, 1 row affected (0.00 sec)

mysql>
mysql> CREATE TABLE
    -> `hadoop_bigdata`.`users` (
    -> `user_id` INT NOT NULL AUTO_INCREMENT ,
    -> `email` VARCHAR(200) NOT NULL ,
    -> `date_of_joining` DATE NOT NULL ,
    -> `date_of_birth` DATE NOT NULL ,
    -> `first_name` VARCHAR(200) NOT NULL ,
    -> PRIMARY KEY (`user_id`)
    -> ) ENGINE = InnoDB;
Query OK, 0 rows affected (0.02 sec)

mysql>
```

Sqoop provides `import` command to import data from relational database to HDFS. Following are generic commands used for importing data using Sqoop:

```
sqoop import (generic-args) (import-args)
sqoop-import (generic-args) (import-args)
```

- `generic-args` are common parameter for export such as providing JDBC connection string, JDBC driver name, username and password for connecting to database.
- `import-args` are various parameters supported by Sqoop for importing data from relational database.

To connect with a database, we can use the following command:

```
sqoop import --driver {driverClassForConnection} --connect
{ConnectionString}
```

Here, `driverClassForConnection` is the name of the class that is part of MySQL connector that we have already downloaded. `ConnectionString` is the parameter that we will use to connect with MySQL host using `jdbc` driver.

Below command will connect on `myhost.com` host with MySQL server with users database:

```
sqoop import --connect jdbc:mysql://myhost.com/hadoop_bigdata
```

If the MySQL connection requires authentication, we need to use username and password as input parameters of the connection string to connect with the desired database:

```
sqoop import --connect jdbc:mysql://myhost.com/hadoop_bigdata --username
root --password mysql@123
```

Now we are connected with the database `hadoop_bigdata`. We can now choose data that needs to be replicated on HDFS.

We can choose the table that needs to be replicated from the `hadoop_bigdata` table:

```
sqoop import --connect jdbc:mysql://myhost.com/hadoop_bigdata --username
root --password mysql@123 --table users
```

In case we need to copy selected columns from the table users, we can specify the list of columns that need to be copied from MySQL 8:

```
sqoop import --connect jdbc:mysql://myhost.com/hadoop_bigdata
--username root --password mysql@123
--table users
--columns "user_id,email,date_of_joining,date_of_birth"
```

We can also specify where condition in the same preceding syntax to copy specific database from MySQL to HDFS:

```
sqoop import --connect jdbc:mysql://myhost.com/hadoop_bigdata --username
root --password mysql@123 --table users --where "date_of_birth >
'1979-12-31'"
```

This syntax will tell Sqoop to copy all the `users` table data where the user's birth date is after 31st December, 1979.

It is also possible to use MySQL queries instead of the syntax for specifying tablename, column or where condition in Sqoop. In case of using direct SQL queries to copy data, we have to specify the destination directory where the output of the query would be copied. As Sqoop does parallel processing of the data, it adds boundary condition and splitting column to the queries used to fetch data from source database.

In case of not using direct query, Sqoop automatically identifies and adds boundary conditions and split by filter before firing the query. A splitting column is generally a primary key of the table. In case of using direct queries, we must provide split by condition, which will be used to split the query output for processing. Also, we must include a static token `$CONDITIONS` in the `WHERE` query. `$CONDITION` token will be replaced by Sqoop with the boundary condition.

Below is an example for using direct query for import:

```
sqoop import
--query 'SELECT * FROM users WHERE $CONDITIONS'
--split-by users.id
--target-dir /hduser/hadoop_bigdata/users/userdata
```

Being self explanatory, the preceding query will get all records from the `users` table. Default value for Hadoop's parallel operation is four. This means that by default, Hadoop will use four parallel operations to copy data from the source database to HDFS. This value is configurable and can be changed while using import command with the `-m` or `--num-mappers` parameter. While increasing the value of the parameter can increase performance of copy operations, it requires proper fine tuning of the parameter before setting any value as number of parallel operations that can be done changes based on the cluster's configuration as well number of thread supported by any relational databases.

Using Sqoop, we can import all tables from a database. Following are the commands used to import all tables from a database:

```
sqoop import-all-tables (generic-args) (import-args)
sqoop-import-all-tables (generic-args) (import-args)
```

`generic-args` remain the same as Sqoop's import commands. We can specify one or more columns that need to be skipped while importing the whole table. The `--exclude-tables` parameter can be used with the `import-all-tables` command to specify the list of tables to be excluded from the list:

```
sqoop import-all-tables
--connect jdbc:mysql://localhost/hadoop_bigdata
--username root --password Pass@123
--exclude-tables login_history
```

The preceding command will import all the tables from the `hadoop_bigdata` database, except `login_history`. If you want to exclude more than one database table, then you need to provide comma separated names of the tables.

Incremental imports using Sqoop

As we are dealing with Big Data, it is general tendency that data in the source tables keep on increasing. Sqoop provides the option to incrementally import such data, so that import command can run the import from the last data imported from the source database. For using incremental imports, following are the three parameters that can be used with Sqoop `import` commands:

`--check-column (col)`	A column that needs to be specified, where Sqoop will check id of the last imported records
`--incremental (mode)`	It is a type of incremental import.
`--last-value (value)`	Sqoop will use this parameter to identify new records inserted in database since last data imported from source table.

As mentioned in the preceding table, Sqoop incremental import can be done either in the append mode or in the last modified mode. When incremental import is done in the append mode, the `--check-columns` parameter will contain column name where sqoop will compare the id value that has been imported last. Sqoop will use the `--last-value` parameter to find out which row was imported last.

If incremental mode is defined as last modified, Sqoop will compare the date mentioned in `--last-value` to find out the last value inserted. and all data which was modified after the date mentioned in `--last-value` will be imported into Hadoop HDFS.

Loading structured data to MySQL using Apache Sqoop

So by now, we have imported all data into HDFS and the data has been processed using MapReduce. Now we need to transfer the data back to MySQL. Apache Sqoop provides the export feature to export data from HDFS storage to relational database like MySQL.

Sqoop export for storing structured data from MySQL 8

Apache Sqoop's export feature can transfer data back to the relational database using the following three methods:

- In insert mode, Sqoop will generate insert queries for the data to be inserted into MySQL. Insert is the default mode of transferring data from HDFS using Sqoop.
- In update mode, Sqoop will provide update statements to update data into the existing records in the destination database.
- In call mode, Sqoop will have a stored procedure call in iteration for the data in HDFS.

Following are generic commands available for exporting data using Sqoop:

```
sqoop export (generic-args) (export-args)
sqoop-export (generic-args) (export-args)
```

`generic-args`, as we learnt earlier in the Sqoop import topic, are common parameters for exporting data from HDFS such as providing JDBC connection string, JDBC driver name, username and password for connecting to database.

`export-args` are lists of parameters that provide different ways for exporting data to the destination database. Following is a list of few parameters that can be used while exporting. The complete list of `export-args` can be found at `sqoop.apache.org`.

`--columns`	Defines the names of columns that we need to export from HDFS. The column names have to be passed in comma separated manner.
`--export-dir directoryname`	Defines the source path of HDFS, from where the data will be exported using Sqoop.
`--num-mappers`	Number of parallel operations to be allowed for exporting data.
`--table`	Defines the name of the table in which the exported data will be placed.
`--call`	If export is done using MySQL's stored procedure, `--call` parameter will be used to define name of stored procedure .
`--update-key`	If export is done by replacing existing data in target table, then update-key parameter will be used to define primary key. Sqoop identify existing records in the target table by --update-key parameter.
`--update-mode`	Default export mode is to append the new data at the end of the table. If export is done by replacing existing data in target table, then we need to explicitly define the export mode as the update mode.

Sqoop's export of data from HDFS is done in parallel. Each of the exports is done using bulk insert method. Each of the Sqoop's export processes creates one bulk insert query of 100 records. The export operation uses transactions to import export data. Export command commits data to the target table after every 100 insert statements and each bulk insert query contains 100 records; this means after every 10k records, one insert operation is committed to the database.

Let's understand the export command using an example. In topic *Sqoop import for fetching data from MySQL 8*, we had imported some data from the `users` table. Let's export that data back to the `users` table using the `export` command:

```
sqoop export
 --connect jdbc:mysql://myhost.com/hadoop_bigdata
--username root --password mysql@123
--table users
--export-dir /hduser/hadoop_bigdata/users/userdata
```

Alternatively, we can use the following command if there are fixed number of columns that we need to export:

```
sqoop export
--connect jdbc:mysql://myhost.com/hadoop_bigdata
--username root --password mysql@123 --table users
--columns "col1,col2,col3"
--export-dir /hduser/hadoop_bigdata/users/userdata
```

Sqoop saved jobs

Importing and exporting of data, which we learned in the previous steps, can be stored as jobs that can be repeated multiple times to perform the same operation again and again. Saved job can also be configured to perform the incremental import operation. In such cases, information regarding last imported rows is stored in Sqoop, which helps Sqoop to restart the import process from where it was stopped last. Following is the syntax for using Sqoop's job command to store import and export operation:

```
sqoop job (generic-args) (job-args) [-- [subtool-name] (subtool-args)]
sqoop-job (generic-args) (job-args) [-- [subtool-name] (subtool-args)]
```

- `generic-args` gives the option to create new jobs, delete existing jobs, list all the existing jobs, or execute created jobs.
- `job-args` is the name of the job for which we want to run the `job` command. It can be the name of the job that we need to create, show, delete or execute.
- `subtool-name` is the name of the operation for which we want to create job. It can be either import or export.
- `subtool-args` are parameters that we use to import or export data when job is executed.

Consider the following example where we are creating a job for importing data from the `users` table:

```
sqoop job
--create userimport
import --connect jdbc:mysql://myhost.com/hadoop_bigdata
--username root --password mysql@123
--table users
```

Similarly, we can create job for exporting data from the `users` table:

```
 sqoop job
--create userexport
export --connect jdbc:mysql://myhost.com/hadoop_bigdata
--username root --password mysql@123
--table users
--columns "col1,col2,col3"
--export-dir /hduser/hadoop_bigdata/users/userdata
```

Similarly, we can list all the existing jobs using the following command:

```
sqoop job --list
```

Or, to run an existing job, we can fire the following `sqoop` command, which will start execution of the process:

```
sqoop job --exec userimport
```

By executing above command, we can run the saved job `userimport`. So without writing complete syntax of the import or export command again and again we can run them using saved jobs easily.

Summary

In this chapter, we understood how log analysis can help an e-commerce store to convert its visitors log information into increasing the sales volume and enhancing user experience, in turn increasing the profit from the business. We found out how MySQL 8 and Hadoop can be used to generate reports for user behavior. We went through how Sqoop can be very useful in exchanging data between MySQL 8 and Hadoop HDFS. We had a brief explanation about Hadoop, went through in detail about Apache Sqoop, and learnt how to use import and export operations of Sqoop.

In the next chapter, we will learn what is real time processing of data and how MySQL's applier can be used for real time processing of the data.

10

Case study: Part II - Real time event processing using MySQL applier

In previous chapter, we discussed an overview of Hadoop along with installation of Hadoop in Linux environment. We also learnt about Apache Sqoop to integrate Hadoop with MySQL 8 to import/export data using batch processing. We also discussed an example where we can use Apache Sqoop in a real-time scenario.

In this chapter, we will discuss about MySQL Applier, which we will use to import data from MySQL 8 to Hadoop using real-time processing. We will cover the following topics:

- Case study Overview
- MySQL Applier overview
- Real time integration with MySQL Applier
- Organizing and analyzing data into Hadoop

Case study overview

MySQL is a proven solution to store transactional data that is used to maintain ACID properties during write operations. Starting from MySQL 5.6, it also includes the new `NoSQL Memcached` API for InnoDB, which improves performance for high volume data ingestion. Hadoop is used to store a huge amount of data (in petabytes) and processing it for many scenarios such as storing archived data or various historical data. Analytical processing of data was handled offline and was not an integrated part of the data processing. However, the technology has evolved and nowadays, Hadoop is an active part of data flows for many use cases where we require real-time data processing and provisioning of data to the user.

We can use MySQL to store the transnational data and Hadoop to store huge amount of data which can easily process the data using a map-reduce algorithm. We can take advantages of both technology to unlock the Big Data analysis. There are various use cases where we need to use real-time integration with the Hadoop and MySQL.

- E-commerce recommendation engine
- Sentiment analysis
- Marketing campaign analysis
- Fraud detection

In our case, let's discuss real-time data processing to develop the recommendation engine for customer when they visit the e-commerce portal. Customers purchase items from e-commerce portal which is stored in order history of customer. During purchase, customer navigates the different pages from e-commerce portal; such browsing history should be stored as it will be needed for further analysis. Customer preferences like preference of brands on various social media platform like Facebook, Google Plus, Twitter, and so on, should be fetched to analyze as well. Based on the order history, browsing history or social media data, you can develop algorithm to display the recommended products to customers.

Data processing needs to be done real-time for accurate recommendation result and achieve better output in terms of selling what customers prefer on e-commerce store. Following is pictorial representation of the workflow on which recommendations would be done.

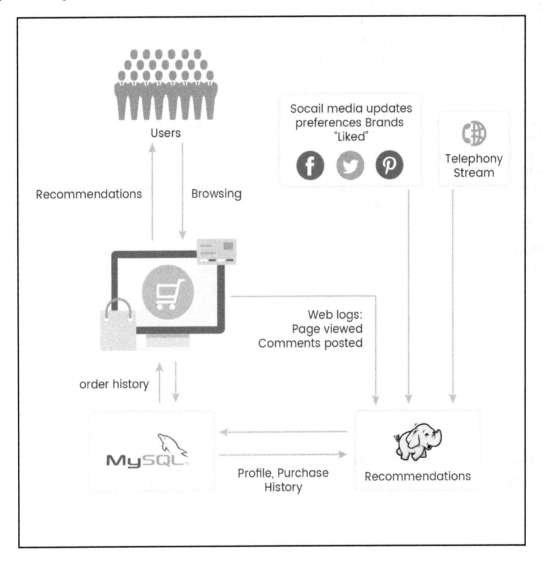

Hadoop is one of the suitable platform to perform analysis on user site visits, social media data, order history, and so on. We can use e-commerce solution like Magento, as an e-commerce portal. E-commerce portal uses MySQL database to store catalog, customer details, order history, and many more. Hadoop can be used to store page navigation data and social media preferences. There are various `APIs` available to pull social media data which can be leveraged to fetch customer brand preferences. Using Hadoop `MapReduce` process we can develop the recommendation engine where Hadoop process order history, view logs and social media data to identify recommended items for the customer.

But how we can transfer data between MySQL and Hadoop to perform analysis in real time? While integrating MySQL with Hadoop, we would need to transfer captured data from MySQL to Hadoop and vice versa, so that analytics on Big Data can take place. The data existing in MySQL needs to moved to **Hadoop Distributed File System** (**HDFS**) on which analytics result will be performed and these analytical results needs to be moved back to MySQL from Hadoop. There are various ways we can load the data between MySQL and Hadoop. Let's see how it can be achieved and what will be an efficient way to do this.

There are multiple solutions and technologies available to dump and load the data from MySQL 8 to Hadoop. We will quickly glance through some of them here.

MySQL Applier

For real-time data integration between MySQL and Hadoop, we can use MySQL Applier. The Applier works as middleware between MySQL 8 and Hadoop for replication of data. The Applier reads the binlog event, decodes the rows in format, and applies those events to the Hive table.

SQL Dump and Import

In this process, we have to write a custom script to extract data from MySQL in the format that we can import to Hadoop using the script. This process relies on existing database tools available to extract data.

Let's see the flow of importing and exporting data using this technique. For example, we have a user table with the below data structure. We will export this `users` table from MySQL and import into Hadoop.

user_id	first_name	last_name	email
1	Chintan	Patel	chintan.patel@gmail.com
2	Jaydeep	sharman	jaydeep.sharman@gmail.com

To export data to the CSV file the following query can be used:

```
SELECT user_id, first_name, last_name, email into OUTFILE 'users.csv'
FIELDS TERMINATED BY ',' FROM users;
```

Copy this file to the Hadoop server to load this file to Hadoop with help of following command:

```
$ hdfs dfs mkdir users
$ hdfs dfs -copyFromLocal users.csv users
```

This is the manual process of importing users table as `.csv` file and import the same file in Hadoop. An advantage of this solution is flexibility; we can create custom formats for data extraction and do not require replication. There would be database query overhead for export which needs to be considered for a large amount of data.

This technique may take a longer time to export/import large amount of data. Also, this file operation will consume more resources which causes slow performance in other areas.

Sqoop

Apache Sqoop is used for the effective transferring of a bulk of data between Apache Hadoop and relational databases like MySQL, Oracle, and Postgres. Sqoop can import or export data in parallel to speed up data transmission between the source and destination database. Sqoop provides batch processing to exchange data between MySQL and Hadoop. We have discussed these technique in `Chapter 9`, *Case study: Part I - Apache Sqoop for Exchanging Data between MySQL and Hadoop*.

Benefit of using Sqoop is, it allows flexible data selection, automated transfer, and does not require replication to be enabled on MySQL.

Limitation with Apache Sqoop is, it uses batch transfer so we would have to transfer data each time whenever we want to update the database. This will create overhead to the operating system and memory which impacts performance. Also, it's not an efficient way to transfer the bulk of data in a case where only a few changes need to update. This will take a long time to update few changes.

Tungsten replicator

Tungsten replicator is an open source replication engine that works with a number of different source and target databases. This functionality allows for replication between MySQL, Oracle, Hadoop among others.

Apache Kafka

Apache Kafka is used to build real-time streaming data pipelines that reliably gets data between systems or applications.

Talend

Talend is an ETL tool used to transfer data from various sources to multiple destinations. Using this solution, we can make use of the Sqoop connector to build a simplified extraction and migration interface. Talend has similar limitations as what we discussed for Sqoop.

Dell Shareplex

A commercial tool that provides replication of data from the Oracle archive logs to Hadoop in almost real-time.

Comparison of Tools

So far, we have seen mainly three solutions to achieve export/import between MySQL and Hadoop. Each tool has its own pros and cons. Let's compare these three solutions to identify which one is suitable for our need.

	SQL Dump and Import	Sqoop	MySQL Applier
Process	Manual / Scripted	Manual / Scripted	Fully Automated
Incremental Loading	Possible with **Data Definition Language** (DDL) changes	Required **Data Definition Language** (DDL) Changes	Fully Supported
Latency	Heavy-load	Intermittent	Real-time
Extraction requirement	Full table scan	Full and partial table scan	Low-impact binlog scan

Basically, *SQL Dump and Import* technique is used rarely and not feasible for large data sets. To overcome manual management and long time, Apache Sqoop can help by providing a better way to transfer data between Hadoop and MySQL automatically.

But as we have seen, Apache Sqoop is also loading the bulk of data rather than the changes. This would take longer time depending on data size. This is where real-time data processing comes into the picture which means automatically loading data whenever new changes occurs and updates it, rather than loading the whole data again. MySQL 8 has capabilities to handle such real-time data processing using MySQL Applier. Let's take a brief of MySQL Applier which helps in real-time data processing.

MySQL Applier overview

MySQL Applier provides real-time data processing between MySQL and Hadoop. This is quite an efficient way to load data because of its performance and real-time processing. This will load the data which has been changed rather than loading whole data. Hence, **No More Bulk Transfer** needed!

MySQL Applier replicates rows inserted into MySQL to the HDFS with help of MySQL binlog. This will use binary log and insert data in real-time; based on events in MySQL. All the events occurred in MySQL Server is available in binlog and Applier takes these changes from the events and applies same in Hadoop. This way we can rapidly acquire new data from the MySQL.

MySQL Applier uses API provided by `libhdfs` which is `C` library. This library is pre-compiled with Hadoop distributions for connecting MySQL master or read a `binlog` file of MySQL. It is responsible for various operations as listed in the following points:

- Get the events (insert, update, delete) occurred on the MySQL Server.
- Decodes events by reading `binlog` and extracts data which is used by events to make changes in Hadoop.
- Use content handlers to get in the format required and appends it to a text file in HDFS.

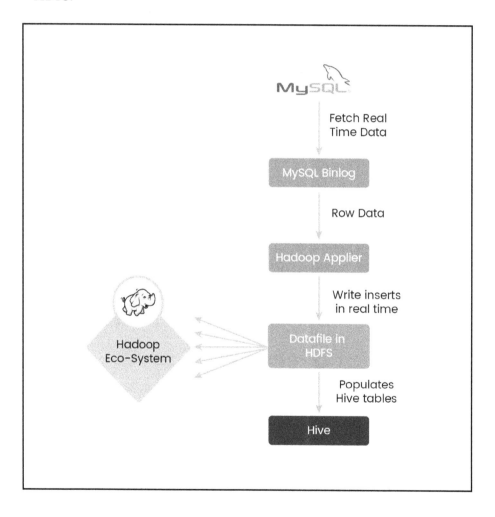

As you can see in earlier diagram that explains how the process takes place while integrating with the MySQL Applier. Whenever any operations is performed on MySQL Server it goes to the binary log. This will have the table raw information which has been changed or added. MySQL Applier will take this raw information and immediately apply changes in HDFS.

With MySQL Applier, we can have real-time connectivity between MySQL and Hadoop which solves many Big Data Analytics use-cases like sales campaign, sentiment analysis, log analysis, and so on.

MySQL Applier installation

Now let's discuss MySQL Applier installation and configuration for real-time data processing.

Below are the prerequisites for Mysql Applier:

- MySQL Applier package
- Hadoop
- Java
- `libhdfs`
- `cmake`
- `libmysqlclient`
- `gcc` which required for run C++ program.
- MySQL Server
- `FindHDFS.cmake`
- Hive

Some of the pre-requisites like Hadoop, Java, MySQL server and MySQL client installation has already been discussed in the `Chapter 9`, *Case study: Part I - Apache Sqoop for Exchanging Data between MySQL and Hadoop*. Let's take a look at the installation for rest of the prerequisites.

libhdfs

This is a precompiled library with Hadoop. You can find `libhdfs.so` file in `[Hadoop]/lib/native` path. We have to export the environment variable for this library using following command:

```
export HDFS_LIBS=/usr/local/hadoop/lib/native
```

cmake

`cmake` is a cross-platform build system. You can create a simple configuration file in the source directory `CMakeLists.txt`.

To install on the server, you can download the latest version from `https://cmake.org/download/` . Run the following command from the Linux terminal to install:

```
$ wget https://cmake.org/files/v3.9/cmake-3.9.4.tar.gz
$ tar xzf cmake-3.9.4.tar.gz
$ cd cmake-3.9.4.tar.gz
$ ./configure --prefix=/opt/cmake
$ make
$ make install
$ export PATH=/opt/cmake/bin/
```

You can verify the installation using the following command:

```
cmake -version
```

This returns the version of the installed cmake.

gcc

gcc is used to run the C++ program. You can install it by performing the following steps:

```
$ sudo yum install gcc
```

You can verify the installation using the following command:

```
$ gcc --version
```

FindHDFS.cmake

Find the HDFS.cmake file to find the libhdfs library while compiling. You can download this file from `https://github.com/cloudera/Impala/blob/master/cmake_modules/FindHDFS.cmake`. After downloading, export the `CMAKE_MODULE_PATH` variable using the following command:

```
$ export CMAKE_MODULE_PATH=/usr/local/MySQL-replication-
listener/FindHDFS.cmake
```

Hive

Hive is a data warehouse infrastructure built on Hadoop that uses its storage and execution model. It was initially developed by Facebook. It provides a query language that is similar to SQL and is known as the **Hive query language** (**HQL**). Using this language, we can analyze large datasets stored in file systems, such as HDFS. Hive also provides an indexing feature. It is designed to support ad hoc queries and easy data summarization as well as to analyze large volumes of data.

Hive tables are similar to the one in a relational database that are made up of partitions. We can use HiveQL to access data. Tables are serialized and have the corresponding HDFS directory within a database. Hive allows you to explore and structure this data, analyze it, and then turn it into business insight.

To install Hive on the server, download the package from `archive.apache.org` and extract it to Hadoop home:

```
$ cd /usr/local/hadoop
$ wget
http://archive.apache.org/dist/hive/hive-0.12.0/hive-0.12.0-bin.tar.gz
$ tar xzf hive-0.12.0-bin.tar.gz
$ mv hive-0.12.0-bin hive
```

To create the Hive directory in Hadoop and give the permission to the folder, following are the commands:

```
$ cd /usr/local/hadoop/hive
$ $HADOOP_HOME/bin/hadoop fs -mkdir /tmp
$ $HADOOP_HOME/bin/hadoop fs -mkdir /user/hive/warehouse
$ $HADOOP_HOME/bin/hadoop fs -chmod g+w /tmp
$ $HADOOP_HOME/bin/hadoop fs -chmod g+w /user/hive/warehouse
```

You can set up the environment variables using the following command:

```
$ export HIVE_HOME="/usr/local/hadoop/hive"
$ PATH=$PATH:$HIVE_HOME/bin
$ export PATH
```

To load the Hive terminal, just use the hive command:

```
[root@ip-172-31-22-58 hive]# hive
17/10/11 01:56:27 INFO Configuration.deprecation: mapred.input.dir.recursive is deprecated. Instead, use mapreduce.input.fileinputformat.input.dir.recursive
17/10/11 01:56:27 INFO Configuration.deprecation: mapred.max.split.size is deprecated. Instead, use mapreduce.input.fileinputformat.split.maxsize
17/10/11 01:56:27 INFO Configuration.deprecation: mapred.min.split.size is deprecated. Instead, use mapreduce.input.fileinputformat.split.minsize
17/10/11 01:56:27 INFO Configuration.deprecation: mapred.min.split.size.per.rack is deprecated. Instead, use mapreduce.input.fileinputformat.split.minsize.per.rack
17/10/11 01:56:27 INFO Configuration.deprecation: mapred.min.split.size.per.node is deprecated. Instead, use mapreduce.input.fileinputformat.split.minsize.per.node
17/10/11 01:56:27 INFO Configuration.deprecation: mapred.reduce.tasks is deprecated. Instead, use mapreduce.job.reduces
17/10/11 01:56:27 INFO Configuration.deprecation: mapred.reduce.tasks.speculative.execution is deprecated. Instead, use mapreduce.reduce.speculative

Logging initialized using configuration in jar:file:/usr/local/hadoop/hive/lib/hive-common-0.12.0.jar!/hive-log4j.properties
SLF4J: Class path contains multiple SLF4J bindings.
SLF4J: Found binding in [jar:file:/usr/local/hadoop/share/hadoop/common/lib/slf4j-log4j12-1.7.5.jar!/org/slf4j/impl/StaticLoggerBinder.class]
SLF4J: Found binding in [jar:file:/usr/local/hadoop/hive/lib/slf4j-log4j12-1.6.1.jar!/org/slf4j/impl/StaticLoggerBinder.class]
SLF4J: See http://www.slf4j.org/codes.html#multiple_bindings for an explanation.
SLF4J: Actual binding is of type [org.slf4j.impl.Log4jLoggerFactory]
hive>
```

Now you can use SQL command to create the directories and documents as mentioned in the following code:

```
hive>  CREATE TABLE user (id int, name string);
OK
```

Real-time integration with MySQL Applier

There are many MySQL applier packages available on GitHub. We can use any of them which provides framework for replication and an example of real-time replication:

- Flipkart/MySQL-replication-listener
- SponsorPay/MySQL-replication-listener
- bullsoft/MySQL-replication-listener

For our configuration, let's use Flipkart/MySQL-replication-listener. You can clone the Git library using the following command:

```
$ git clone https://github.com/Flipkart/MySQL-replication-listener.git
```

Here are some environment variables required by the package. Make sure that all are set properly.

- HADOOP_HOME: The Hadoop root directory path
- CMAKE_MODULE_PATH: The path of the root directory where FindHDFS.cmake and FindJNI.cmake files are located in HDFS
- HDFS_LIB_PATHS: The path of the libhdfs.so file available in HADOOP
- JAVA_HOME: You need to set the Java home path for this variable

Now build and compile all the libraries using the following command:

```
$ cd src
$ cmake . -DCMAKE_MODULE_PATH:String=/usr/local/cmake-3.10.0-rc1/Modules
$ make -j8
```

Package generated from earlier command would be used to set up replication from MySQL 8 to Hadoop. By compiling this package, we will get the executable command happlier, which we will use to start replication:

```
$ cd examples/mysql2hdfs/
$ cmake .
$ make -j8
```

Now before starting the replication we have to understand how we would map MySQL and Hadoop data structure with help of following figure.

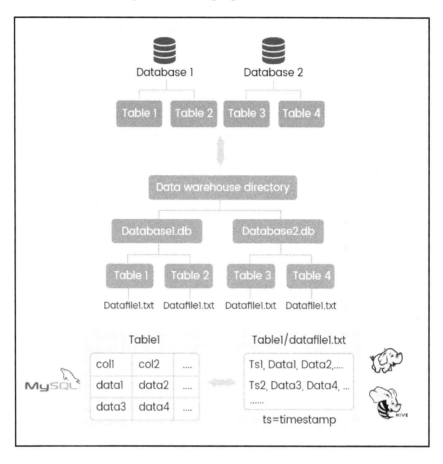

The preceding image explains the data structure mapping for MySQL 8 and Hadoop. In Hadoop, the data is stored as a data file. Applier is not allowed to run the DLL statement so we have to create a database and table on both sides. For MySQL, we can run the SQL statement to CREATE table while in Hadoop we can use HIVE to create a database and table.

Following is the SQL query to create a table, which we have to run on the MySQL server:

```
CREATE TABLE chintantable (i INT);
```

Follwing is the Hive query to create a table, which we have to run from the HIVE command line:

```
CREATE TABLE chintantable ( time_stamp INT, i INT) [ROW FORMAT DELIMITED]
STORED AS TEXTFILE;
```

Once you create the database and table on MySQL and Hive following command is used to start replication:

```
./happlier mysql://root@127.0.0.1:3306 hdfs://localhost:8088
```

MySQL details in `happlier` command is optional. By default, it uses `mysql://user@127.0.0.1:3306` and for HDFS details are configured in the `core-site/core-default.xml` file. Now each row added to MySQL database it's corresponding rows would be created in HDFS.

When any insert operation is performed in the MySQL database, the same corresponding row is replicated in the Hadoop table. We can also create an `API` to replicate update and delete operations from the `binlog API`.

Organizing and analyzing data in Hadoop

As we learned in the `Chapter 9`, *Case study: Part I - Apache Sqoop for exchanging data between MySQL and Hadoop*, Hadoop can be used for processing unstructured data generated through relational databases like MySQL. In this topic, we will find out how we can use Hadoop for analyzing the unstructured data generated in MySQL 8. Based on our case study of e-commerce store, we will try to find out the bestselling product among the customers based on the order history of customers in e-commerce store. We will transfer the order data generated in MySQL 8 into Apache Hive using MySQL applier. Than we will use **Hive Query Language (Hive-QL)** for analyzing required data.

`Hive-QL` uses map-reduce algorithm which makes it much faster to analyze millions of data within seconds. Data generated in Hive can be transferred back to the MySQL 8 as a flat table.

Consider following table of user's order history generated in MySQL 8:

```
CREATE TABLE IF NOT EXISTS `orderHistory` (
 `orderId` INT(11) NOT NULL PRIMARY KEY AUTO_INCREMENT,
 `customerName` VARCHAR (100) NOT NULL,
 `customerBirthDate` DATE NULL,
 `customerCountry` VARCHAR(50),
 `orderDate` DATE,
 `orderItemName` VARCHAR (100),
 `orderQuantity` DECIMAL(10,2),
 `orderTotal` DECIMAL(10,2),
 `orderStatus` CHAR(2)
) ENGINE=InnoDB DEFAULT CHARSET=latin1 COMMENT='USER ORDER HISTORY
information' AUTO_INCREMENT=1;
```

This table stores information about customer's name, birthdate, region as well information about the order like order date, item name, quantity, price and status of the order.

Let's insert some sample data in this table which we will use to transfer into Apache Hive with help of following example mentioned:

```
mysql> INSERT INTO orderHistory ( orderId, customerName, customerBirthDate,
customerCountry, orderDate, orderItemName, orderQuantity, orderTotal,
orderStatus)
VALUES (111, "Jaydip", "1990-08-06", "USA", "2017-08-06", "Chair", 1, 500,
1);
mysql> INSERT INTO orderHistory ( orderId, customerName, customerBirthDate,
customerCountry, orderDate, orderItemName, orderQuantity, orderTotal,
orderStatus)
VALUES (222, "Shabbir", "1985-02-10", "India", "2017-09-06", "Table", 3,
1200, 1);
mysql> INSERT INTO orderHistory ( orderId, customerName, customerBirthDate,
customerCountry, orderDate, orderItemName, orderQuantity, orderTotal,
orderStatus)
VALUES (333, "Kandarp", "1987-04-15", "India", "2017-09-06", "Computer", 1,
43000, 1);
```

Following is the output `orderHistory` table which would be used for further analysis:

```
mysql> select * from orderHistory\G;
*************************** 1. row ***************************
 orderId: 111
 customerName: Jaydip
customerBirthDate: 1990-08-06
 customerCountry: USA
 orderDate: 2017-08-06
 orderItemName: Chair
 orderQuantity: 1.00
```

```
  orderTotal: 500.00
  orderStatus: 1
*************************** 2. row ***************************
      orderId: 222
 customerName: Shabbir
customerBirthDate: 1985-02-10
customerCountry: India
    orderDate: 2017-09-06
 orderItemName: Table
orderQuantity: 3.00
  orderTotal: 1200.00
 orderStatus: 1
*************************** 3. row ***************************
      orderId: 333
 customerName: Kandarp
customerBirthDate: 1987-04-15
customerCountry: India
    orderDate: 2017-09-06
 orderItemName: Computer
orderQuantity: 1.00
  orderTotal: 43000.00
 orderStatus: 1
3 rows in set (0.00 sec)
```

Now before we transfer data from MySQL to Hive, let's create similar schema in Apache Hive.

Following is the example to create table in Hive:

```
CREATE TABLE orderHistory (
  orderId INT,
  customerName STRING,
  customerBirthDate DATE,
  customerCountry STRING,
  orderedDate DATE,
  orderItemName STRING,
  orderQuantity DECIMAL(10,2),
  orderTotal DECIMAL(10,2),
  orderStatus CHAR(2)
) ROW FORMAT DELIMITED
FIELDS TERMINATED BY ',';
```

With help of this step we have MySQL `orderHistory` table with data that need to be transferred and Apache Hive's `orderHistory` table which is ready to receive input data. Let's start transferring data from MySQL to hive using MySQL applier.

Following command will start MySQL applier and start transferring data from MySQL to Hive.

```
./happlier mysql://root@127.0.0.1:3306 hdfs://localhost:8088
```

We will have all the rows of order history table in Apache Hive. We can use `Hive-QL` to fetch bestselling product form order history. Following is the query to get maximum selling product:

```
SELECT
 orderItemName,SUM(orderQuantity),SUM(orderTotal)
FROM
 orderHistory
GROUP BY orderQuantity;
```

This query will give sum of quantity sold for each products and their total sale price. Output of this data can be stored into comma delimited text files. This text files can now be exported back to MySQL using Apache Sqoop. We have learned about Apache Sqoop in `Chapter 9`, *Case study: Part I - Apache Sqoop for exchanging data between MySQL and Hadoop.*

Output generated for best selling product in Hive can be exported to a flat table in MySQL8 which can be used to display best selling product easily. Similarly, we can use `orderHistory` table for generating other reports like:

- Best selling products in different age group
- Region wise best selling products
- Month wise best selling products.

Order history is one part of the customer activity on an e-commerce application. There are lot of other activities like social sharing, bookmarks, referrals which we can use for building a strong recommendation engine using humongous amount of data being generated. That's the place you can use power of having MySQL for Big Data!

Summary

In this chapter, we have gone through case study of recommendation engine in an e-commerce application. We found different tools for transferring data from MySQL to big data technologies like Hadoop. We learnt exciting topic of MySQL applier overview along with installation and it's integration. Then, we understood how to use MySQL applier for real time processing of data. We also learnt on how we can organize and analyze data in Hadoop's Hive and transfer data from MySQL to Hadoop using MySQL Applier.

Index

PHP, using 211
prerequisites 208
Python, using 212
Not Only SQL (No SQL)
big data 205
change management 204
less management 205
NDB Cluster API 215
scaling 205
using, with Memcached API layer 207
versus SQL 206

O

optimizer 185
Oracle MySQL cloud service 153
ORDER BY clause 51

P

partition option
pruning 142
using, with DELETE query 146
using, with INSERT query 148
using, with UPDATE query 147
partition selections
providing, with query 143
partition
pruning 139, 141
partitioned data
about 120
querying on 142, 145
partitioning types
horizontal partitioning 121
vertical partitioning 121
partitioning
about 120
types 121
performance 104
PHP
Memcached 116
prerequisites, MySQL Applier
cmake 258
FindHDFS.cmake 259
gcc 258
Hive 259
libhdfs 258

primary index
about 81
defining 81
natural keys, versus surrogate keys 82
pruning
about 140
with key partitioning 142
with list partitioning 141
Python Memcached
reference 118

R

real-time event processing
case study 250
Relational Database Management System
(RDBMS) 38, 204
replace statement 59
Replication User
configuring 178
replication
best practices 198
binary logs, using 156
configuration 157
global transaction ID, using 161
global transaction identifiers, using 156
master configuration 158
methods 156
MySQL multi-source replication 165
slave configuration 160
statement-based, versus row-based replication
173
with binary log file 157
Return on Investment (ROI) 10

S

SaaS (Software as a Service) 21
Select statement, MySQL 8
LIMIT clause 52
optimizing 57
ORDER BY clause 51
SQL JOINS 52
UNION query 55
using 48
WHERE clause 49
Sloan Digital Sky Survey (SDSS) 11

www.ingramcontent.com/pod-product-compliance
Lightning Source LLC
Chambersburg PA
CBHW080629060326
40690CB00021B/4864